THE RHETORIC OF JOHN DONNE'S VERSE.

BY

WIGHTMAN FLETCHER MELTON.

A Dissertation

SUBMITTED TO THE BOARD OF UNIVERSITY STUDIES OF THE JOHNS HOPKINS UNIVERSITY
IN CONFORMITY WITH THE REQUIREMENTS FOR THE DEGREE OF
DOCTOR OF PHILOSOPHY

1906

BALTIMORE
J. H. FURST COMPANY
1906

Publishing Statement:

This important reprint was made from an old and scarce book.

Therefore, it may have defects such as missing pages, erroneous pagination, blurred pages, missing text, poor pictures, markings, marginalia and other issues beyond our control.

Because this is such an important and rare work, we believe it is best to reproduce this book regardless of its original condition.

Thank you for your understanding and enjoy this unique book!

THIS DISSERTATION

IS AFFECTIONATELY DEDICATED TO MY WIFE AND CHILDREN,

WHOSE SACRIFICES HAVE ENABLED ME,—

AFTER TEACHING FIFTEEN YEARS,—TO SPEND THREE YEARS IN THE

UNIVERSITY.

WITHOUT THEIR SYMPATHY

THIS WORK COULD NOT HAVE BEEN ACCOMPLISHED.

TABLE OF CONTENTS.

	PAGE
INTRODUCTION	1
SOME OF DONNE'S CRITICS	8
SECONDARY ACCENT IN DONNE'S VERSE	58

THE RHETORIC OF VERSE IN DONNE.

I.	THE TITLE DEFINED	103
II.	THE MYSTERY OF DONNE'S ART	108
III.	THE ENDS TO BE ATTAINED BY THIS PECULIARITY:	
	(1) 'Artistic Monotone'	112
	(2) Lipogrammatic Verse	116
	(3) Special Stress	117
	(4) Obscurity	118
	(5) Affinity to Prose	122
IV.	MONOSYLLABIC DICTION NOT CONDUCIVE TO HARSHNESS WHEN THE VERSE-PATTERN IS KNOWN	124
V.	DONNE'S EAR FOR RHYTHM	125
VI.	DONNE'S 'SECRET'	127
VII.	DONNE'S VERSE-REFERENCES TO POETRY:	
	(1) 'Poeticness'	134
	(2) 'The Measure Changed'	134
	(3) Donne Imitates Abraham Fraunce	135
VIII.	WHAT JONSON MEANT BY 'KEEPING OF ACCENT'	137
IX.	ARSIS-THESIS VARIATION OF REPEATED SOUNDS, SYLLABLES, AND WORDS	142
X.	DONNE'S RULE	148
	(1) A Line Begins and Ends with the same Word	148
	(2) A Line Begins and Ends with the same Sound or Syllable	151
	(3) Arsis-Thesis Variation of Repeated Sounds and Syllables in the Midst of the Line	152
	(4) Arsis-Thesis Variation of Repeated Words	163
	(5) Donne's Rule Stated, and Operation Observed	164
XI.	PUTTING DONNE'S METRICAL PECULIARITY TO THE TEST	169
	(1) Donne's Authorship of Doubtful Poems Determined	170
	(2) Was Joseph Hall 'the harbenger to Donne's Anniversarie'?	173
	(3) The Missing Word Supplied	174
	(4) The Superfluous Word Recognized	176
	(5) The Correct Variant Selected	177
	(6) Difficult Lines Scanned	181
	(7) Donne's Part in Dialogue Poems Recognized	183

Table of Contents.

XII.	INVESTIGATION OF THE SOURCES OF DONNE'S METRICAL PECULIARITY...............	186
XIII.	IN THE MATTER OF RHYTHM, DONNE DID NOT FOUND A SCHOOL................	193
XIV.	A GROUP OF ADDITIONAL POINTS...............	195
XV.	A FURTHER APPLICATION OF DONNE'S MEASURE...............	196
XVI.	WHEN ARSIS-THESIS VARIATIONS DO NOT OCCUR...............	201
XVII.	WHEN ARSIS-THESIS VARIATION IS POSSIBLE...............	203
XVIII.	WHEN ARSIS-THESIS VARIATION IS IMPOSSIBLE...............	203
XIX.	LACK OF ARSIS-THESIS VARIATION DUE TO CORRUPT TEXT.......	204
XX.	APPARENT LACK OF ARSIS-THESIS VARIATION EXPLAINED.......	205
	NOTE...............	206

THE RHETORIC OF JOHN DONNE'S VERSE.

INTRODUCTION.

According to Goldsmith, all those 'misguided innovators' who succeeded, but did not understand Dryden, Addison, and Pope, 'are silent, and those who make out their meaning are willing to praise, to show their understanding.'[1]

There are so many literary historians, and writers on versification, who make no mention of John Donne, that we may take it for granted that he was either not understood, or not appreciated by them. Of those who do mention him, to praise or to condemn, it cannot be said that all, or any, fully understand him,—that praise and condemnation are sometimes offered to 'show understanding' there can be no doubt.

Our first chapter makes no pretense to being an exhaustive study of Donne's critics, for the reason that our concern is only with the metrical side of his poetry.[2] Even with this end in view, some important authorities may have been overlooked; but the showing is sufficient to enable one to trace the current of opinion from Ben Jonson to the present time. Occasionally when one critic quotes or refers to another, no further special mention will be made of the one so quoted or referred to.

The second chapter is merely an application, to the poetry of Donne, of the theory of 'secondary word-accent in English verse,' as advanced by Professor Bright and applied in the dissertations of his pupils, Huguenin, Brown, and Miller. The last of these has cited numerous examples from Donne; but it seems necessary, as a preliminary to our third chapter, that a more particular, or more

---

[1] *The Poetical Works of Thomas Parnell*, (Aldine ed.), pp. 52–3.

[2] A study of the critics who are concerned specially with the style and thought-matter of Donne may be found in the forthcoming work of Professor Martin G. Brumbaugh (University of Pennsylvania) : *A Study of the Poetry of John Donne.*

extended view of Donne's accent be offered, and a comparison made of his 'ruggedness' with the smoothness of his contemporaries and successors, and especially of those who are his critics.

The third chapter deals with a yet practically untouched aspect of the criticism of English verse. The revelation of Donne's 'secret' came to me suddenly after three years of daily, almost hourly, entreating, caressing, and wheedling of each line of his poetry.[1] At first the thing seemed improbable; but, at the same time, it was so real and so plain as to give one that uncanny feeling experienced by those who dare to meddle with the affairs of 'some old lover's ghost.'

In this connection, I wish to say that this discovery came to me as a result of the 'secondary word-accent' theory taught by Professor Bright, and while I was actually engaged in applying it to Donne's verse. Were this theory in need of a final, clinching argument, the poetry of Donne would supply it. Furthermore, it may be said that the man whose ear is too dull to catch the music of the ripples, and even the eddies, of rhythm, and who insists upon white-capped wave after wave, the inevitable long, (just so long and no longer),—and the inevitable short, (just so short and no shorter), can never, till he has been redeemed, appreciate the delicacy of Donne's lighter verse, or the straight thrust of his satire.

The temptation is strong to follow the line of thought suggested by Carpenter,[2] and Trost,[3] and add a chapter on *Conceits*; and even stronger to devote a chapter to *Platonism* in Donne;[4] but it seems advisable, on deliberation, to confine the discussion to the purely metrical.

---

[1] Dowden, in his chapter on 'The Poetry of John Donne,' says (p. 91): 'Some [poets] must be taken by storm, some must be entreated, caressed, wheedled into acquiescence.'—Edward Dowden, *New Studies in Literature*, Boston and New York, 1895, pp. 90–120.

[2] Frederic Ives Carpenter, *English Lyric Poetry*, London, 1897, p. lxi.

[3] Wilhelm Trost, *Beiträge zur Kenntnis des Stils von John Donne in seinen 'Poetical Works*,' Marburg, 1904, pp. 34–38.

[4] For an interesting beginning on this subject, as it applies to Donne, see James Smith Harrison, *Platonism in English Poetry, etc.*, New York, 1903, Chapter II.

The text employed for reference is Chambers' edition, which, while it is probably the best to be had, and is most accessible to the greatest number, is not enough better than the Grolier Club edition to deserve the high praise given it by Professor Norton and others. This is not meant as an adverse criticism, either of Norton or of Chambers, for the former is modest and sincere, and the latter has done the best, with some minor exceptions, that could be done,—with the text of Donne as it has come down to us, — by one unacquainted with the author's peculiarity.

There are hundreds of lines that Donne himself would refuse to father if he could see them to-day. It is easy to realize why this is so: copyists and printers, not understanding the meaning, or the scansion of the verse, undertook to *Pope* it or *Purnell* it, and left some lines lame, others puzzling, and yet others partially, if not absolutely, meaningless.

Professor Norton says, 'No poems require more care in printing, for the thought is often intricate, the diction often involved, so that for understanding them every help is needed that can be given by the press. Even with such help many passages remain difficult and some seem corrupt.'[1]

Of the few poems published in Donne's life-time (1611, 1612, 1621, 1625) Grosart cites errors occurring in the second edition that were corrected in the third and fourth,—but more in the third and fourth that were not in the second,[2]—showing, to adopt a phrase from van Dam and Stoffel's title, 'high-handed ways of . . . . . Jacobean printers.'[3]

Grosart says (i, xii), '. . . such collating and utilization of manuscripts, public and private, have enabled me to correct the swarming errors and bewilderments of previous editions.'

John Donne, the younger, in the dedicatory letter (ed. of 1650) to William Lord Craven (see Chambers, i, xlix), drops a bit of irony that is full of significance. Instead of quoting the letter,

---

[1] Grolier Club ed., i, vii.
[2] The ed. of 1611 contains only the first part of *An Anatomy. First Anniversary*. It might be better, therefore, not to refer to the ed. of 1612 as the second edition.
[3] *Anglistische Forschungen*, Heidelberg, 1902, vol. 10, p. 1.

we may note the remark of Gosse (i, 60) on the subject: 'John Donne the younger . . . remarked that in previous impressions of his father's poems "the kindness of the printer" had "added something too much, lest a spark of this sacred fire might perish undiscerned." But in his own later editions he left out scarcely anything, and this phrase is perhaps merely an apology for what might seem, though genuine, trifling.'

Gosse's statement needs examples, and a goodly number of them, to sustain it. What does he mean by 'scarcely anything'?

To illustrate: a fellow-student once inquired, 'Have you ever noticed how seldom Donne employs the article "a"'?

Following a suggestion, he came back next day, saying, 'I counted up to 900 and quit.'

Even in this day of printing-house facilities, and proof-reading privileges, men who write about Donne continue to make mistakes.

Furst,[1] quoting Coleridge,

'Donne, whose muse on dromedary trots.'

puts it down

'Donne, whose muse or dromedary trots.'

which is quite a different situation. On page 25, at the beginning of a sentence, where it seems almost impossible for a mistake to evade the eye, we read, 'Hope and Parnell . . . attempted the revision.'

In this study, use has been made of a number of editions of the poetry of Donne. For critical comparison the Grosart, Chambers, and Grolier Club editions have been consulted, and each is the best in its own way: Grosart for manuscript variants; Chambers for chronological and general notes; Grolier for seventeenth century (printed) variants.

Norton speaks of 'blunders [in Grosart] proceeding from carelessness and from lack of intelligence,'[2] citing enough examples

---

[1] Clyde Furst, *A Group of Old Authors*, Philadelphia, 1899, p. 1.
[2] C. E. Norton, 'The Text of Donne's Poems,' *Studies and Notes in Philology and Literature*, Vol. v. (Harvard University Studies: Child Memorial Volume), Boston, 1896, p. 3.

seemingly to warrant the charge; but my debt to Grosart is so great that I shall ever be ready to offer a general defence in his behalf.

To be sure, it is somewhat vexing, and at the same time amusing, to read in Grosart, *Good Friday*, 30:

'Uppon His Mother cast mine eye.'

and turning to his note to find, 'I prefer " distress'd " [Mother], (69) to "miserable" [Mother], of our MS. (Addl. 18647).'

Such blunders are very rare and need annoy none but the careless investigator, who, as does Richter, overlooks the note, and charges Donne with 'fremde Verse... unter die Fünftakter.'[1]

Of course it is to be deplored that Grosart 'silently corrected' some lines in a few of the poems. That he has no ear for rhythm is attested scores of times; and, with this serious defect, it is a marvel that he has done as well as he has. One example will suffice.

The Lamentations of Jeremy (389–390):

'For oughtest thou, O Lord, despise us thus
And to be utterly enragèd at us.'

Grosart's note:
'It will be seen that Donne in this scriptural lament affects the accented -èd, as more solemn. I also read the last line so.'

To so accent the word in this couplet is neither 'scriptural' nor 'solemn,' but it is extremely *lamentable*.

The 'minor exceptions,' in Chambers, previously referred to, may be too insignificant to deserve notice; but it is to be hoped that future editions will be consistent in accenting the *-ed* of participles, and in the use of either capitals or small letters in pronouns referring to the Deity.

Probably the most glaring blunder in Chambers is found in (ii, 136) *The Second Anniversary*, 263–5:

---

[1] Rudolph Richter, 'Über den Vers bei Dr. John Donne,' in *Beiträgen zur Neueren Philologie* (Jakob Schipper Festschrift), Wien und Leipzig, 1902, p. 400.

> Have not all souls thought
> For many ages, that our bodies wrought
> Of air, and fire, and other elements?

Grosart and Grolier editions have 'body is,' which is clearly the sense; and with elision of the 'y' the scansion is perfect.

We are pleased to note the correction of the figures in the 'List of First Lines' (vol. ii, pp. 319–326) in the reprint of Chambers, recently brought out by George Routledge & Sons, London. The outcry against the 1896 edition, on this account, will be remembered.

It is a pity that the Grolier edition was limited. Mrs. Burnett, —daughter of James Russell Lowell,—and Professor Norton, in collating the seventeenth century editions, have placed all students of Donne under obligations to them. Less than a half dozen times in the nearly 10,000 lines I noticed the use of some unaccounted-for particle, not to be found in the 1633 edition on which theirs is based. This contingency was anticipated by Professor Norton (p. ix): 'Though much care has been taken in the collation of the texts, and the printing of the present edition, it is possible that some variant readings and some errors may have escaped notice.'

It affords me particular pleasure to record my gratitude to Professor Charles Eliot Norton, of Harvard University; Professor Martin G. Brumbaugh, of the University of Pennsylvania; Professor H. M. Belden, of the University of Missouri; and Librarian William C. Lane, of Harvard University.

Professor Norton, in addition to much wise counsel, allowed me access to the 'Norton Collection,' in the Harvard Library, where I found and eagerly examined the three MSS. described in 'The Text of Donne's Poems'; and the following editions of the poems: 1633, 1635, 1639, 1649, 1654, 1669, and 1719.

Besides kindly sympathy and generous encouragement, Professor Brumbaugh placed at my disposal his editions of the poems, 1633 and 1650, the former of which probably belonged to Izaak Walton, and contains, either in his or in a contemporary's handwriting, marginal references of great value in determining the chronology of the poems, and other facts. I was also allowed the privilege of reading and making extracts from his interesting work, *A Study of the Poetry of John Donne,* which is soon to be published.

Professor Belden, on request, promptly sent me his unpublished paper on 'Donne's Prosody,' which I have found very helpful, as subsequent quotations will show.

Mr. Lane was very courteous and attentive while I worked in the Harvard Library, and has since taken pains in gathering information for me, and in replying promptly to inquiries by mail.

CHAPTER I.

SOME OF DONNE'S CRITICS.

The *Retrospective Review* gives 'a few evidences of the estimation in which Donne was held during his life; taking them, however (in order to avoid the charge of partiality or flattery), from what was not written till after his death,'[1]

The lines there quoted are from Hyde, Porter, and others, some of whom are as visionary as Donne has been accused of being in *An Anatomy*.

Since the purpose of this study is to investigate the mechanism of Donne's verse, and not the mystery of his life, we may very well steer clear of contemporary flattery and post-mortem extravagance. After Jonson and Drummond, whose criticisms furnish the starting point, the nearest next that will be noticed is Dryden, who was born the same year the Dean of St. Paul's died.

An effort has been made to present the criticisms in their chronological order; but, occasionally, the date of an utterance can only be approximated. Only those views that seem to demand comment will receive it.

To the close student of Donne it becomes more and more apparent that the charge of 'ruggedness' and 'harshness', which has been made against his verse for nearly three centuries, is due, (barring misprints), either to the influence of Ben Jonson's remark to Drummond (1618), or to the fact that critics have failed to compare the word-accents employed by him and by his contemporaries and successors. Since, however, *Drummond's Works* was not published till 1711, and since we have no evidence that all Donne's seventeenth century critics were acquainted with the manuscript (though its contents must have been the gossip of the Literati for the ninety-three years), there must be assigned a

[1] Vol. viii (1828), pp. 33, 34.

third cause for the charge : dullness of ear, or inability to appreciate delicate word-tone.

Jonson said, 'That Done, for not keeping of accent, deserved hanging.'[1]

In so far as word-accent is concerned, it may be shown, and will be in Chapter II, that Donne did not place a word or syllable,—proper names alone excepted,—in position to receive the ictus, that may not be matched in the verse of Shakespeare, Jonson, and other contemporaries. Furthermore, examples will be presented from Dryden, Pope, Milton, Tennyson, and other successors, showing that the critics, of three hundred years, have accepted from other poets, with explained satisfaction, the very word-accents Donne has been severely criticised for employing.

It is difficult to understand how Jonson, even playfully, or 'over his wine cup,'[2] could have said Donne 'deserved hanging' on account of 'accents' which he, himself, and his most illustrious contemporary made use of.

Gosse calls attention to the 'curious fact that Jonson alone, of those who in the first half of the seventeenth century discussed the characteristics of Donne's style, commented on the peculiarities of his metre.'[3]

Another opinion, on this subject, by Gosse (ii, 331), is worthy of attention : 'Ben Jonson was not isolated in the sense that Donne was; but he too . . . desired to break away from the melody and pastoral sweetness . . . of the age into which he was born.'

Johnson (Chalmers, *Eng. Poets*, vii. 13) speaks of '. . . Jonson, whose manner resembled that of Donne, more in the ruggedness of the lines, than in the cast of his sentiment.'

Carpenter expresses a kindred view : 'The truth is that neither

---

[1] *Notes of Ben Jonson's Conversations with William Drummond of Hawthornden*, ed. by David Laing, London, 1842, p. 3.

[2] Alexander B. Grosart, *The Complete Poems of John Donne, etc.*, in two vols., London, 1872 (The Fuller Worthies' Library), ii, xlviii. Hereafter cited as Grosart.

[3] Edmund Gosse, *The Life and Letters of John Donne, etc.*, in two vols., London, 1899, ii, 333. Hereafter cited as Gosse.

Jonson nor Donne was by temperament fundamentally lyrical, and that fact was an unhappy augury for the lyrical spirit of the succeeding age.'[1]

For the present, it may be said that Jonson evidently meant more by 'keeping' than by 'accent.'

Supposing Jonson to have meant what has been understood by so many faint warblers,—and what our examples will prove to be foundationless,—we may, at this point, present other censures which Drummond records, thereby placing the criticism of Donne in its proper setting, and determining the amount of consideration which his alleged censure of Donne would deserve.

Beginning on page 2, of the *Conversations:* 'Spenser's stanzas pleased him not, nor his matter . . . Samuel Daniel was a good man . . . but no poet. That Michael Drayton's . . . long verses pleased him not. That Silvester's translation of Du Bartas was not well done; . . . Nor that of Fairfax his. . . (p. 3) That Done for not keeping of accent deserved hanging. That Shakespeer wanted arte. (p. 4) That Sharpham, Day, Dicker were all rogues; and that Minshew was one. That Abram Francis, in his English Hexameters, was a foole. That next himself, only Fletcher and Chapman could make a mask. . . (p. 5) That Bonefonius Vigilium Veneris was excellent. . . (p. 7) That [my verses] were all good especiallie my Epitaphe of the Prince, save that it smelled too much of the Schooles [Greek and Latin]; . . . yett that he wished, to please the King, that piece of Forth Feasting had been his own. (p. 8) He esteemeth John Done the first poet in the world in some things: his verses of the Lost Chaine he heth by heart; and that passage of the Calme, *That dust and feathers doe not stirr, all was so quiet.* . . . Sir Edward (Henry) Watton's verses of a happy lyfe, he hath by heart; and a piece of Chapman's translation of the 13 of the Iliads, which he thinketh well done. That Done said to him, he wrott that Epitaph on Prince Henry, *Look to me, Faith,* to match Sir Ed. Herbert in obscureness. (p. 9) He hath by heart some verses of Spenser's *Calender,* about wyne, between

---

[1] *Eng. Lyr. Poetry,* p. lv.

Coline and Percye... That since [Done] was made Doctor [he] repenteth highlie and seeketh to destroy all his poems... (p. 10) Daniel was at jealousies with him, (Ft. n:... though he bore no ill will on his part). Drayton feared him; and he esteemed him not. That Francis Beaumont loved too much himself and his own verses. That Sir John Roe loved him... He beat Marston, and took his pistoll from him. Sir W. Alexander was not half kinde unto him, and neglected him because a friend to Drayton. That Sir Aiton loved him dearly... That Markham... was not of the number of the Faithfull, i. (e.) Poets, and but a base fellow. (p. 12) That such were Day and Middleton. That Chapman and Fletcher were loved of him. Overby was his friend and turn'd his mortall enemie... (p. 15) That Done himself, for not being understood would perish. That Sir W. Raughley esteemed more of fame than of conscience... (p. 16) Marston wrott his Father-in-lawes preachings, and his Father-in-law his comedies. Shakespear, in a play, brought in a number of men saying they had suffered shipwrack in Bohemia, wher ther is no sea neer by some 100 miles. Daniel wrott Civill Warres, and yett hath not one batle in all his book. The Countess of Rutland was nothing inferior to her Father Sir P. Sidney in poesie... (p. 17) Flesher and Beaumont ten yeers since, hath written the Faithful Shipheardesse, a Tragi-comedie, well done... Sir P. Sidney was no pleasant man in countenance, his face being spoiled with pimples... (p. 19) He was Master of Arts in both the Universities, by their favour, not his studie. He married a wife who was a shrew, yet honest... (p. 22) He heth consumed a whole night in lying looking to his great toe, about which he hath seen Tartars and Turks, Romans and Carthaginians, feight in his imagination. ... (p. 24) Salisbury never cared for any man longer nor he could make use of him... (p. 26) That verses stood by sense without either colours or accent; *which yet other tymes he denied...* (p. 32) What is that, the more you out of it groweth still the longer—A ditch... (p. 35) He said to me that I was too good and simple, and that oft a man's modestie made a fool of his witt... (p. 36) Tailor was sent along here to scorn him... Joseph Hall the harbenger to Done's Anniversarie... (p. 37) [He said] *They* is still the nominative, *those* accusative, *them* newter... [That] He was better versed and knew more in Greek and Latin, than all the Poets in England, and quintessence their braines... Of all styles he loved most to be named Honest, and hath of that ane hundreth letters so naming him... (p. 38) He went... homeward the 25 of January 1619, in a pair of shoes which, he told, lasted him since he came from Darnton...'

Drummond concludes (pp. 40–41) '*He [Jonson] is a great lover and praiser of himself; a contemner and scorner of others; given rather to loose a friend than a jest... His inventions are smooth and easie; but above all he excelleth in a Translation.*'

Laing (p. 5) cites Gifford[1] (i, cxxiv) as quoting Drummond's remarks and saying, 'it is observable that every addition by Drummond is tinctured with spleen...'; but Drummond's conclusions are so in keeping with the conversations that he need not have given them.

We have faithfully presented enough of the critical portions of the *Conversations* to show their general trend. Some bits of gossip are also admitted as showing what Drummond regarded as worth recording. Some things are omitted which are quite as vulgar as any line to be found in the worst of Donne's poetry,—and be it remembered, Donne's ugly poetry was no more intended to be printed and preserved than were Jonson's conversations.

---

[1] In Gifford's 'Memoir,' i, xliii (*The Works of Ben Jonson*, edited by Lieut. Col. Francis Cunningham, London, 1870), under 'Heads of Conversations, &c.,' all that Jonson said of Donne is quoted, except the censure 'for not keeping of accent,' which is neither mentioned nor referred to. On p. 474, however, it is restored to its place and commented upon. After the quotations (p. xliii) Gifford concludes (p. xliv): 'Such are the remarks of Jonson on his contemporaries: set down [by Drummond] in malice, abridged without judgment, and published without shame.'

Saintsbury (*A History of Criticism*. London and Edinburgh, 1902, ii, 199, note) takes a more rational view of the matter: 'The dicta, thus juxtaposed, should make all argument about apparently one-sided judgments superfluous. If Drummond had omitted the first ['for not keeping of accent deserved hanging'] or the last ['the first poet in the land in some things'] we should have been utterly wrong in arguing from the remainder.

Chambers remarks, 'It has been thought that there was some jealously between the two poets, and that the allusion to the Countess of Bedford's "better verser" in Jonson's Epistle to the Countess of Rutland, is a hit at Donne. Probably, however, Daniel is the "verser" referred to.'[1]

It seems wholly unnecessary to undertake to establish any reason or excuse for Jonson's remarks to Drummond, seeing that he mentions Donne oftener than any other, and always with compliment, except in the one instance cited. Should we fail to prove what we believe he meant by that censure, we have yet two alternatives upon which to rest. One is that Drummond made the suggestion and Jonson, his guest, half-willingly agreed to it;[2] the other, that Jonson had just 'awoke' from gazing all night towards his great toe.

Drummond (1619):

'Donne, among the Anacreontick lyrics, is second to none, and far from all second; but as Anacreon doth not approach Callimachus, tho' he excels in his own kind, nor Horace to Virgil, no more can I be brought to think him to excel either Alexander's or Sidney's verses: They can hardly be compared together trading diverse paths; the one flying swift, but low, the other, like the eagle, surpassing the clouds. I think, if he would, he might easily be the best Epigrammatist we have found in English; of which I have not yet seen any come near the Ancients. Compare the Song *Marry and Love* [*Thy Flavia*] with Tasso's stanzas about beauty; one shall hardly know who hath the best.'[3]

This view is interesting as showing that Jonson's dicta had no influence upon a better versifier than himself.

Dryden's remark, in the preface to *Eleanor* (1692), 'Doctor Donne, the greatest wit, though not the best poet of our nation, etc.' is quoted by Grosart (ii, xxxiv), Gosse (ii, 350), and many others, some of whom comment upon it.

---

[1] E. K. Chambers, *Poems of John Donne*, 2 vols., London and New York, ii, 224, Note. Hereafter cited as Chambers.

[2] Barrett Wendell, *The Temper of the Seventeenth Century in English Literature*, New York, 1904, p. 118: 'Whether this emphasis came of Jonson's own motion or because of questions from Drummond, we can never know.'

[3] *Conversations*, p. 50.

James Russell Lowell says, 'Dryden, with his wonted perspicacity follows Jonson' in this opinion, and that 'he [Dryden] shows little of that finer instinct which suggests so much more than it tells, and works the more powerfully as it taxes more the imagination of the reader . . .'[1]

Hartley Coleridge, after quoting the same from Dryden, adds: 'I cannot think that Donne as a wit was at all to be compared to Butler . . . But Donne was an impassioned poet—Butler only a profound wit.'[2]

Dryden's next criticism (1693) is more to our purpose:

'Would not Donne's Satires, which abound with so much wit, appear more charming if he had taken care of his words and his numbers? But he followed Horace so very close, that of necessity he must fall with him; and I may safely say it of this present age, that, if we are not so great wits as Donne, yet, certainly, we are better poets.'[3]

If Dryden was also speaking for himself, may it not be asked, If he was a better poet than Donne, why did he need, in his *Eleanora*, to copy Donne to such an extent as to make an acknowledgement, in the preface, imperative? 'I have followed [Donne's] footsteps in the design of his panegyric, [*An Anatomy*].'[4]

The next criticism bears about equally upon matter and metre, and may be presented in the language of Gosse (ii, 350, 361):

'When, in a regrettable passage of undiluted eulogy, Dryden wished to flatter Lord Dorset to the top of his bent, he told him that Donne alone, of all the English poets, had equalled him in talent, and that even the Dean of St. Paul's "was not happy enough to arrive at [Dorset's] versification." Again, that laudation may reach its acme, Dryden declares that Dorset "equals Donne in the variety, multiplicity, and choice of thoughts, and excels him in the manner and the words. I read you both with the same admiration." This is tantamount to saying that especially in the department of "wit", Dryden admired Donne more than he admired any other British poet. And this more than

---

[1] *Among my Books*, cited by Grosart, ii, xxxiv.
[2] *Essays and Marginalia*, ed. by Derwent Coleridge, London, 1851, ii, 47.
[3] *Essay on Satire*, prefixed to 'Juvenal,' 1693, cited by Gosse, ii, 350.
[4] *Ibid.*, ii, 350.

sixty years after Donne's death, and across more than one complete revolution in taste and literary fashion! For those who were sagacious enough to read between the lines, and discount the flattery of Dorset, this was praise for Donne of an extraordinary quality. He has never since found an admirer so strenuous among critics of a like authority with Dryden.'

It is noteworthy that, while Dryden thought Donne's Satires would have appeared more charming (and this means that he thought them charming anyhow), he had better judgment than to undertake to Pope them, or to Parnell them.

Gosse (ii, 326) suggests that it was 'somewhere about 1717' that the Earl of Oxford and the Duke of Shrewsbury 'commended the *Satires* of Donne to the revising hand of Pope and Parnell.'

Goldsmith, Gilfillan, and the various other biographers of Parnell do not give a date for his 'versifying' of Donne's third Satire; but Parnell and Pope were together, at Bath, in 1715, when they probably talked over the project, which was carried out,—Parnell's part at least,—soon afterward, for he died in 1718.

Parnell has left no reason for taking part in this affair, beyond the title which he gives to his production: 'Dr. Donne's third Satire *Versified.*'[1] Pope's title is: 'The Satires of Dr. John Donne *Versified.*'[1]

When we come to consider Pope in connection with this matter, it will appear that Parnell was merely an instrument in the hands of his younger but stronger fellow-versifier.

It may be noted, in passing, that Parnell, in his version of this Satire, frequently places the particles (articles, conjunctions, and prepositions) in position to receive the ictus; furthermore, we meet such accents as the following, which were, no doubt, and which *are*, certainly, objected to in Donne:

    53. Seek thou Religion *primitívely* sound.

    153. For every *contrarý* in such degree.

    137. Nor were submission *humbleness* exprest.

    139. Power *fróm* above, *subordinátely* spread.

---

[1] The Italics are mine.

Notwithstanding such accents, however, Goldsmith says of Parnell,[1] 'His poetical language is not less correct than his subjects[2] are pleasing. He found it at that period at which it was brought to its highest pitch of refinement.'

Of this performance Norton remarks:

'In Parnell's hands this Satire (III.), one of the most direct, serious, and masculine of Donne's poems, full of real emotion and the expression of sincere conviction, becomes a piece of artificial diction, feeble in substance and poor in form.'[3]

Gilfillan, speaking generally of Parnell's poetry, says it 'is slipshod, easy, and pleasing.'[4]

Campbell, also speaking of the whole body of Parnell's verse, says ' . . . Its tone is peculiarly delightful: not from mere correctness of expression to which some critics have stinted its praises, but from the graceful and reserved sensibility that accompanied his polished phraseology.'[5]

According to Coleridge, this Satire (III.) needed no 'versifying':

'If you would teach a scholar in the highest form how to *read*, take Donne, and of Donne this Satire (III.). When he has learned to read Donne, with all the force and meaning which are involved in the words, then send him to Milton, and he will stalk-on like a master, *enjoying* his walk.'[6]

Pope's 'versifying' of Donne's *Satires* (II. and IV.) will ever stand as proof that even a great man can do a little, mean thing.

Examining the evidence closely, it appears, First: That, probably, Pope suggested to Parnell, at Bath, or elsewhere, 'You

---

[1] *The Works of Oliver Goldsmith*, ed. by Peter Cunningham, London, 1854, vol. iv ('Life of Parnell,' pp. 127-146, reprint of 1770), p. 141.

[2] Mitford, 'Life of Parnell', in the *The Poetical Works* of Thomas Parnell, (Aldine ed.) London, 1866, p. 52, quoting Goldsmith says, '... than his *couplets* are pleasing.'

[3] Charles Eliot Norton, *The Poems of John Donne*, 2 vols. (From the text of the ed. of 1633, revised by James Russell Lowell), ed. for the Grolier Club, New York, 1895, i, xxv. Hereafter cited as Norton.

[4] *The Poetical Works of Johnson, Parnell, Gray and Smollet*, ed. by George Gilfillan, New York, 1855, p. 89.

[5] *Specimens of the British Poets*, Thomas Campbell, London, 1819, iv, 409.

[6] *Notes Theological, Political and Miscellaneous*, quoted by Grosart, ii, xliv.

versify Donne's third Satire, and I will versify the second and fourth.' This was in order that he might have a 'divine' to share with him whatever of blame might attach to the performance. That Pope could and did use Parnell is borne out by many letters and references. Two will suffice here:

'When Pope had a Miscellany to publish, he applied to Parnell for poetical assistance, and the latter as implicitly submitted to him for correction.'[1]

When Pope was being assisted, by Parnell, in his translation of Homer, he wrote to him, 'My business depends entirely upon you . . . , Dear Sir, not only as you are a friend and a good natured man, but as you are a Christian and a divine, come back speedily, and prevent the increase of my sins; for at the rate I have begun to rave, I shall not only damn all poets and commentators who have gone before, but be damned myself by all who come after me.'[2]

Second: Pope published his 'Imitations' to satisfy a grievance; and selected Donne as an example of 'so eminent a divine' as showing 'with what indignation and contempt a Christian may treat vice or folly, in ever so low, or ever so high a station.'[3]

Third: Pope declares that he 'versified' Donne's Satires at the desire of the Earl of Oxford and of the Duke of Shrewsbury,[4]—the integrity of which *declaration* has been questioned.[5]

Fourth: Dr. Johnson says, 'Pope seems to have known their imbecility, and therefore suppressed them while he was yet contending to rise in reputation, but ventured them when he thought their deficiencies more likely to be imputed to Donne than to himself.'[6]

Pope's editor (same page) defends his imitation of *Satire* IV. against the 'contemptious treatment it received from Johnson'. This would indicate that his editor thought the imitation of *Satire* II. deserved such treatment. His argument, in Pope's defense, is

---

[1] Goldsmith, *op. cit.*, p. 139.
[2] *The Works of the British Poets*, Robert Anderson, M. D., London, 1795, vii, iv.
[3] *The Works of Alexander Pope*, new ed. Elwin and Courthope, London, 1881, iii, 287.
[4] *Ibid.*, 287.   [5] *Ibid.*, 424.   [6] *Ibid.*, 424.

that if these imitations had been executed immediately on the suggestion of Lord Oxford and the Duke of Shrewsbury they would have been 'published in the first volume of his collected works (1717)'.

When we remember that the second of these was not published till 1733, and then anonymously 'By an Eminent Hand,'[1]—that they were not printed as Pope's till their authorship became known in the quarto volume of 1735,—and, that, according to Warburton,[2] they were versified long before they were published, —we are constrained to accept the suggestions of Pope's editor[3] as to revisions in the lines (to bring them down to the date of publication), and that 'the poet, who had no scruples' confided to Warburton the whole truth which had not been published in the 'Advertisement'. This seems to point back, very definitely, to 1615-1618, when Parnell also 'versified'.

Fifth: In *Satire* II. 'Versified', Pope deliberately covers up one of his tracks. Line 68 of *Windsor Forest* reads,

'The hollow winds through naked temples roar.'[4]

In a foot-note, Wakefield, without comment, quotes Donne, *Sat.* II, 60,

'Than when winds in our ruin'd abbeys roar.'

Turning to Pope's *Sat.*, II, 62, 'Versified', we find,

'More rough than forty Germans when they scold.'[5]

In a foot-note, on *this* line, the editor says,
'Donne's verse is,

"Than when winds in our ruin'd abbeys roar,"

a reflection on the destruction of the Monasteries. Pope alters this to introduce a sneer against the King's countrymen.'

The editor is *inexcusably* mistaken as to the line altered, which is line 59, in Donne.

[1] *Ibid.*, 425.   [2] *Ibid.*, 424.   [3] *Ibid.*, 425.
[4] *Ibid.*, i, 344.   [5] *Ibid.*, iii, 429.

'More, more, than ten Sclavonians scolding more.'

Line 60, one of the most characteristic, poetic, and beautiful lines ever written by Donne, Pope appropriated, and so he alters it in his 'Versified' *Satire* by leaving it out.

The evidence of another, but less successful, performance of this kind leaves no room to doubt that it was deliberate in both instances.

In the *Essay on Man*, IV, 39-42, we read,

> There's not a blessing individuals find,
> But some way leans and harkens to its kind;
> No bandit fierce, no tyrant mad with pride,
> No caverned hermit rests self-satisfied.

The editor gives this foot-note: 'The image is drawn from a person leaning towards another and listening to what he says. Pope took the expression from the simile of the compasses in Donne's Songs and Sonnets:

> " And though it in the centre sit,
>   Yet when the other far doth roam,
> It leans and harkens after it,
>   And grows erect as that comes home."'

The editor then gives the Manuscript reading of the eight lines following line 40, but does not call attention to the fact that the original is much nearer to Donne than the printed lines. Putting lines 39 and 40, of the printed copy, with 41 and 42 of the manuscript, Donne's compasses stand up partially restored, at least with the rivet replaced:

> There's not a blessing individuals find,
> But some way leans and hearkens to its kind;
> 'Tis not in self it can begin and end,
> The bliss of one must with another blend.

Sixth: Pope's purpose could not have been to make Donne 'nicer' reading. (See Donne, *Sat.* IV, 109-111, and Pope, IV, 153-4.) The first is bad enough, the second worse.

Seventh: If by 'Versifying' Donne, Pope meant to show his disapproval of the word-accents employed by the former, why such lines as these:

Satire II.

2. This town, I had the sense to hate it *tóo*.
8. It brought (no doubt) the Excise and Army *ín*.
35. I pass o'er all those *Cónfessórs* and martyrs: Charters.
44. In what commandment's large *conténts* they dwell.
49. And brings all *nátural* events to pass.
52. More pert, more proud, more *posítive* than he.
59. Call *hímsélf barríster* to every wench.
90. Satan *hímself* feels far less joy than they.
72. He starves with cold to save them *fróm* the fire.
75. For you he sweats and labours *át* the laws.
83. In shillings *ánd* in pence at first they deal.
92. Glean *ón*, and gather *úp* the whole estate.
94. Indentures, covenants, *árticlés* they draw,
102. O'er *a* learn'd, *unintélligible* place.
109. The lands are bought; but where are *tó* be found.
114. The good old landlord's *hospítable* door.

Satire IV.

2. Adieu to all the follies *óf* the age.
19. So was I punished, *ás* if full as proud.
31. Nay, all that lying *travélers* can feign.
60. With royal *favorítes* in flattery vie.
103. He dwells amidst the royal *famíly*: I.

110. "How *elegánt* your Frenchmen!" "Mine, d'ye mean?"
125. New eunuchs, harlequins, and *óperás*: plays.
135. Or quickened *á* reversion *bý* a drug.
137. And whether *tó* a bishop *ór* a whore.
149. What squire his lands, what *citizén* his wife.
159. Silence or hurt, he libels *thé* great man.
175. Stood just a-tilt, the *ministér* came by.
178. Not Fannius self more *impudéntly* near.
179. When half his nose is *ín* his Prince's ear.
196. Shall I the terror *óf* this sinful town.
207. It ought to bring all courtiers *ón* their backs.
225. And all in splendid *povérty* at best.
226. Painted for sight, and essenced *fór* the smell.
236. 'Twould burst e'en Hereclitus *wíth* the spleen.
252. Sweeter than Sharon, *ín* immaculate trim.
253. Neatness itself *impertínent* in him.
267. As Herod's hangdogs in old *tapéstry* : awry.
272. Frighted, I quit the room; but leave it *so:* go.

Should the point be raised that, as Pope was paraphrasing, it was impossible to rid the lines of all Donne's secondary accents, the examples in our Chapter II, will show that he exercised even as great freedom, in this respect, in his other productions.

Eighth: If Pope was sincere in *An Essay on Criticism*, he did not object to the so-called 'roughness,' or 'harshness' in Donne. Hear him (338-357):

'But most by numbers judge a poet's song,
And smooth or rough, with them, is right or wrong:

In the bright muse, though thousand charms conspire,
Her voice is all these tuneful fools admire;
Who haunt Parnassus but to please their ear,
Not mend their minds; as some to church repair
Not for the doctrine, but the music there.
These equal syllables alone require,
Tho' oft the ear the open vowels tire;
While expletives their feeble aid do join;
And ten low words oft creep in one dull line:
While they ring round the same unvaried chimes,
With sure returns of still expected rhymes;
Where'er you find "the cooling western breeze,"
In the next line, it "whispers through the trees:"
If crystal streams "with pleasing murmurs creep,"
The readers threatened, not in vain, with "sleep:"
Then, at the last and only couplet fraught
With some unmeaning thing they call a thought,
A needless Alexandrine ends the song,
That, like a wounded snake, drags its slow length along.'

One familiar with Donne's heroic verse, meeting these lines for the first time, would believe them written in his defense.

Even more decided are some earlier lines in this *Essay*, (233-236):

'A perfect judge will read each work of wit
With the same spirit that its author writ:
Survey the whole, nor seek slight faults to find
Where nature moves, and rapture warms the mind.'

We may now present a few opinions of Pope's 'translations' of Donne.

John Done: 'It is plain Roguerie to discurte or mispoint [another's] writings.'[1]

Gosse (ii, 351-2): 'It is easy to see that Pope, while far too

---

[1] *Polydoron*, 1631, p. 88. While this was said before Pope's day, it is a universal truth.

acute not to perceive the masculine force of Donne, was completely out of sympathy with his style. He was even more conscious than Dryden had been of the rugosities of Donne's metre, and he was incapable of appreciating any method in satire except that of polished and pointed antithesis . . . Where the diction of Pope is richest and most idiomatic we see, or may think we see, the suffused influence of the Dean of St. Paul's . . .'

Warburton: ' . . . Our Poet hath admirably *versified*, as he expresses it, two or three [?] Satires of Dr. Donne.'[1]

Warton: 'Pope succeeded in giving harmony to a writer, more rough and rugged than any of his age, and who profited so little by the example Spenser has set, of a most musical and mellifluous versification. . .'[2]

Arnold: 'The satires of Donne and Hall (the first of which received the honour of modernization from Pope) are too rough and harsh to have much poetic value.'[3]

Grosart (i, xxviii, xxix): 'One of the "Curiosities of Literature" more fantastically curious than any in D'Israeli, is, that Pope and Parnell reversified the Satires of Donne. I know not that I can do better than allow here an openeyed writer (the late Dr. Samuel Brown of Edinburg, I believe) to put the thing as follows:[4]

'Pope took it upon himself to "improve" some of Donne's Satires; and he did it, but in much the same style as the sailor, who, having obtained a curiosity in the form of the weapon of a sword-fish, "improved" it by scraping off and rubbing down all the protuberances by which it was distinguishable from any other bone. Fortunately, however, in most editions of Pope's writings, the original crudities [!] are printed side by side with the polished improvement upon them; as sometimes we see, uphung in triumph at the doors of writing-masters, pairs of documents to some such effect as this: I. "This is my handwriting *before* taking lessons of Mr. Pope. Signed, John Donne." II. "This is my hand-

---

[1] *Pope's Works*, iii, 424.
[2] *Ibid.*, 424.
[3] Thos. Arnold, *Manual of English Literature*, London, 1867, p. 393.
[4] Furst (*op. cit.*, p. 25) gives an extract from the same.

writing *after* taking lessons of Mr. Pope. Signed, John Donne"
...'[1]

Grosart concludes (p. xxx), 'Few will differ from this drastic verdict; and, indeed, apart from Elwin's demonstration of the rottenness of Pope as a man, it were easy to prove, by the improvements on Donne and the like, that, while a matchless Verser, he was no Poet in any deep sense of the much abused word.'

Coleridge: 'Read them [the Satires] as Donne meant them to be read, and as sense and passion demand, and you will find in the lines a manly harmony.'[2]

Norton quotes the first four lines of Satire II., and remarks, 'Pope, translating this into more flowing lines vulgarizes it ...'[3]

Having lingered thus long with Pope and Parnell, because the subject seemed to demand it, we may now go forward more rapidly.

Niceron (1729):

'Ces Poësies qu'il Jean Donne composa à l'âge de 18 ans sont pleines d'esprit. Une partie e été traduite en *Flamand* par Constantin Hugonius, à la solicitation du Roi Charles II. qui croyoit que le stil e de *Donne* etoit inimitable à l'égard des Hollandois & des Allemans.'[4]

Theobald (1733):

'The ostentatious Affectations of obstruse Learning, peculiar to that Time, the Love that Men naturally have to every Thing that looks like Mystery, fixed them down to this Habit of Obscurity. Thus became the Poetry of Donne (tho' the wittiest Man of that Age) nothing but a continued Heap of Riddles.'[5]

---

[1] Grosart quotes from *Gallery of Poets*: No. 1, 'John Donne,' in Lowes' *Edinburgh Magazine*, vol. i., pp. 228–236.

[2] *Lectures and Notes on Shakespeare and other English Poets*, collected by Th. Ashe, London, 1883, p. 427. Quoted by Norton, i, 220.

[3] *Ibid.*, xxv.

[4] Jean Pierre Niceron, *Memoires des Hommes Illustres*, Paris, 1729, viii, 151.
This statement follows a reference to Donne's *Juvenilia or Certaine Paradoxes and Problemes*, 1633.

[5] Mr. Theobald, *The Works of Shakspeare*, London, 1733, i, xlvi. (Referred to but not quoted by *Retrospective Review*, viii, 31.)

To which the *Retrospective Review* replies (viii, 31): 'Theobald, in his egregious preface to Shakspeare, calls Donne's Poems "nothing but a continued heap of riddles." We shall presently show that he knew as little about Donne as he himself has shown that he knew about Shakspeare.'

Hume (1759):

'In Donne's satires, when carefully inspected, there appear some flashes of wit and ingenuity; but these totally suffocated and burried, by the hardest and most uncouth expression that is anywhere to be met with...

'Jonson possessed all the learning which was wanting in Shakespeare, and wanted all the genius of which the other was possessed. Both of them were equally deficient in taste and elegance, in harmony and correctness.'[1]

Coleridge alone excepted, it is possible that no one, in his writings, ever referred to Donne oftener than Dr. Samuel Johnson. His 'Life of Cowley' has the appearance of a picture painted with Donne as a background. The following is a fair example of Johnson's opinion of Donne, expressed of him individually:

'It was the same admirable critic [Johnson] who observes that, if Donne was "upon common subjects unnecessarily and unpoetically subtle, yet where scholastic speculation can be properly admitted, his copiousness and acuteness may justly be admired."'[2]

Several times, in connection with the Metaphysical [?] School, Donne's verse is harshly criticised by Johnson. A representative expression is this:

'The metaphysical poets were men of learning, and to show their learning was their whole endeavor; but, unluckily resolving to show it in rhyme, instead of writing poetry they only wrote verses, and very often such verses, as stood the trial of the finger better than the ear; for the modulation was so imperfect, that they were only found to be verses by counting the syllables.'[3]

---

[1] David Hume, *The History of England*, new ed., London, 1841, iv, 389, 390.

Norton (i, xxiv) quotes the criticism of Donne, but not of Shakespeare and Jonson, which is here given, because our Chapter II. is, in a manner, a comparative study.

[2] Gosse, *op. cit.*, ii, 342.

[3] 'Life of Cowley,' Chalmers, *Eng. Poets*, vii, 12.

Elsewhere he says: 'Though the following lines of Donne on the last night of the year [' *The twilight of two years, etc.*'] have something in them too scholastick, they are not inelegant.'[1]

Anderson (1795):

'All [Donne's] contemporaries are lavish in his praise. Prejudiced, perhaps, by the style of writing which was then fashionable, they seem to have rated his performances beyond their just value. To the praise of wit and subtilty his title is unquestionable. In all his pieces he displays a prodigious richness of fancy and elaborate minuteness of description; but his thoughts are seldom natural, obvious, or just, and much debased by the carelessness of his versification.'[2]

Southey (1807):

'Donne could never have become a poet, unless Apollo taking his ears under his divine care, would have wrought as miraculous change in their external structure, as of old he wrought in the external of those of Midas. The power of versifying is a distinct talent, and a metrical ear has little more connexion with intellect than a musical one. Of this Donne is a sufficient example.'[3]

Norton, citing the same volume and page, quotes the first sentence above, as follows:

'Nothing indeed could have made Donne a poet, unless as great a change had been wrought in the structure of his ears as was wrought in the elongation of those of Midas.'[4]

To which he replies, 'Surely it could only be the ears of Midas himself that would not find music and poetry in,—

"Little think'st thou, poor flower,"
(&c. quoting eight lines.)

'And in *The Relic* there is a metrical felicity which corresponds with the intimate poetic sentiment and gives perfect expression to it:

---

[1] *The Works of Samuel Johnson*, a new ed.; edited by Arthur Murphy, London, 1810, ix, 25.
[2] *British Poets*, ed. by Robert Anderson, M. D., London, 1795, iv, 4–5.
[3] *Specimens of the Later English Poets*, ed. by Robert Southey, London, 1807, i, xxiv.   [4] Norton, i, xxviii.

"When my grave is broke up again,"'
(&c. quoting nine lines.)

In Southey's awkward sentences his double purpose seems to be to compliment Donne's intellect, or talent, and to condemn the rhythm or metre of his verse. Be it remembered that Southey is extremely nice in his distinctions, as on page iii, 'I have said "*it is certain* that Chaucer wrote rhythmically rather than metrically, etc."'

Chalmers (1810):

'Donne's numbers, if they may be so called, are certainly the most rugged and uncouth of any of our poets. He appears either to have had no ear, or to have been utterly regardless of harmony. Yet Spenser preceded him, and Drummond, the first polished versifer, was his contemporary; but it must be allowed that before Drummond appeared, Donne had relinquished his pursuit of the Muses, nor would it be just to include the whole of his poetry under the general censure which has been usually passed. Dr. Warton seems to think that if he had taken pains he might not have proved so inferior to his contemporaries; but what inducement could he have to take pains, as he published nothing, and seems not desirous of public fame? He was certainly not ignorant or unskilled in the higher attributes of style, for he wrote elegantly in Latin, and displays considerable taste in some of his smaller pieces and epigrams.'[1]

Aikin (1811):

'Donne is so rugged a versifier, that scarcely any of his productions are reducible to regular measure without some alteration. His language, also, is generally far from elegant or refined, and his thoughts are extremely strained and artificial. The foregoing piece [*The Message*], however, has not required much correction to entitle it to a distinguished place among ingenious songs.'[2]

Aikin simply changes the strophic form from eight to six lines, probably to make it suit some song-scheme he had in mind. A skilful musician to whom the original and altered forms were recently submitted expressed a decided preference for the original.

---

[1] Chalmers, *English Poets*, London, 1810, v, 124.
[2] John Aikin, *Vocal Poetry*, Boston, 1811, p. 231, note.

It is really amusing to see how successfully Donne anticipated his critics. One wonders if Dr. Aikin ever read these lines:

> Some man his voice and art to show,
> Doth set and sing my pain.
> *The Triple Fool*, 13–14.

Campbell (1819):

In a brief introduction (pp. 73–4) to three poems, and a part of another, which he presents as specimens of Donne's verse, Campbell ventures the courageous opinion, 'The life of Donne is more interesting than his poetry.'[1]

Sanford (1819):

'Donne is considered as a great wit, a tolerable divine, and something of a poet. Poetry, indeed, in the highest sense of the word, we can almost say, he had none . . . Of Donne, it may be said, that he was more witty than learned; and more learned than poetical.'[2]

Retrospective Review (viii, 31,–1823–):

'[Donne was] imbued with . . . a mode of expression singularly terse, simple and condensed—an exquisite ear for the melody of versification—and a wit, admirable as well for its caustic severity as its playful quickness . . .'

On p. 51, the *Review* quotes *Elegy XVII* ('By our first strange and fatal interview'), with the comment:

'There is a solemn and sincere earnestness about it, which will cause it to be read with great interest, even by those who may not be capable of appreciating, in detail, the rich and pompous flow of the verse, and the fine harmony of its music; the elegant simplicity of the language; and the extreme beauty of some of the thoughts and images.'

De Quincy (1828):

'Few writers have shown a more extraordinary compass of powers than Donne; for he combined, what no other man has ever done—the last sublimation of dialectical subtlety and address

---

[1] Campbell, *op. cit.*, iii, 73.
[2] Sanford and Walsh, *British Poets*, Philadelphia, 1819, iv, 137.

with the most impassioned majesty. Massy diamonds compose the very substance of his poem on the Metempsychosis, thoughts and descriptions which have the fervent and gloomy sublimity of Ezekiel or Æschylus, whilst a diamond-dust of rhetorical brilliances is showered over the whole of his occasional verses and his prose. No criticism was ever more unhappy than that of Dr. Johnson, which denounces all this artificial display as so much perversion of taste. There cannot be a falser thought than this; for, upon that principle, a whole class of compositions might be vicious, by conforming to its ideal.'[1]

Jameson (1829):

'What is good [in Donne] is the result of truth, of passion, of a strong mind, and a brilliant wit: what is bad, is the effect of a most perverse taste, and a total want of harmony.'[2]

This criticism follows a quotation of the first two lines of Coleridge's celebrated 'dromedary' quatrain, which she misconstrues (for I can never believe it was meant in the nature of a harsh criticism), and which must have influenced her to some extent, for on pages 103-4-5, *Elegy XVII. Elegy on his Mistress* is quoted, with this comment:

'I would not have the heart of one who could read these lines, and think only on their rugged style, and faults of expression.'

The further Mrs. Jameson gets from Coleridge's lines, the tenderer she grows towards Donne: (p. 108) 'Among Donne's earlier poetry may be distinguished the following little song,[3] which has so much more harmony and elegance than his other pieces, that it is scarcely a specimen of his style. It was long popular, and I can remember when a child, hearing it sung to very beautiful music.'

---

[1] 'On Whateley's Rhetoric,' *Blackwood's Mag.*, Dec., 1828, vol. xxiv, pp. 892-3, quoted by Grosart, ii, xxxix, and referred to by Gosse, i, 139. (One feature of DeQuincy's criticism, which is not noticed by either Grosart or Gosse, will be presented in Chapter III.)

[2] Mrs. Anna Murphy Jameson: *Memoirs of the Loves of the Poets*, 2nd. ed., London, 1831, vol. ii, (pp. 94-109: 'Story of Dr. Donne and His Wife.'), p. 95.

[3] *The Message.*

Coleridge (1811-1834).[1]

Grosart (ii. xxxviii) observes, 'Coleridge, (*the* Coleridge) has almost to superlative, marked out the greatness of Donne's thought. "After all," he says, in annotating 'Woman's Constacy,' "there is but one Donne. And now tell me yet wherein, in *his own kind*, he differs from the similar power in Shakespeare? Shakespeare was all men potentially, except Milton; and they differ from him by negation, or privation, or both."'

Usually, however, Coleridge's remarks bear more directly upon the metre of Donne's verse.

Gosse (i, 282) publishes for the first time Coleridge's note, written in 1811, on *Song*: ('Sweetest love I do not go'),—'This beautiful and perfect poem proves by its title "*Song*," that *all* Donne's Poems are equally metrical (misprints allowed for), tho' *smoothness*, that is to say, the metre necessitating the proper reading, be deemed appropriate to *Songs*; but, in Poems where the Author *thinks*, and expects the Reader to do so, the sense must be understood in order to ascertain the metre.'

A part of this opinion seems to have remained fixed in the mind of Coleridge:

'To read Dryden, Pope, etc., you need only count syllables; but to read Donne you must measure *time*, and discover the time of each word by the sense of the passion ... In poems where the writer *thinks*, and expects the reader to do so, the sense must be understood to understand the metre.'[2]

About another opinion, if opinion it may be called, Grosart (i, xi) raises a question. It is the following quatrain, usually quoted from Coleridge, without initials, and with the statement that he wrote it in *a* (sometimes *his*) copy of Donne:

---

[1] Coleridge (S. T.) mentions Donne so frequently that it would be difficult to fix the date of each utterance. Especially is this true with reference to those MSS. not published till some years after his death. The date '1811-1834' is so put down, because the earliest recorded expression was written in 1811, and he seems to have continued to admire and to defend Donne up to the year of his death, 1834.

[2] *Notes Theological, &c.*, 1853, pp. 249-50. Quoted by Norton, i, xxx.

> 'With Donne, whose muse on dromedary trots,
> Wreathe iron pokers into true love-knots;
> Rhyme's sturdy cripple, fancy's maze and clue,
> Wit's forge and fire-blast, meaning's press and screw.'[1]

After speaking of Coleridge's 'somewhat paradoxical theory of Donne's measures and accentuations,' Grosart adds (i, xi): 'By the way, the name of Coleridge reminds me that even well informed critics and literary authorities, *e. g.*, Mrs. Jameson in her 'Loves of the Poets,' and Lieut. Col. Cunningham in his edition of the Works of Ben Johnson, and others, continually quote the empty burlesque lines on Donne of *Hartley* Coleridge, as *the* Coleridge's, in the teeth of the latter's abundant expressions of his lofty estimate and love for Donne as a poet.'

It happens that Hartley Coleridge also highly esteemed Donne. We have already quoted his opinion, in discussing Dryden, that 'Donne was an impassioned poet.'

Grosart does not give his authority, and it seems clear that he is mistaken. But for the fact that Cunningham quotes the full quatrain, as above, and Mrs. Jameson the first two lines of it, it might be supposed that Grosart has confused father and son. Hartley Coleridge wrote:

> '[Donne]
> Of stubborn thoughts a garland thought to twine;
> To his fair maid brought cabalistic poses,
> And sung fair ditties of metempsychosis:
> Twists iron pokers into true love-knots,
> Coining hard words not found in polyglots.'[2]

Aside from the more reasonable supposition that Hartley imitated his father,—borrowing one of the lines almost bodily,—instead of writing two sets of lines on the same subject, duplicating one of his own lines,—the matter is settled definitely by Henry Nelson Coleridge, who was familiar with the hand-writing

---

[1] Norton (i, xxvi), quoting this, remarks, 'Even Coleridge, gifted as he was with sensibility and acute critical perceptions, does imperfect justice to its quality [the quality of Donne's verse] in his quatrain.'

[2] W. Davenport Adams, *Dictionary of English Literature*, p. 203.

of both uncle and cousin, and who was the literary executor of his uncle, Samuel Taylor Coleridge.

Accompanying 'Lecture X. Donne—Dante—Milton—Paradise Lost' there is this editorial note: 'Nothing remains of what was said on Donne in this lecture. Here, therefore, as in previous like instances, the gap is filled up with some notes written by Mr. Coleridge in a volume of Chalmers' Poets, belonging to Mr. Gillman. The verses were added in pencil to the collection of commendatory lines.'[1] The editor publishes two sets of lines, designated as 'I' and 'II,' the former the quatrain in question, and with the note: 'No. I, is Mr. C's.'

Cunningham (1836):

'[Donne's] satires are pungent and forcible, but exceedingly rugged and uncouth in their versification... [His sermons] abound in all kinds of learning, and contain many striking thoughts, but are exceedingly rough in style.'[2]

The Penny Cyclopaedia (ix, 85-1837-):

'As a poet, Donne was one of those writers whom Johnson has (to use Wordsworth's expression) "strangely" designated metaphysical poets: a more infelicitous expression could not have well been devised.

'In the biography of Cowley, Johnson has committed an unintentional injustice towards Donne. By representing Cowley's faults as the faults of a school, he brings forward parallel passages from other authors containing like faults, and Donne is one of them. He has previously described the school as a set of cold unfeeling pedants, and hence the reader finding Donne's worst

---

[1] Henry Nelson Coleridge, *The Literary Remains of Samuel Taylor Coleridge*, London, 1836, i, 148. The same may be found in Coleridge's *Complete Works*, ed. by Shedd, iv, 286-7. Campbell (Globe ed., p. 190) prints the quatrain, with the date '? 1818'.

Query: May not Grosart have had in mind Lamb's copy of Donne referred to by Gosse (ii, 335, note) in which Coleridge 'scribbled ... some interesting notes in 1811', and which probably does not contain the quotation? Gosse says, 'This valuable copy is now in the possession of Mr. W. H. Arnold, of New York.' There are several W. H. Arnolds now (1906) living in New York; but none of them own, or ever owned, this copy of Donne.

[2] George Godfrey Cunningham, *Lives of Eminent and Illustrious Englishmen,* Glasgow, 1836, iii, 242.

lines cited in illustration of that remark, may easily imagine that he never did any thing better, and set him down as a mere pedantic rhymer.

'The fact is, that "quaint conceits" are only the deformities of Donne's poetical spirit: the man himself has a rich vein of poetry, which was rarely concealed even when most laboriously encumbered, while some of his pieces, both for thought and even [for?] melody, are absolutely gems. His fault, far from being coldness, is too much erotic fervour: he allows his imagination to run loose into the most prurient expressions; and in some of his amatory pieces, the conceit stands as a corrective to their excessive warmth. His satires, though written in a measure inconceivably harsh, are models of strength and energy. Their merits were discovered by Pope, who (to use his own odd phrase) translated them into English...

'We beg to call the attention of the readers who study the progress of their own language to one fact, and that is, that whilst many of the pieces of Donne, written in lyric measures, are absolute music, what he has composed in the heroic measure is painfully uncouth and barbarous. Thus, though the invention of heroic verses took place at an early period (it is attributed to Chaucer), we find that a language must be in a highly cultivated state before this kind of verse can be written in perfection.'

Craik[1] considers only the last paragraph, above quoted, and with this comment: 'Pope has given us a translation of [Donne's] four[2] Satires into modern language, which he calls *The Satires of Dr. Donne Versified.* Their harshness, as contrasted with the music of his lyrics, has also been referred to as proving that the English language, at the time when Donne wrote, had not been brought to a sufficiently advanced state for the writing of heroic verse in perfection. That this last notion is wholly unfounded, numerous examples sufficiently testify: not to speak of the blank verse of the dramatists, the rhymed heroics of Shakespeare, of

---

[1] Geo. L. Craik, *A Compendious History of English Literature*, &c., London, 1871, p. 579.

[2] A singular slip: Pope *deformed* only two of the Satires (II. and IV.); and Donne is supposed to be the author of seven.

Fletcher, of Johnson, of Spenser, and of other writers contemporary with and of earlier date than Donne, are, for the most part, as perfectly smooth and regular as any that have since been written; at all events, whatever irregularity may be detected in them, if they be tested by Pope's narrow gamut, is clearly not to be imputed to any immaturity in the language. These writers evidently preferred and cultivated, deliberately and on principle, a wider compass, and freer and more varied flow of melody than Pope had a taste or an ear for. Nor can it be questioned, we think, that the peculiar construction of Donne's verse in his satires and many of his other[1] later poems was also adopted on choice and system.'

Drake (1838):

'A more refined age, however, and a more chastised taste, have very justly consigned his [Donne's] poetical labours to the shelf of the philologer. A total want of harmony in versification, and a total want of simplicity both in thought and expression are the vital defects of Donne. Wit he has in abundance, and even erudition, but they are miserably misplaced; and even his amatory pieces exhibit little else than cold conceits and metaphysical subtleties. . .'[2]

Alford (1839):

'This labor of compression [laborious condensation of thought] on his [Donne's] part has tended to make his lines harsh and unpleasing; and the corresponding effort required on the reader's part to follow him, renders most persons insensible to his real merits. That he had and could turn to account a fine musical ear is amply proved by some of . . . his pieces.'[3]

Craik (1845):

'Herbert (Rev. George) was an intimate friend of Donne, and no doubt a great admirer of his poetry; but his own has been to a great extent preserved from the imitation of Donne's peculiar style, into which it might in other circumstances have fallen, in

---

[1] *Satires* and *other later* poems (?).
[2] Nathan Drake, *Shakespeare & His Times*, Paris, 1838, p. 298.
[3] Henry Alford, *Dr. Donne's Works*, London, 1839, i, xxiii.

all probability by its having been composed with little effort or elaboration, and chiefly to relieve and amuse his own mind by the melodious expression of his favorite fancies and contemplations.'[1]

Landor (1846):

> 'Frost-bitten and lumbaginous, when Donne,
> With verses gnarl'd and knotty, hobbled on,
> Thro' listening palaces did rhymeless South
> Pour sparkling waters from his golden mouth.'
>
> *Satirists*, 19–22.

Farr (1847):

['Donne's] great offence appears to be harshness of versification; but admitting that he is frequently rugged and sometimes obscure, this once favourite writer may nevertheless be pronounced to be a true and often delightful poet.'[2]

Cleveland (1852):

'The "Retrospective Review," viii, 31, gives [Donne's] poetry higher praise than we think it deserves...'[3]

Mrs. Thompson[4] (1861):

'He became an admirable preacher, but was more known as a poet than a divine; yet of his poems it has been said:—

> "'Twas then plain Donne in honest vengeance rose,
> His wit harmonious, but his rhyme was prose."[5]

---

[1] Geo. L. Craik, *Sketches of the History of Literature, &c.*, London, 1845; Series II, iv, 17.

[2] Edward Farr, *Select Poetry ... of the Reign of James the First*, Cambridge, 1847, p. xii.

[3] Charles D. Cleveland, *A Compendium of English Literature*, Philadelphia, 1852, p. 166, note.

[4] Mrs. K. B. Thompson, *Celebrated Friendships*, London, 1861, i, 306. ('Magdalen Herbert and Dr. Donne,' pp. 297 ff.)

[5] Mrs. Thompson gives no reference, but she is quoting Dr. John Brown's *Essay on Satire* (Part III, 401-4) addressed to Warburton:

> 'Twas then plain Donne in honest vengeance rose,
> His wit refulgent, though his rhyme was prose;
> He midst an age of puns and pedants wrote
> With genuine sense, and *Roman* strength of thought.

See *Dodsley's Collection*, iii, 335.

'Satire was Donne's forte; but as Dryden observed, his "thoughts were debased by his versification."'

Craik (1861):

'On a superficial inspection, Donne's verses look like so many riddles. They seem to be written upon the principle of making the meaning as difficult to find out as possible,—of using all the resources of language, not to express thought but to conceal it. . .

'But, running through all this bewilderment, a deeper insight detects not only a vein of the most exuberant wit, but often the sunniest and most delicate fancy, and the truest and tenderest feeling. . .

'Donne's later poetry, in addition to the same abundance of originality of thought, often running into a wildness and extravagance not so excusable here as in his erotic verses, is famous for the singular movement of the versification, which has been usually described as the extreme degree of the rugged and the tuneless. . .

'His lines, though they will not suit the see-saw style of reading verse,—to which he probably intended that they should be invincibly impracticable,—are not without a deep and subtle music of their own, in which the cadences respond to the sentiment, when enunciated with a true feeling of all that they convey. They are not smooth and luscious verses, certainly; nor is it contended that the endeavor to raise them to as vigorous and impressive a tone as possible, by depriving them of all over-sweetness or liquidity, has not been carried too far; but we cannot doubt that whatever harshness they have was designedly given to them, and was conceived to infuse into them an essential part of their relish.

'Here is one of Donne's Songs:—

"Sweetest love, I do not go, . . ."

'Somewhat fantastic as this may be thought, it is surely, notwithstanding, full of feeling; and nothing can be more delicate than the execution. Nor is it possible that the writer of such verses can have wanted an ear for melody, however capriciously he may sometimes have experimented upon language, in the effort, as we conceive, to bring a deeper, more expressive music out of it than it would really yield.'¹

Craik is quoted thus at length, here and elsewhere, because it seems that he has approached nearer to an understanding of Donne's principle of versification than any Englishman,—Coleridge alone excepted,—that has yet studied him.

Taine (1864):

'Plusieurs ont du talent néanmoins, Quarles, Herbert, Habington,² surtout Donne, un satirique poignant, d'une crudité terrible, un puissant poëte d'une imagination précise et intense, et qui grande encore quelque chose de l'energie et du frémissement de la première inspiration. Mais il gâte tous ces dons de parti pris, et réussit, à force de peine, à fabriquer du galimatias.'³

While this criticism, '*crudité terrible*,' includes others, besides Donne, and seems pointed at his *Satires*, it comes nearer to touching on the mechanism of his verse than anything else said by Taine.

Arnold (1867):

'As a writer, the great popularity which he [Donne] enjoyed in his own day has long since given way before the repulsive harshness and involved obscurity of his style.'⁴

Macdonald (1868)⁵:

'It is not surprising that, their author [Donne] being so inartistic with regard to their object, his verses themselves should be harsh and unmusical beyond the worst we would imagine fit to be called verse. He enjoys the unenviable distinction of having no rival in ruggedness of metrical movement and associated sounds.

---

[1] Geo. L. Craik, *A Compendious History of Eng. Lit.*, &c., London, 1871, i, 597, 580. (Craik died in 1866. The preface to this work bears the date, 1861, as above.)

[2] Babington.

[3] H. Taine, *Histoire de la Litterature Anglaise*, Paris, 1903, onzième édition, i, 362-3.

[4] Thos. Arnold, *op. cit.*, p. 131.

[5] George Macdonald, *England's Antiphon*, p. 115: Quoted by Grosart, ii, xliii, from p. 116. (Grosart refers indiscriminately to 'Antiphon,' ii, xxxvi, and xlvii, and to 'Dr. Macdonald,' xxxvii, and xxxix. His page reference may be correct. The only available copy here is an edition bearing no date. The date assigned for the criticism is that of the original ed. of the *Antiphon* in England.)

This is clearly the result of indifference; an indifference, however, which grows more strange to us when we find that he *can* write a lovely verse and even an exquisite stanza.'

Grosart fails to note Macdonald's contradiction (p. 113) of the charge of 'indifference' cited above: 'Faulty as they are [Donne's Poems] . . . they are not the less the work of a great and earnest man.'

On *Hymn to God, my God, in my Sickness*, Macdonald comments (p 118): 'The three stanzas together [4, 5, 6] make us lovingly regret that Dr. Donne should have ridden his Pegasus over quarry and housetop, instead of teaching him his paces.'

Quoting *Holy Sonnets*, I., VIII., and X., Macdonald remarks (p. 121): 'Rhymed after the true Petrarchian fashion, their rhythm is often as bad as it can be to be called rhythm at all. Yet these [three] are very fine.'

Corser (1873):

'. . . Donne left English poetry worse than he found it. The Editor is free to confess, along with many others, that Donne as a writer of poetry is no favorite of his. When he considers the pedantry, obscurity and metaphysical conceits introduced into his lighter poetry, the rugged discordant diction, and inharmonious versification of his Satires, and the dullness and utter want of sensibility in his Elegies and religious Poems, as compared with the beauty, the tenderness and graceful simplicity of many of the writers, of his own age, he is immediately struck with the contrast they exhibit. . .'[1]

Grosart (1873, ii, xliv.):

'But after all, I fear it must be conceded that it is as Thinker and Imaginator, and Artist of ideas rather than words in verse, we have to assert Donne's incomparable genius. He has nothing of the "smoothness" of various contemporaries, and very little of the ever-changing music of *the* Poet of "all time." Nevertheless, the various-readings and perpetual fluctuation of text in the MSS. lift up a united protest against any such charge as that of "indiffer-

---

[1] Thomas Corser, *Collectanea Anglo-Poetica*, 1873, Part V, p. 223. (*Chetham Society Publications*, vol. xci.)

ence." He must have worked laboriously, even in his versification. What satisfied Ben Jonson ought to be sympathetically studied by us ... (p. xlv). On reading the verse Letters, and Elegies, and Funeral Elegies, and the class entitled "Lyrical," there reach [reaches?] my ear occasionally Shakespearean melody, and now and again as I study I am conscious of an indefinable something suggestive of Shakespeare.'

Lightfoot (1877):

'[Donne's] versatility is a constant theme of admiration with those who knew him. At the age of twenty he wrote poems which his contemporaries regarded as masterpieces. His fame as a poet was greater in his own age than it has ever been since. During the last century, which had no toleration for subtle conceits and rugged rhythms, it was unduly depreciated; but now again it has emerged from its eclipse. No quaintness of conception and no recklessness of style and no harshness of metre can hide the true poetic genius which flashes out from his nobler pieces.'[1]

Kempe (1877):

'The tenderness, the fervour and the poetry of Donne... reconcile ... us to his fancies, extravagances and affectations...'[2]

Adams (1877):[3]

'The Funeral Elegies exhibit all Dr. Donne's subtlety of thought and ruggedness of versification, and many passages have a sonorous dignity, like the prose of Bacon or Sir Thomas Browne.'

On page 203 Adams quotes Hazlitt as having said, 'Of Donne I know nothing but some beautiful verses to his wife, dissuading her from accompanying him on his travels abroad, and some quaint riddles, in verse, which the sphinx could not unravel.'

Browning (1878):

---

[1] Joseph Barber Lightfoot, *Historical Essays*, London, 1895, pp. 244–5. 'Donne, the Poet-Preacher,' pp. 221-245. (This is one of a course of lectures on 'The Classic Preachers of the English Church,' delivered at St. James Church, Westminster, in 1887.)

[2] Lightfoot's Lectures, *The Classic Preachers of the English Church*, with Introduction by J. Edward Kempe, London, 1877, p. xix.

[3] W. Davenport Adams, *Dictionary of English Literature* (no date), p. 263. (Allibone gives '1877.')

> *He's greatest now and to de-struc-ti-on*
>   *Nearest.* Attend the solemn words I quote
> O Paul! *There's no pause at per-fec-ti-on.*
> Thus knolls thy knell the Doctor's bronzèd throat!
> *Greatness a period hath, no sta-ti-on!*
> Better and truer verse none ever wrote
> (Despite the antique outstretched *a-i-on*)
> Than thou, revered and magisterial Donne.
> *The Two Poets of Croisic*, cxiv.

'The modern appreciation of Donne seems to begin with Robert Browning, who met with the poems when he was still a boy (about 1827), and was greatly influenced by them. He put the Mandrake song to music. He quoted and praised the Dean so constantly in later years that Miss Barrett noticed it early in their acquaintance; "your Donne," she says on several occasions.'[1]

Minto (1880):

'The terrible crudeness and power which some critics have seen in [Donne's] satires is not a churlish crudeness; it is nothing but the boisterous extravagance of youth, the delight of a fresh untamed intellect in its own strength...

'If we take talent to be the power of adroitly manipulating common materials into common forms, no man had less of it than Donne. He had an invincible repugnance to the commonplace. Everything is his own, alike the thought and the instrument by which it is expressed. He is no man's debtor. He digs his own ore, and uses it according to his own fancy.'[2]

Hales (1880):

'For the most part we look on [Donne's work] with amazement, rather than with pleasure. It reminds us rather of a "pyrotechnic display", with its unexpected flashes and explosions, than of a sure and constant light... We weary of such unmitigated cleverness — such ceaseless straining after novelty and surprise. We long for something simply said.

---

[1] Gosse, ii, 353.

[2] William Minto, 'John Donne,' *The Nineteenth Century Review*, vol. vii (1880, pp. 845–863), pp. 853 and 862.

'His natural gifts were certainly great. He possesses a real energy and fervour. He loved, and he suffered much, and he writes with a passion which is perceptible through all his artificialities...

'Two of his Satires (II. and IV.) were reproduced—"versified"—in the last century by Pope, acting on the suggestion of Dryden; No. III. was similarly treated by Parnell. In these versions, along with the roughness of the metre, disappears much of the general vigour; and it should be remembered that the metrical roughness was no result of incapacity, but was designed. Thus the charge of metrical uncouthness so often brought against Donne on the ground of his satires is altogether mistaken. How fluently and smoothly he could write if he pleased, is attested over and over again by his lyrical pieces.'[1]

Schipper (1888):

'So correct und wohllautend im Ganzen der fünftaktige, gereimte Vers der zuletzt genannten, hervorragenden Dichter [Shakspere] gebaut ist, so incorrect und holperig ist in der Regel derjenige John Donnes, während seine zum Theil in kürzeren Versarten geschriebenen, strophischen Dichtungen meistens einen fliessenderen Rythmus haben.'[2]

Schipper's service to the student of English poetry, in tabulating and illustrating the strophic forms of verse, is not to be undervalued; but he is inconsistent in his views concerning the availability for ictus of syllables bearing secondary accent. He also goes astray in allowing inversions, other than initial and caesural, in a heroic line.

Swinburne (1889):

'That chance is the ruler of the world I should be sorry to believe and reluctant to affirm; but it would be difficult for any competent and careful student to maintain that chance is not the ruler of letters. Gray's odes are still, I suppose, familiar to

---

[1] *The English Poets*, ed. by Thomas Humphrey Ward, London and New York, 1880. (Introduction to Donne, pp. 558–60, by John W. Hales), p. 560.

[2] Jakob Schipper, *Neu englische Metrik*, Bonn, 1888, ii, 204. (Given in Trost's Bibliography as 'Englische Metrik,')

thousands who know nothing of Donne's Anniversaries; and Bacon's Essays are conventionally if not actually familiar to thousands who know nothing of Ben Jonson's *Discoveries*. And yet it is certain that in fervour of inspiration, in depth and force and glow of thought and emotion and expression, Donne's verses are as far above Gray's as Jonson's notes or observations on men and morals . . . are superior to Bacon's in truth of insight . . . and in concision of Eloquence.'[1]

Collier (1890):

'Beneath the artificial incrustations which characterize this school [Metaphysical], Donne displays a fine poetic feeling. He is also noted in our literary history as the first writer of satire in rhyming couplets.'[2]

Chambers (1895):

'One does not like the expression, "a school of poetry;" but it is difficult to dissociate the tendencies or tempers in question from the influence of two representative and dominant personalities, those of Spenser the musical, and of Donne the imaginative. On the one hand there is a body of poetry, transparent, sensuous, melodious, dealing with all the fresh and simple elements of life, fond of the picture and the story, rejoicing in love and youth, in the morning and the spring; on the other a more complex note, a deeper thrill of passion, an affectation for the sombre, the obscure, the intricate, alike in rhythm and in thought. . . Certainly Spenser and Donne are the typical exponents of their respective groups; certainly the personal influence of either would be hard to overestimate; certainly the poetry of melody began earlier than the poetry of imagination; . . . still to the last they appear side by side, often directing in this mood and in that the harmonies of the same pen.'[3]

Dowden (1895):

---

[1] *A Study of Ben Jonson*, New York, 1889, p, 129.

[2] William Francis Collier, *A History of English Literature in a Series of Biographical Sketches*, London, 1890, p. 168.

[3] *English Pastorals*, selected and with an Introduction by Edmund K. Chambers, London, 1895, pp. xxvii, xviii. (Warwick Library.)

'Touches of dramatic power are rare in Donne, whose genius was lyrical and meditative, not that of a dramatist. . .

'The meter of *The Extasie* is the same as that of *The Angel in the House*, and the manner in which meaning and metre move together closely resembles that of Mr. Patmore's *Preludes*.'[1]

The Extasie is a four-accent strophic poem, and as this is the only statement, on the metrical aspect of Donne's verse, in Dowden's delightful chapter on Donne, it is quoted in the hope of provoking him to a fuller expression. It may be said, however, that this poem, smooth-flowing as it may be regarded, is characteristic of Donne.

Norton[2] (1895):

'I do not impugn Ben Jonson's opinion that Donne deserved hanging for not keeping of accent. His sins in this respect are, indeed, unpardonable and unaccountable. He puts accent where he likes, forcing it from one syllable to another as if it had no settled place of its own.[3] Some of the transpositions are astounding, as, for instance:

"Blasted with sighs, and surrounded with tears."

"As fresh and sweet there apparels be, as be
The fields they sold to buy them. . ."

"At their best
Sweetness and wit, they're but mummy possesst."

---

[1] *New Studies in Literature*, pp. 103, 114. (This may also be found in *The Fortnightly Review*, vol. xlvii, no. 3, pp. 791-808; *Littell's Living Age*, vol. clxxxvi, pp. 195-205; and in the *Eclectic Magazine*, vol. cxv, pp. 234-244.)

[2] Grolier Club, ed. i, xxix.

[3] Ten years later (*Donne's Love Poems*, p. vii.) Professor Norton practically repeats this opinion, including Jonson's dictum, and with the important additon: '. . . Some of the faults of rhythm attributed to him are due to the reader rather than to the poet.'

Since the Grolier Club edition was prepared, Professor Norton has obtained three contemporary manuscript collections of Donne's poems, which, though full of errors themselves, afford correction of some errors in the printed texts. (See his account of them in *Harvard Studies and Notes on Philology and Literature*, vol. v, 1897.)

Norton seems to have become reconciled to the accent on the first syllable of 'surrounded,' as he gives a note of explanations (p. 81, *The Love Poems of John Donne*, 1905), justifying the author in so using the word. A discussion of this troublesome line must be postponed to Chapters II. and III.

Concerning the second example, it is a pity that Professor Norton did not observe that this line should be scanned:

As fresh and sweet their appárels be, as be
The fields they sold to buy them.

Since Chaucer said 'monéye;' Wyatt, 'beaúty;' Kyd, 'Coúntrey;' Herrick, 'rósemary;' Shakespeare, 'nobódy;' and Milton, 'lády' (See our chapter II.), why object to Donne's saying 'múmmy?'

Saintsbury (1896):

'It was the opinion of the late seventeenth and of the whole of the eighteenth century that Donne, though a clever man, had no ear. Chalmers, a very industrious student, and not such a bad critic, says so in so many words; Johnson undoubtedly thought so; Pope demonstrated his belief by his fresh "tagging" of the Satires. They all to some extent no doubt really believed what they said; their ears had fallen deaf to that particular concord. But they all also no doubt founded their belief to a certain extent on certain words of Dryden's which did not exactly import or comport what Mr. Pope and the rest took them to mean. Dryden had the knack, a knack of great value to a critic, but sometimes productive of sore misguiding to a critic's readers—of adjusting his comments solely to one point of view, to a single scheme in metric and other things. Now, from the point of view of the scheme which both his authority and his example made popular, Donne was rather formless. But nearly all the eighteenth-century critics and criticasters concentrated their attention on the Satires; and in the Satires Donne certainly takes singular liberties no matter what scheme be preferred. . . The opening stanzas especially [of 'Jeremiah'] have a fine melancholy clang not unknown, I think, as a model to Mr. Swinburne. . . But if Donne cannot receive the praise due to the accomplished poetical artist, he has that not perhaps higher but certainly rarer, of the inspired poetical creator.'[1]

Jessopp (1897):

'I have never been able to feel much enthusiasm for Donne as a poet; and it is as a poet that Donne's fame has chiefly come down to us. Who was I that I should undertake to deal with the life of the man whose poetry I had not the power of appreciating at its worth? There must be some deficiency, some obliquity in my own mind. . . There is no man in England who has written so exquisitely on Donne as he [Edmund Gosse] or shown such subtle sympathy with his poetic genius.'[2]

Mosher (1897):

'There is an inspired breath of the Renaissance in [Donne's] verse, flashes of supreme insight as in the world of tragic art Webster only knew; single lines of beauty unsurpassed discoverable in this man's work and nowhere else.'[3]

Carpenter (1897):

'Donne's poetry, it cannot be denied, is denuded of most of the habits and ornaments which up till then had been considered *de rigueur* for polite verse.'[4]

This quotation does not fully express Carpenter's view; and it may be doubted if he is considering, at this point, the matter of accent. A careful reading of his thoughtful and skillfully-executed Introduction brings one in close touch with Donne's metaphysics and conceits.

The Academy (1897):

'The typical modern, who wants to lie and let the plums of poetry fall into his mouth, had better hold aloof from Donne . . .

---

[1] Chambers, i, xix-xx, xxvii, xxxiii.
[2] Augustus Jessopp, *John Donne*, Boston and New York, 1897, p. viii.
[3] Thos. B. Mosher, *The Bibelot*, Portland, Me., vol. iii, no. 4, (April, 1897) p. 106.
[4] *Eng. Lyr. Poetry*, lvi.

read him, read all he wrote, for he is a mine of rough but priceless ore.'¹

Alden (1899):

'The measure [of the Satires] is characterized by approximation to the common speech of conversation; it is this that throws both syllable counting and observance of regular accent into the background... The style is like the metre: rugged, free and conversational in construction, and yet extremely compact, almost always vigorous, occasionally obscure either through conciseness or Latinized construction. It is marked by the curiously concrete vocabulary, the intellectual mood and the outflashing insight (often cynical in tone) which mark the body of the early poetry of the author. Quite naturally, it shows the elements of cynicism, coarseness, and dramatic interpretation, to a greater degree than his other poems.'²

Furst³ (1899):

'It must be acknowledged that Donne's verses, on superficial reading seem like riddles made to conceal the thought instead of expressing it; but it is none the less true that a more careful study will always show wit, fancy, tenderness and deep feeling. Although his lines will not allow themselves to be read in the liquid way which modern criticism insists upon for model verse, they have, in compensation, a deep and subtle music which adds true feeling to the thought, and a dignity and movement which, like that of Milton's verse, does much to replace the wanting smoothness.'⁴

Gosse (1899):

'In his own words, Dr. Jessopp "has never been able to feel much enthusiasm for Donne as a poet," whereas to me, even to

---

[1] Vol. lii, p. 475.

[2] Raymond Macdonald Alden, *The Rise of Formal Satire in England, Etc.*, Philadelphia, 1899, p. 83.

[3] *A Group of Old Authors*, p. 15. (The first chapter: 'A Gentleman of King James' Day: Dr. John Donne,' appeared originally in *The Citizen*, Philadelphia, September, 1896.)

[4] By reference to the quotation from Craik (pp. 36, 37) it will be observed that Furst agrees with and paraphrases him.

his last seraphical hour in his bedchamber at St. Paul's, Donne is quintessentially a poet.'[1]

For a more particular view of Gosse on Donne's verse, we go back to 1894:[2] 'The terms "irregular," "unintelligible," and "viciously rugged," are commonly used in describing Donne's Poetry, and it seems even to be supposed by some critics that Donne did not know how to scan. This last supposition may be rejected at once; what there was to know about poetry was known to Donne. But it seems certain that he intentionally introduced a revolution into English versification. It was doubtless as a rebellion against the smooth and somewhat nerveless iambic flow of Spenser and the earliest contemporaries of Shakespeare that Donne invented his violent mode of breaking up the line into quick and slow beats. The best critic of his own generation, Ben Jonson, hated the innovation, and told Drummond "that Donne, for not keeping of accent, deserved hanging." It is difficult to stem a current of censure which has set without intermission since the very days of Donne itself, but I may be permitted to point out what I imagine was the poet's own view of the matter.

'He found, as I have said, the verse of his youth, say 1590, exceedingly mellifluous, sinuous, and inclining to flaccidity. A five-syllable iambic line of Spenser or of Daniel trots along with the gentlest amble of inevitable shorts and longs. It seems to have vexed the ear of Donne by its tendency to feebleness, and it doubtless appeared to him that the very gifted writers who immediately preceded him had carried the softness of it as far as it would go. He desired new and more varied effects. . . The iambic rhymed line of Donne has audacities such as are permitted to his blank verse by Milton, and although the felicities are rare in the older poet, instead of being almost incessant, as in the latter, Donne at his best is not less melodious than Milton. When he writes—

---

[1] Edmund Gosse, *The Life and Letters of John Donne*, (2 vols.) London, 1899, i, xi.

[2] *The Jacobean Poets*, New York, 1894, pp. 61–64. Partially reproduced in *The Life and Letters of John Donne*, (1889), ii, 334–5.

        Blasted with sighs, and surrounded with tears,

we must not dismiss this as not being iambic verse at all, nor—much less—attempt to read it—

        Blásted with síghs, and surroúnded with teárs,

but recognize in it the poet's attempt to identify the beat of his verse with his bewildered and dejected condition, reading it somewhat in this notation:—

        Blasted | with sighs ‖ and surrounded | with tears.

The violence of Donne's transposition of accent is most curiously to be observed in his earliest satires, and in some of his later poems is almost entirely absent. Doubtless his theory became modified with advancing years. No poet is more difficult to read aloud. Such a passage as the following may excusably defy a novice:—

> No token of worth but 'Queen's man,' and fine
> Living, barrels of beef, and flagons of wine,
> I shook like a spied spy. Preachers, which are
> Seas of wits and arts, you can then dare
> Drown the sins of this place, for, for me,
> Which am but a scant brook, it enough shall be
> To wash the stains away.

But tread the five-foot verse not as a fixed and unalterable sequence of cadencies, but as a norm around which a musician weaves his variations, and the riddle is soon read—

> No token | of worth | but Queen's | man | and fine
> Living | barrels of | beef and | flaggons of | wine.
> I shook | like a spied | spy. | Preachers | which are
> Seas | of wit | and arts, | you can then | dare
> Drown | the sins | of this place, | for, | for me,
> Which am | but a scant | brook, | it enough | shall be
> To wash | the stains | away.'

Concerning the line,

> Blasted with sighs, and surrounded with tears.

we shall speak later.

Disregarding the variant of 1633, Gosse follows 1669, in which one of the lines has an extra syllable. Two of the lines lack a syllable. Thus we see out of six and a half lines selected by him to illustrate a theory, three of the lines are crippled—and Donne did not write lame verse.

His example is taken from *Satire* IV. and comprises lines 235 to the period in 241. According to the ed. of 1633, 236, reads,

> Living, barrels of beef, flagons of wine,

James Russell Lowell, in the Grolier Club edition of Donne, suggests as a reading for 238 and 239,

> Seas of [all] wits and arts, you can then dare
> Drown the sins of this place, for [as] for me.

I accept Lowell's emendation of line 238, but suggest for the next line,

> Drown the sins of this place, [yet] for, for me.

While it may be a half-way anticipation of the theory which is to be advanced, fully discussed, and illustrated in subsequent pages, I will now say paleontologically : I cannot, from a given bone, construct Donne's animal; but given the animal, with a missing or dislocated bone, I find no trouble in supplying or articulating that bone.

Since we shall have to come back to these lines, we may leave them for the present.

Gosse continues (p. 64):

'The poetry of Donne possesses in no small degree that "unusual and indefinable witchery" which Dr. Jessopp has noted as characteristic of the man himself. But our enjoyment of it is marred by the violence of the writer, by his want of what seems to us to be good taste, and by a quality which has been overlooked by those who have written about him, but which seems to provide the key to the mystery of his position. Donne was, I would venture to suggest, by far the most modern and contemporaneous of the writers of his time. He rejected all the classical togs and imagery of the Elizabethans, he borrowed nothing from French or Italian tradition. He arrived at an access of actuality in style, and it was because he struck them as so novel and so completely in touch with his own age that his immediate coevals were so much fascinated with him.'

The Church Quarterly Review (1900):

' [Our readers] will find much upon Donne's poetry which will enable them to understand the unique marks of his genius.'

The *Review's* personal opinion of Donne, as a poet, is possibly expressed in a subsequent statement, beginning: ' The husband, or as Mr. Gosse will call him " the poet," etc.'[1]

Stephen (1900):

'Mr. Gosse, in the " Life" which has just appeared, professes his belief that Donne contains the quintessence of poetry; but even Dr. Jessopp—an enthusiastic admirer of the prose—honestly confesses that the poems are not to his taste. I may, therefore, take courage to confess that I too find them rather undigestible. They contain, I do not doubt, the true spirit; but I rarely get to the end, even of the shortest, without being repelled by some strange discord in form or in substance which sets my teeth on edge. Yet I am as much attracted as I am repelled. The man himself excites my curiosity.'[2]

The Academy (1900):

'Metaphysical, rugged, and obscure, dowered with a *macabre* imagination and a white heat of passion, he [Donne] was an entirely new note in a literature dominated, outside the drama, by the distant influence of Spenser.'[3]

Sanders (1900):

'The want of the Art-Spirit which is conspicuous in his

---

[1] Vol. l. ('John Donne,' pp. 91-106), pp. 98-9.
[2] Leslie Stephen, *The National Review*, vol. xxxiv, ('John Donne,' pp. 595-613), p. 595. The Grolier Club edition of Donne's poems, ed. by C. E. Norton, 1895, is dated in this article, by typograpical error, 1795.
[3] Vol. lix., p. 608.

[Donne's] life, is perhaps one of the causes why his poems are so unequal and so full of irregularities, and eccentricities and absurdities... Some of his poems are conspicuously beautiful and well wrought throughout; others and these the majority, have their completeness spoilt by carelessness or wilful eccentricity.'[1]

Chadwick (1900):

'That Donne could be so undramatic in a period of intense dramatic realization, that he could be so rough in a period of "suggared sonnets" and mellifluous verse, is eloquent of his stiff-necked individuality...

'How daintily this ponderous elephant could dance is shown by the "Song" ['Sweetest love I do not go.'] he wrote when he was going over to Paris in 1612.'[2]

Richter (1902):

'Dass Donne in den Satiren und den fünftaktigen Gedichten der Jugend das Metrum wirklich absichtlich vernachlässigte, ist wohl als sicher anzunehmen, und die Meinung mancher Kritiker, er habe eben nicht bessere Verse machen können, mag von vornherein abgewiesen werden.'[3]

This is one of the most rational statements in Richter's article, and it is selected in an attempt to do him justice. Should Donne ever be forgotten, as Jonson said, 'for not being understood' the seat of Chief Misunderstander should be reserved for our friend of Elbogen.

The primary purpose of Richter's study is to prove, both by internal evidence and changes in the style or structural form of Donne's poems, that his life or poetry may be divided into three distinct periods. This suggestion had been made, six years before, by Saintsbury;[4] but Richter was evidently not aware of the existence of this edition of the poems, for he makes no reference to it

[1] H. M. Sanders, *Temple Bar*, vol. cxxi. ('John Donne,' pp. 614-628,) pp. 622-23.
[2] John White Chadwick, 'John Donne Poet and Preacher,' in *The New World: A Quarterly Review of Religion, Ethics, Theology.* Vol. ix., no. 43, (March, 1900) Boston, pp. 35 and 41.
[3] 'Über den Vers bei Dr. John Donne,' p. 413.
[4] Chambers, i, xix.

and falls into grave errors from which such a knowledge would have saved him.

In the twenty-five pages there are a few more than ninety typographical and other errors, many of which can but be attributed to lack of care on the part of the author, and to his slight acquaintance with the English language, and with Donne.

As illustrations of carelessness: (p. 403), we find twenty-seven examples of slurring under the heading " many a ;" this combination occurs in only two of the examples, in the first of which the 'a' is omitted; the second is given just as it appears in Grosart, from which it is taken, but makes no sense, besides being ungrammatical:

> But as oft alchemists doe coyners proue,
> Soe manie a selfe-despiseinge gett self-loue.
> *The Cross*, 37, 38,

No variants are given in Grosart, or Chambers, but the latter very sensibly corrects the line:

> So may a self-despising get self-love.

If Richter is redeemed from this error, because he followed his text, it remains that he made an unfortunate selection of an example.

On page 404, near the foot, he gives the -*ion* of 'religion' as '*einsilbig*,' and on page 405, near the top, he gives the same syllable of the same word, in the same line and poem as '*zweisilbig*.'

As illustrations of ignorance of English: On p. 400 we find this example of '*Fehlende Senkung im Innern*,' accented as here:

> "This féllow chúseth mé"? He sáith, "Sír."
> *Satire* II, 51.

Of course the line should be scanned

> "This féllow chúseth me?" He sáith, "Sír."

On pp. 405-6 there are forty-six examples of '*vollgemessene Participformen*,' thirty-five of which are marked for accent by Grosart (twelve of the thirty-five also required by rime),—Richter follows him and is right. In these forty-six examples Grosart makes three mistakes,—Richter follows him and is wrong. In the remaining eight Richter has no guide and makes six mistakes.

On page 405 we find 'theater,' 'humble,' 'chronicles,' and 'knoweth' offered in illustrations of 'Zerdehnung.'

On page 410, as an example of 'schwebende Betonung im Reime' is given 'rely mit awry.'

As to ignorance of Donne, we find (pp. 394-5) under the head of 'Taktumstellung' this statement, 'Ganz vereinzelt aber kommt diese Freiheit in einigen von Donne's letzten Dichtungen vor, so in der 10. Elegie *The Autumnal*, in *A Hymn to God the Father* und in *Lament for his wife*.'

As Richter had not seen the Chambers ed. of Donne, it would hardly be just to charge him with not knowing that this Elegy was written in what he would call Donne's first period; and that *Lament for his Wife* was written by William Browne (See Chambers i, 238-9 and ii, 304-5), leaving only one of the two poems by Donne in the third period; but it does play havoc with his theory. He might as well have said, Because Jonah was three nights in the whale's belly, and because Daniel was cast into a den of three lions, it is evident that the life and poetry of Donne should be divided into three periods.

An effort is made (pp. 414 ff.) to refute the claim of Gosse, that Donne attempted an innovation in verse. To this end a number of conventional expressions in Donne's lines are quoted, but everything that the poet said favorable to his work is overlooked, reminding us again that 'the traveler sees what he looks for.'

Courthope (1903):

'Nor can [Donne] be reckoned among the poets who, by their sense of harmony and proportion, have helped to carry forward the refinement of our language from one social stage to another.'[1]

Trost (1904):

As the title of Trost's dissertation indicates, he is not concerned with the word accent, or scansion of Donne's verse.[2] His chapter

---

[1] W. J. Courthope, *History of English Poetry*, London, 1903, iii, 168.
[2] *Beiträge zur Kenntnis des Stils von John Donne*, &c.

and paragraph subjects comprise: '*Donne s Motive und ihre Variationen*' '*Der Stil im allgemeinen;*' '*Wörter;*' '*Wortspiele;*' '*Sätze;*' '*Redefiguren*' (Conceits); '*Bilder;*' '*Personifikationen;*' '*Vergleiche;*' '*Klimax;*' '*Oxymoron;*' '*Epizeuxis;*' and '*Alliteration.*'

While Trost's study is not exhaustive, it is a distinct contribution to the literature on Donne. The only blunder to which attention need be called, occurs on p. 3 :

'Rudolf Richter, (1902) hat in seiner Abhandlung über den Vers bei Donne die Dichtungen desselben in drei grosse Abschnitte zerlegt. . . Ich hatte dieselbe Dreiteilung wie Richter durgeführt ehe mir der betreffende Band zur Einsicht vorlag; ich glaube mich daher umsomehr berechtigt, diese Gruppierung beizubehalten.'

Unlike Richter, Trost saw and quoted from Chambers, but overlooked Saintsbury's (Introduction, pp. xviii-xix, vol. i.) three-period suggestion made in 1896. Furthermore, he weakens his own investigation by endorsing a theory that has no foundation.

Gwynne (1904):

[1] 'No one disputes the supreme excellence of his [Browning's] work at its best, as for instance in *Men and Women;* but, on the other hand, no one denies the vices of style which make his principal work, *The Ring and the Book*, so difficult of reading. He may vanish from general view, as Donne, a man of very similar qualities and defects has vanished, or as Cowley vanished half a century later.'

While this does not concern Donne's metre, it is interesting to notice how persistently he lives in the face of the evil prophecies of 'The Tribe of Ben.'

Wendell (1904):

'Spenser frankly set forth in English poetry the influence of classical Italian. Jonson sturdily expounded and practiced the permanent poetic principles of the enduring classics of antiquity. Donne wrote with utter disregard of both these influences; and, although he was manifestly influenced by the decadent ingenuities

---

[1] Stephen Gwynne, *The Masters of English Literature*, New York, 1904, p. 400.

which had become fashionable in Italy and Spain, his English manner was, almost rudely his own...

'To us ... [Donne's poems] cannot have the sort of surprising quality which, in their own day attracted instant attention. So far as I can discover, their approach to popularity came not so much from their aggressive peculiarity of form as from the fact that, in contrast to the literature about them, they must have appeared amazingly veracious. The lack of conventional grace, when other men were so apt to be conventionally graceful, makes them seem astonishingly genuine: they seem to express not fancy, but fact, and in a temper very like that of the art which modern cant calls realistic...

'His obscurity is not a matter of language; his vocabulary is almost as pure as Jonson's own. The difficulties of him spring rather from the pervasive intensity, which strives, deliberately or instinctively, to charge his lines with a heavier burden of thought and feeling than any lines could unbendingly carry. Accordingly he seems, once for all, to disdain the oddities into which the lines distort themselves under the strain...

'For not keeping of accent, no doubt Donne deserved hanging; but he could plead in confession and avoidance this intensity which was all his own...'[1]

Citing examples of beauty (p. 125) Wendell seems to apologize for even half-way agreeing with Jonson: 'Better, still, take the haunting melody of those two lines of Donne which are most familiar ...:

> I long to talk with some old lover's ghost,
> Who died before the god of love was born.'

Babbott (1905):

'There are few poems in the English language that have a purer lyrical ring than Donne's best. Keats and Milton and even Shakespeare flash through their lines on the reader's mind and

---

[1] Barrett Wendell, *The Temper of the Seventeenth Century in English Literature*, New York, 1904, pp. 120-125.

reflect the same heavenly source. One can go back to them again and again without losing any of their inimitable witchery.'[1]

Belden (1906):

'[Donne's] verse is possibly mad, . . . but there was method in his madness, and a definite purpose which he very effectually accomplished... The verse-rythm of Donne's poetry is the natural outward and visible form of his mental temper. He writes so because he can best express his thoughts and his feeling. This I take it is the meaning of Coleridge's rather mysterious dictum that in Donne 'the sense, including the passion, leads to the metre.' But I should rather say that in Donne the meaning, straining against the rhythm of the fore-established metre in the reader's mind, reproduces there the slow, tense emphasis of Donne's thought. The melodists, from Greene and Marlowe to Swinburne, are always in danger (if it is a danger) of lulling the mind to sleep with the music of the sense. The verse pattern is caught at once; we get the tune; and the melodist never ventures far from it, however much he may adorn it with alliteration, assonance, and vowel-series. Such things we say sing themselves, —which can seldom if ever be said of Donne's poetry. It is the test of lyric as distinguished from other poetry that it does so sing itself. Donne's verse (with possibly one or two exceptions) is never lyric in this sense. Instead, he leaves you, line after line and phrase after phrase in doubt of the pattern, or of how the line is to be fitted to the pattern, producing thereby a searching pause on almost every syllable,—a sort of perpetual " hovering accent." This is the real idiosyncrasy of Donne's verses, and in it consists, no doubt, much of the peculiar charm of Donne's poetry for certain minds.'[2]

Looking back over this array of criticism,[3] and realizing that

---

[1] Frank L. Babbott, *Poems of Donne*, (The Marion Press) Jamaica, Queensborough, N. Y., 1905, pp. vi, vii.

[2] Prof. H. M. Belden, (University of Missouri), *Donne's Prosody*. (A paper recently read before the Central Branch of the Modern Language Association, at the University of Wisconsin.)

[3] Other criticisms may be found in Chapter III. Chapters on 'John Donne' in *Leisure Hours*, vol. 13, and *The Argosy*, vol. 32, are not accessible.

Donne's poetry, as a whole, can be but one thing, we are impressed with the fact that his critics, the majority of them at least, have (to use one of Donne's conceits) shivered his verse and given to the world definite reflections of themselves in the numerous sparkling fragments.

CHAPTER II.

SECONDARY ACCENT IN DONNE'S VERSE.

A Comparative Study.

'Iterated acknowledgement is due Sievers for his fine discrimination in classifying secondary word-accents and in proving their rhythmic function in Anglo-Saxon... But, although Sievers has opened the way, no one has hitherto consistently and completely pursued the rhythmic function of secondary word-accents along the entire course of English versification.'[1]

Professor Bright contributed another study on this subject in 1901.[2] The same year Dr. Julian Huguenin and Dr. G. D. Brown made special application of the principle of secondary accent, the former to Anglo-Saxon verse[3] and the latter to the poetry of Milton.[4] In 1904 Dr. Raymond D. Miller, 'pursued the rhythmic function of secondary word-accent along the... course of English versification' from Chaucer to Dryden.[5] Miller cites a number of examples from John Donne, but it is impossible to pursue this study without looking more extensively, and at the same time more narrowly, into the principle of secondary accent as it manifests itself in the verse of Donne.

Professor Bright discusses three opinions, or doctrines, as to the manner in which poetry should be read.[6] The first, the sense-doctrine, requires that it be 'read as one reads prose... its advocates maintaining that [this method] alone enables the reader to

---

[1] James W. Bright, 'Proper Names in Old English Verse,' *Pub. Mod. Lang. Asso. of America*, (1899) xiv, 356-7.

[2] 'Concerning Grammatical Ictus in English Verse.' *An English Miscellany*, Oxford, 1901, pp. 22-33.

[3] *Secondary Stress in Anglo-Saxon*, Baltimore, 1901.

[4] *Syllabification and Accent in the Paradise Lost*, Baltimore, 1901.

[5] *Secondary Accent in Modern English Verse* (Chaucer to Dryden), Baltimore, 1904.

[6] *Proper Names, etc.*, pp. 361-2.

"bring out" the meaning. It is thus that the relation of the art of poetry to music is ruthlessly pushed aside by the assumption that the harmony of "numbers" must not be regarded as much as the logic of the sense.'

Sometimes this method of scansion does not conflict with rhythm, as in the line,

From hi´gher po´wers; from Go´d reli´gion flo´ws.[1]

but in the succeeding line the rhythm is violated:

Wi´sdom and ho´nour from the u´se of ki´ngs.

No theory which ignores the music of verse can be correct.

The second doctrine (*third* in Professor Bright's discussion) is the ictus-doctrine, which requires the reader to stress strongly every word or syllable standing under the ictus; and to stress no other word or syllable. This method of scansion (commonly designated 'routine scansion') is sure to give a rhythmic, or rather a galloping reading, which may not interfere with the sense, as in

Go´ and ca´tch a fa´lling sta´r.[2]

but at times the sense is violated. Thus in the line

I sing the progress of a deathless soul.[3]

of though an arsis, deserves only a weak stress; while in

The flail-finn'd thresher, and steel-beaked sword-fish.[4]

-finn'd, steel-, and *sword-,* though only theses, must be stressed to 'bring out' the sense; *and* like *of,* in the line above, though an arsis, deserves only a weak stress.

Just as the sense-doctrine disregards rhythm for sense, so the ictus-doctrine ignores sense for rhythm; and both may be dismissed.

The third doctrine, (*second* in Professor Bright's discussion) is

---

[1] Donne, *Eclogue*, 67.
[2] Donne, *Song*, 1.
[3] Donne, *The Progress of the Soul*, 1.
[4] *Ibid.*, 351.

the rhythm-, or pitch-doctrine, which has due regard to both sense and ictus.

Before illustrating this doctrine, it is well to inquire why the harmonies of verse are not generally perceived. Professor Bright gives a satisfactory answer: 'On the one hand we are apt to misunderstand the artistic quality of what is commonly described as "monotony," and then a second barrier is set up in the growing tendency in pronunciation to subordinate as uniformly unstressed all other syllables to those which have the chief word-stress.'[1]

In his lectures Professor Bright has called attention to the fact that simple 'duration' in the enunciation of words or syllables falling under the ictus, is conducive to 'artistic monotone.' He thereby intends to modify his previous description of the ictus, to the extent of substituting *duration* for *pitch* as the characteristic element in the rhythmic quality of secondary-accent syllables when under the ictus.

In the poems of Alexander Smith,[2] we meet lines in which the sense-doctrine and the ictus-doctrine come in conflict, and in which the author italicizes the word in thesis that requires sense-accent or emphasis for meaning:

'Tis the deep soul that's touched, *it* bears the wound.
                              Page 8, verse 14.

Our ears, Sir Bookworm, hunger for *thy* song.   22, 17.

I'd rush across this waiting world
And cry, '*He* comes!' . . .   26, 3.
Lay it upon *her* grave. . .   118, 9.
But few request *my* prayers. . .   136, 3.

Deep in the mists of sorrow long I lay,
Hopeless and still, when suddenly *this* truth
Like a slant sunbeam quivered through the mist
And turned it into radiance. . .   158, 2-5.

In these lines the author has indicated the words which the sense-doctrine requires to be stressed—each time the word is in

---

[1] *Concerning Grammatical Ictus, etc.*, p. 26.
[2] *A Life-Drama and Other Poems*, Boston, 1865.

thesis; but the ictus-doctrine, ignoring the sense, requires the stress to fall upon the succeeding word, which is in arsis. In such cases the rhythm- or pitch-doctrine offers the only solution; the word in thesis receives a word-accent that is subordinated to the ictus, and so preserves the rhythm.

To illustrate the principle:

Butler writes:

> Those whose interest lies between
> His keeping *out* and bringing *in*.[1]

Francis Scott Key:

> But the dwellings of earth, whether high or low,
> Or mighty and massive their walls,
> Cannot keep *in* joy or keep *out* woe
> They must open when misery calls.[2]

In the first example sense-, ictus-, and rhythm-doctrines agree; in the second, in which the sense is practically the same as in the first, Key's lines become prose, and awkward prose at that, if read as we have read Butler's. In Key's line the subordination of the word-accent to an adjacent ictus ('conflict') preserves the sense and does not destroy but rather enriches the rhythm.

The explanation of the lines of Key and Butler applies equally to the following examples from Donne:

> And sleep which locks *up* sense, doth lock *out* all.[3]

> In looking *up* to God, or *down* to us.[4]

> And heat of taking *up*, but cold lay *down*.[5]

Other examples from Donne, which are so plain as to need no comment:

---

[1] *Hudibras*, Part III, Canto II, 1189-90.
[2] *Poems*, New York, 1857; 'The Nobleman's Son,' p. 140, 5-8.
[3] *Elegy X. The Dream*, 16.
[4] *Obsequies of Lord Harrington, etc.*, 5.
[5] *Elegy XV. A Tale of a Citizen and His Wife*, 43.

Here I *un*swear and overswear them thus.¹
Open to all searchers, unprized if *un*known.²
That what they have *mis*done
Or m*i*ssaid, we to that may not adhere.³
That hate *towards* them breeds pity *towards* the rest.⁴
Empaled himself to keep them out *not* in: been.⁵
Shall so much faster ebb *out* than *flow in.*⁶

While, as we have seen, Alexander Smith places emphatic words, falling in thesis, in italics, to indicate the manner in which he means his lines to be read, and to show their meaning, it is unnecessary for the poet to resort to such a scheme except it be to guide dull ear or slothful intellect. However, since the prose writer, whose meaning can be in no danger of conflict with accent, employs italics, has not the poet the same privilege?

Johnson writes, '[Cowley's] two metrical disquisitions *for* and *against* Reason are no mean specimens of metaphysical poetry.'⁷

Smith:

> 'And it will fit *one* heart, yea, as the cry
> Of the lone plover fits the dismal heath.⁸

The object of each seems practically the same: to prevent the flow of the sentence or the pattern of the verse from obscuring the meaning.

In the examples now to be cited from Donne's verse, we shall begin with the particles (articles, prepositions, conjunctions, etc.).

---

¹ *Elegy XVII. Elegy on His Mistress*, 11.
² *Elegy III. Change*, 6.
³ *A Litany*, 114-15.
⁴ *Satire* II, 4.
⁵ *To Sir Edward Herbert, etc.*, 11.
⁶ *Obsequies of the Lord Harrington, etc.*, 160.
⁷ 'Life of Cowley,' Chalmers' *Eng. Poets*, vii, 25.
⁸ '*A Life Drama,*' III, 29, 30.

Usually these examples will be given in blocks of five lines,[1] (a particle in ictus in each foot of the line) showing that the poet seldom, if ever, resorts to inversion, initial or cæsural (and there are no other metrical inversions), in order to relieve such particles from bearing the rhythmic accent.

At the very outset we are confronted with innumerable dissenters, of whom we may better select one representative than to undertake to review all.

Mayor[2] speaks of the prepositions 'of,' 'from,' 'with,' and 'on' in Gray's *Elegy*, lines 16, 20, 46 and 56, as 'scarcely audible prepositions.' He continues, 'Properly read, these lines have only four accents and have therefore no claim to be reckoned specimens of the five-accent verse.'

He offers two scansions:

4-accent: The rúde | forefá | thers of the hám | let sléep.

5-accent: Nó more shall róuse them from their lówly béd.

Men of like views must have lived in the days of Donne:

> To love and grief tribute of verse belongs,
> But not of such as pleases when 'tis read.[3]

These 'scarcely audible prepositions' are vastly more significant than some critics would have us believe.[4] Professor Bright, in his lectures, has called attention to the fact that since we gain our knowledge of things through their relation with other things, and since prepositions are relation-showing words, they are not to be ignored in the scansion of verse. He has also pointed out, as one of the differences between prose and verse, the fact that the poet is more likely to dwell upon relational words, while the prose writer drops them and proceeds to the object of the relation. A

---

[1] Occasionally an adverb, or a propositional-adverb, regarded by all as eligible to receive the ictus, will be admitted merely to complete a set of examples.

[2] *English Metre*, Cambridge, 1901, p. 116.

[3] *The Tripple Fool*, 17, 18.

[4] Great ecclesiastical institutions have turned upon the hinge of a single small preposition: Did John baptise *in* Jordan?

prose writer would have said, 'The fountains, the rivers, and the ocean mingle.' Shelley sings,

> The fountains mingle *with* the river
> And the rivers *with* the ocean.
>
> Love's Philosophy, 1, 2.

To put the matter another way: the prose writer, when he has occasion to use relational words, so constructs his sentence that they may be hurried over. He would say, 'The moping owl complains to the moon;' but Gray writes it:

> The moping owl does *to* the moon complain.
>
> Elegy, 10.

In commercial life there is a growing tendency to dispense with relational words. Such expressions as 'Write me,' and 'Wire me,' are now-a-days accepted without question.

Professor James, discussing 'successive psychoses;' cautions against the undue emphasizing of the more 'substantive parts,' and the failure to register the 'transitive parts' in the stream of thought.[1]

In addition to what has been said, it may be added that prepositions, in showing relation—in marking the flight of thought from one concept to another—answer some important questions. Tennyson's *Morte d'Arthur*, 272 lines, shows almost a hundred prepositions bearing the ictus; some of them telling *where* (what place and what position), others *when, whence, how, why, how far*, etc.

Where?

> So all day long the battle roll'd
> Among the mountains *by* the wintry sea. 1, 2.
> I heard the ripple washing *in* the reeds,
> And the wild waters leaping *on* the crag. 70-1.

---

[1] William James, *The Principles of Psychology*, New York, 1904, i, **244**.

When?

               In act to throw: but *át* the last.   61.

Whence?

               The lights begin to twinkle *fróm* the rocks.
                                           Ulysses, 54.

How?

               Now I see *bý* thine eyes that this is done.
                                           M. d'A., 149.

Why?

               Thou wouldst betray me *fór* the precious hilt.   126.

How far?

               A cry that shiver'd *tó* the tingling stars.   199.

'Perhaps every one has observed that particularly in Shakespeare's later plays he seems absolutely careless as to what kind of words the rhythmic accent may fall on. Sometimes it is on the article *the*, sometimes on the preposition *of*, sometimes the conjunction *and*. . .'[1]

Coleridge remarks: 'But, I say, in this lordliness of opulence, in which *the* positive of Donne agrees with *a* positive of Shakespeare, what is it that makes them homoiousian indeed, yet not homoousian?'[2]

Donne's verse, like Shakespeare's, and like the prose of Coleridge, shows 'insignificant' words stressed to meet the exigencies of rhythm and meaning.

a

      In *á* continuous rage so void of reason: treason.[3]
      Did this soul *á* good way towards heaven direct.[4]
      And with new physic, *á* worse engine far.[5]

---

[1] Sidney Lanier, *The Science of English Verse*, New York, 1880, p. 213.
[2] Coleridge, *Notes Theological, etc.*, 1853, p. 251. Quoted by Grosart, ii, xxxviii.
[3] *Elegy* XV, 52.
[4] *An Anatomy. First Anniv.*, 126.
[5] *Ibid.*, 160.

Love was as subtly catched as á disease.¹
And whisper "By Jesu!" so oft that á: away.²

Others:

A book to á few lines: but it was fit.
        Jonson, *Epistle* [To my Lady Lovell], 3.
I do not set my life at á pin's fee.
        Shakespeare, *H.* I. iv. 65.
Or quickened á revision by a drug.
        Pope, *Donne's Sat.* IV. *Versified*, 135.
Brightening the skirts of á long cloud ran forth.
        Tennyson, *Morte d' Arthur*, 54.
Upon the sea-mark á small boat did wait.
        Shelley, *The Revolt of Islam*, I, xvi, 8.
We walked together on the crown
Of á high mountain which looked down.
        Poe, *Tamerlane*, 138, 9.

While Donne went further than these in placing *a* both in ictus and in rime, the following example from Jonson shows that judge and accused (?) might have occupied the same scaffold:

        When, see (the worst of all lucks)
        They met the second prodigie, would feare a
        Man, that had never heard of a Chimera.³

                the
Donne:
        Where *thé* king's counsels and his secrets rest.⁴
        Then note they *thé* ship's sicknesses, the mast.⁵
        Blood in the streets and *thé* just murderèd.⁶

¹ *Elegy* XVI, 66.
² *Satire* IV, 215.
³ *The Voyage Itself*, 58–60.
⁴ *Eclogue, 1613, December 26*, 90.
⁵ *The Storm*, 53.
⁶ *The Lamentations*, 314.

And in that pleasure lengthen thé short days.¹

In Donne's verse no line ends with *the*, and so, to complete this block of examples, a line must be borrowed from Blake:

> Smile on our loves; and, while thou drawest thé
> Blue curtains of the sky...²

Others:

> Spun out in name of some of thé old nine.
> > Jonson, *Elegie on My Muse*, 6.
> My reason, thé physician to my soul.
> > Shakespeare, *Sonnet*, cxlvii, 5.
> Nor God alone in thé still calm we find.
> > Pope, *An Essay on Man*, 109.

an

Donne:

> 'Twere án ambition to desire to fall.³
> They kill'd once án inglorious man, but I.⁴
> The amorousness of án harmonious soul.⁵

Others:

> We must have án account of that too, gossip.
> > Jonson, *M. L.*, V, vi, 22.
> This blindness springs from án access of light.
> > Parnell, *Donne's Satire* III. *Versified*, 91.

and

Donne:

Thy graces ánd good works my creature be.⁶

---

¹ *Elegy* XVI. *The Expostulation*, 56.
² *The Evening Star*, 5, 6.
³ *Upon the Untimely Death of* ... *Prince Henry*, 50.
⁴ *Holy Sonnets* XI, 7.
⁵ *A Hymn to Christ, etc.*, 18.
⁶ *Elegy* VII, 25.

To hear God's message ánd proclaim His laws.[1]
Or turn their course by travel ánd new lore.[2]
Think he which made your waxen garden, ánd: stand.[3]

Others:
Of eggs and halberds, cradles, ánd a herse,
A pair of scissors, ánd a comb in verse;
Acrostichs, ánd telestichs on jump names.
    Jonson, *An Execration upon Vulcan*, 37-9.
And to be short, for not appearance ánd.
    Shakespeare, *Henry VIII*, IV, i, 30.
In shillings ánd in pence at first they deal.
    Pope, *Donne's Sat.* II, *Versified*, 83.
Thy Maker's vengeance, ánd thy monarch's ire.
    Parnell, *Donne's Sat.* III, *Versified*, 26.
And leaves the world to darkness ánd to me.
    Gray, *Elegy*, 4.
For mid that sunshine, ánd those smiles.
    Poe, *Tamerlane*, 102.

as

Donne:
So ás the influence of those stars may be.[4]
Return and ás of old renew our day.[5]
In all religions ás much care hath been.[6]
Such services I offer ás shall pay.[7]
Sink like a lead without a line; but ás: pass.[8]

Others:
Which though I cannot, ás an architect.
    Jonson, *An Epigram* [To the Lord
        Treasurer of England], 25.

---

[1] *To Mr. Tilman, etc.*, 20.
[2] *Elegy* XII, 60.
[3] *Satire* IV, 169.
[4] *An Anatomy. Second Anniv.*, 393.
[5] *The Lamentations*, 388.
[6] *To the Countess of Bedford* (2), 25.
[7] *Elegy* VI, 8.
[8] *To Sir Henry Watton* (1), 55.

Backward she pushed him, *ás* she would be thrust.
> Shakespeare, *V. and A.*, 34.

Nor be so civil *ás* to prove unjust.
> Pope, *An Essay on Criticism*, 581.

Who reverenced his conscience *ás* the king.
> Tennyson, *Idyls of the King*, 7.

at

Donne:

Nor *át* his board together being sat.[1]
But wonder *át* a greater far to us.[2]
Is not contented *át* one sign to inn.[3]
I tune my instrument here *át* the door.[4]
And he makes me the mark he shooteth *át*.[5]

Others:

Much like a press of people *át* a door.
> Shakespeare, *R. of L.*, 1294.

Glad time is *át* this point arrived.
> Jonson, *Epithalamion* [From Hymenæ], 1.

The fair sat panting *át* a courtier's play.
> Pope, *An Essay on Criticism*, 540.

With incense kindled *át* the Muse's flame.
> Gray, *Elegy*, 72.

Which Grandolph from his tomb-top chuckles *át*.
> Browning, *The Bishop Orders His Tomb*, 66.

but

Donne:

If, *bút* to loathe both, I haunt court or town.[6]
To any *bút* my Lord of Essex' days.[7]
To sea for nothing *bút* to make him sick.[8]

---

[1] *Elegy* I, 19.
[2] *Holy Sonnets*, XII, 11.
[3] *Elegy*, XVIII, 7.
[4] *A Hymn to God, My God, etc.*, 4.
[5] *The Lamentations*, 192.
[6] *To Sir Henry Watton* (2), 6.
[7] *Elegy* XV. *A Tale of a Citizen and His Wife*, 40.
[8] *Elegy* XIX, 3.

Only the stamp is changèd, *bút* no more.[1]

Others:

Were Tarquin night, as he is *bút* night's child.
Shakespeare, *R. of L.*, 785.
Nor are thy vicars, *bút* the hands of fate.
Parnell, *Donne's Sat.* III, *Versified*, 124.
I had no being—*bút* in thee.
Poe, *Tamerlane*, 115.

by

Donne:

When *bý* thy judgment they are dignified.[2]
Why are we *bý* all creatures waited on?[3]
For this they're scattered *bý* Jehovah's face.[4]
Restore Thine anger, so much *bý* Thy grace.[5]
Had correspondence whilst the foe stood *bý*.[6]

Others:

My Shakspeare, rise! I will not lodge thee *bý*
Chaucer, or Spenser, or bid Beaumont lie
A little further, to make thee a room.
Jonson, *To the Memory of My Beloved Mr.
William Shakspeare*, 19-21.

A reverend man that grazed his cattle nigh,
Sometime a blusterer, that the ruffle knew
Of court, of city, and had let go *bý*
The swiftest hours observèd as they flew.
Shakespeare, *A Lover's Complaint*, 57-60.

---

[1] *To Mr. Tilman, etc.*, 14.
[2] *The Storm*, 6.
[3] *Holy Sonnets* XII, 1.
[4] *The Lamentations*, 323.
[5] *Good Friday, etc.*, 41.
[6] *Elegy* XIII, 46.

In a kingdom bý the sea.
>> Poe, *Annabel Lee*, 2.

from

Donne:
> If *fróm* th' embrace of a loved wife you rise.[1]
> They fly not *fróm* that, nor seek precedence.[2]
> So is pride issued *fróm* humility.[3]
> Kindred were not exempted *fróm* the bonds.[4]

Others:
> And beck'ning wooes me *fróm* the fatal tree.
>> Jonson, *An Elegie on the Lady Pawlet*, 3.
>
> He hath, my lord, wrung *fróm* me my slow leave.
>> Shakespeare, *H.*, I, ii, 58.
>
> And wipe the tears forever *fróm* his eyes.
>> Milton, *Lycidas*, 181.
>
> No more shall rouse them *fróm* their lowly bed.
>> Gray, *Elegy*, 20.
>
> We turn'd our foreheads *fróm* the falling sun.
>> Tennyson, *The Brook*, 166.

down

Donne:
> Do but stoop *dówn* to kiss her utmost brow.[5]
> And though beyond is *dówn* the hill again.[6]
> My love descend, and journey *dówn* the hill.[7]
> Therefore that he may raise, the Lord throws *dówn*.[8]

Others:
> His gray visage *dówn* the stream was sent.
>> Milton, *Lycidas*, 62.

---

[1] *To M(r). I. L.*, 8.
[2] *To the Countess of Bedford* (5), 36.
[3] *The Cross*, 40.
[4] *Elegy* XVIII, 41.
[5] *Elegy* VI, 26.
[6] *To the Countess of Huntingdon* (2), 86.
[7] *Elegy* IX. *The Autumnal*, 48.
[8] *A Hymn to God, My God, etc.*, 30.

                                        For a stroke
On my raised head and naked arm came d*ówn*: town.
                    Shelley, *The Revolt of Islam*, III, xi, 2.

                            in
Donne:

For *in* whatever form the message came.[1]
To enter *in* these bonds is to be free.[2]
Which, faint for hunger, *in* the streets do lie.[3]
And made the dark fires languish *in* that vale.[4]
Empaled himself to keep them out, not *in*: been.[5]

Others:
                        Stay, stay, I feel
        A horror *in* me! All my blood is steel.
                    Jonson, *An Elegie on Lady Pawlet*, 8.
He grants salvation centres *in* his own.
                    Parnell, *Donne's Sat.* III, *Versified*, 73.
To sport with Amaryllis *in* the shade.
                                Milton, *Lycidas*, 68.
And silent *in* its dusty vines.
                    Tennyson, *Mariana in the South*, 4.

                            if
Donne:

But *if*—as all th' All must—hopes smoke away.[6]
And stand firm, *if* we by her motion go.[7]
I think it mercy *if* Thou wilt forget.[8]
If poisonous minerals, and *if* that tree.[9]

---

[1] *Elegy* XVIII, 71.
[2] *Elegy* XX, 31.
[3] *The Lamentations*, 164.
[4] *Resurrection*, 7.
[5] *To Sir Edward Herbert, etc.*, 11.
[6] *To M(r). R(owland) W(oodward)*, 27.
[7] *The Annunciation and Passion*, 30.
[8] *Holy Sonnets* IX, 14.
[9] *Ibid.*, 1.

Donne has no line ending in *if*, but an example from Hood, completes the five:

> Stood, an apparent sentinel as *if*: (stiff)
> To guard the water-lily.[1]

Or from Shakespeare:

> Yea, watch
> His pettish lunes, his ebbs, his flows, as *if*
> The passage and whole carriage of this action
> Rode on his tide...
> Shakespeare, *T. & C.*, II, iii, 140.

for

Donne:
> Nor *fór* the luck sake; but the bitter cost.[2]
> And punished *fór* offences not their own.[3]
> Much, much dear treasure *fór* the great rent day.[4]
> Have the remembrance of past joys *fór* relief.[5]
> With us at London, floats our courtiers *fór*: nor.[6]

Others:
> Say that thou didst forsake me *fór* some fault.
> Shakespeare, *Sonnet*, LXXXIX, 1.
> To pluck a garland, *fór* herself or me.
> Jonson, *An Elegie on the Lady Pawlet*, 4.
> Some trifle not worth caring *fór*: or.
> Blake, *The Everlasting Gospel*, 123.
> Whom else could I dare look backward *fór*: Leonor.
> Browning, *By the Fireside*, XXI, 3.

of

Donne:
> Part *óf* our passage; and a hand or eye.[7]

---

[1] *The Haunted House*, 55, 56.
[2] *Elegy* XI. *The Bracelet*, 8.
[3] *Elegy* XI. *The Bracelet*, 20.
[4] *To Mr. Rowland Woodward*, 33.
[5] *Holy Sonnets* III, 11.
[6] *Satire* IV, 175.
[7] *The Storm*, 3.

The daughters óf my people have sinned more.[1]
A virgin squadron óf white confessors.[2]
Have we proved all the secrets óf our art?[3]

Donne has no line ending in 'of'; for this we look to Shelley :

Burns bright or dim, as each are mirrors óf : { (move) (love) (wove) }
The fire for which all thirst.
Adonais, LIV, 8.

Or to Coleridge :
With a strange music that she knows not óf.
Remorse II, i, 42.

Others :

Did I there wound the honour óf the crown,
Or tax the glory óf the church or gown?
Jonson, *An Execration upon Vulcan*, 23-4.
Adieu to all the follies óf the age.
Pope, *Donne's Sat.*, IV, *Versified*, 2.
Or for some idol óf thy fancy draw.
Parnell, *Donne's Sat.*, III, *Versified*, 35.
Under the opening eyelids óf the morn.
Milton, *Lycidas*, 26.
Implores the passing tribute óf a sigh.
Gray, *Elegy*, 80.
To help me óf my weary load.
Tennyson, *Mariana in the South*, 30.
The more than beauty óf a face.
Poe, *Tamerlane*, 77.

on

Donne :

And ón the hatches, as on altars, lies.[4]
Some sitting ón the hatches would seem there.[5]

---

[1] *The Lamentations*, 289.
[2] *A Litany*, 92.
[3] *Elegy* XIII. *His Parting from Her*, 53.
[4] *The Calm*, 25.
[5] *The Storm*, 51.

Our persecutors *on* our necks do sit.¹
Fix we our praises therefore *on* this one.²
Why are we by all creatures waited *on* : upon.³

Others :
                First, then, advance
My drowsie servant, stupid Ignorance
Known by thy scaly vesture ; and bring *on*
Thy fearful sister, wild Suspition.
                Jonson, *Witches' Charms*, 49-52.
She feedeth *on* the steam, as *on* a prey.
                Shakespeare, *V. and A.*, 63.
For never-resting time leads *on* : (gone)
To hideous winter.
                Shakespeare, *Sonnet* V, 5.
        Put *on* (Hee'l say) put *on*
(My rosy love) that thy rich zone.
                Crashaw, *A Hymn to. . . St. Teresa*, 171.
If Jonson's learned sock be *on* : anon.
                Milton, *L'Allegro*, 132.
And waste its sweetness *on* the desert air.
                Gray, *Elegy*, 56.
Ever the weary wind went *on*.
                Tennyson, *The Dying Swan*, 9.
The spacious fields from me to Heaven take *on*
Tremors of change and new significance.
                Sidney Lanier, *Clover*, 62-3.

                or

Donne :
    A witness *or* comparison for thee.⁴
    Dead sods of sadness, *or* light squibs of mirth.⁵
    But is captived, and proves weak *or* untrue.⁶

---

¹ *The Lamentations*, 357.
² *Upon the Translation of the Psalms, etc.*, 7.
³ *Holy Sonnets* XII, 1.
⁴ *The Lamentations*, 138.
⁵ *A Litany*, 128.
⁶ *Holy Sonnets* XIV, 8.

Take such wives as their guardians offer ór : abhor.[1]

Others :

A scarlet piece, or two, stitch'd in : when ór
Diana's grave, or altar, with the bor-
Dring circles of swift waters. . . .
   Jonson, *Horace. Of the Art of Poetrie*, 19–21.
Who should weep most for daughter, ór for wife.
   Shakespeare, *R. of L.*, 1785.
But roars a torrent ór a flood below.
   Parnell, *Donne's Sat.* III, *Versified*, 142.
The cock's shrill clarion, ór the echoing horn.
   Gray, *Elegy*, 19.

    out

Donne :

Give oút for nothing but new injuries.[2]
As angels oút of clouds, from pulpits speak.[3]
He hath broke my bones, worn oút my flesh and skin.[4]
To see God only, I go oút of sight.[5]
As water did in storms, now pitch runs oút : spout.[6]

Others :

Th' Æmilian schoole, in brasse can fashion oút : (about)
The nails. . .
   Jonson, *Horace. Of the Art of Poetrie*, 46.
Fair torch burn oút thy light, and lend it not.
   Shakespeare, *R. of L.*, 183.
Till my bad angel fire my good one oút : about.
   Shakespeare, *Sonnet*, CLIV, 14.
Of linked sweetness long drawn oút : bout.
   Milton, *L'Allegro*, 140.
And every chance brought oút a noble knight.
   Tennyson, *Morte d'Arthur*, 231.

[1] *Satire* III, 61.
[2] *Elegy* XIV, 18.
[3] *To Mr. Tilman, etc.*, 43.
[4] *The Lamentations*, 181.
[5] *A Hymn to Christ, etc.*, 30.
[6] *The Calm*, 11.

so

Donne:

Rise *só* high like a rock, that one might think.¹
Our bodies *só*, but that our souls are tied.²
Restore Thine anger *só* much, by Thy grace.³
Since thou must do the like and *só* must move.⁴
And from our tatter'd sails rags drop down *só* : ago.⁵
O Varius? why am I now envied *só* : loe.
    Jonson, *Horace. Of the Art of Poetrie*, 79.
She says 'tis *só* : they answer all 'tis *só*.
    Shakespeare, *V. and A.*, 851.
And ye have power to touch our senses *só* : blow.
    Milton, *Hymn on Christ's Nativity*, 127.
If búsinéss is battle, name it *só* :
Wár-crimes less will shame it *só*,
And widows less will blame it *só*.
    Sidney Lanier, *The Symphony*, 61-63.

to

Donne:

Life *tó* that name, by which name they must live.⁶
Then are you *tó* yourself a crucifix.⁷
His tongue for thirst cleaves *tó* the upper jaw.⁸
This day when my soul's form bends *tó* the east.⁹
Our turning brain, and both our lips grow *tó* : through.¹⁰

Others:

He ever hastens *tó* the end and so

---

¹ *An Anatomy. Second Anniv.*, 287.
² *Elegy* XIII. *His Parting from Her*, 70.
³ *Good Friday, etc.*, 41.
⁴ *To Mr. Tilman, etc.*, 21.
⁵ *The Storm*, 57.
⁶ *A Funeral Elegy*, 12.
⁷ *The Cross*, 32.
⁸ *The Lamentations*, 282.
⁹ *Good Friday, etc.*, 10.
¹⁰ *Elegy* XIII, 58. 'Grow to' in the sense of growing together.

As if he knew it rapps his hearers tó
The middle of his matter...
Jonson, *Horace. Of the Art of Poetrie*, 211-213.
More studious tó divide than tó untie.
Pope, *An Essay on Man*, 82.
But are not critics tó their judgment too.
Pope, *An Essay on Criticism*, 18.
The path of glory lead but tó the grave.
Gray, *Elegy*, 36.
Close-latticed tó the brooding heat.
Tennyson, *Mariana in the South*, 3.
To lift adoring perfumes tó the sky.
Sidney Lanier, *Corn*, 23.

too

Donne:

And tóo high; beast and angels have been lóved.[1]
In harvest tóo indulgent to your sports.[2]
That spectacle of tóo much weight for me.[3]
Perhaps by golden mouthed Spenser tóo, pardie.[4]
Have both translated and applied it tóo : do.[5]

Others:

Great and good turns, as well could time them tóo : doe.
Jonson, *Epistle to Sir Edward Sackville*, 2.
And I by this will be a gainer tóo : do.
Shakespeare, *Sonnet* LXXXVIII, 9.
Yet she sailed softly tóo : blew.
Coleridge, *Ancient Mariner*, VI, 52.
Cloud, sunset, moonrise, star-shine tóo : drew.
Browning, *The Last Ride Together*, 29.

---

[1] *The Progress of the Soul*, 472.
[2] *To Sir Henry Goodyere*, 20.
[3] *Good Friday, etc.*, 16.
[4] *Satire* VII, 9.
[5] *Upon the Translation of the Psalms, etc.*, 19.

up

Donne:
Built *úp* against me and hath girt me in.[1]
Loth to go *úp* the hill, or labor thus.[2]
For I could muster *úp*, as well as you.[3]
Her soul is gone to usher *úp* her corse.[4]
Of formless curses, projects unmade *úp*.[5]

Others:
Bút as men drink *úp*
In haste the bottome of a med'cinal cup.
     Jonson, *An Elegie*, 3.
A vengeful canker eat him *úp* to death.
     Shakespeare, *Sonnet* XCIX, 12.
Struck *úp* against the blinding wall.
     Tennyson, *Mariana in the South*, 55.
Faint as a new-washed soul but lately *úp*
From out a buried body.
     Sidney Lanier, *Clover*, 32.

with

Donne:
Pace *with* the native stream the fish doth keep.[6]
Nor is it *with* His heart, that He doth smite.[7]
And burn me, O Lord, *with* a fiery zeal.[8]
Her tongue is soft and takes me *with* discourse.[9]

Others:
Perhaps to have been burnèd *with* my books: looks.
Condemn'd me to the ovens *with* the pies.
     Jonson, *An Execration upon Vulcan*, 18, 54.

---

[1] *The Lamentations*, 182.
[2] *An Anatomy. First Anniv.*, 281.
[3] *The Damp*, 17.
[4] *Elegy on Mistress Boulstred*, 46.
[5] *Elegy* XIV, 25.
[6] *The Progress of the Soul*, 251.
[7] *The Lamentations*, 226.
[8] *Holy Sonnets* V, 13.
[9] *Elegy* XVIII, 30.

'Twould burst e'en Heraclitus *with* the spleen.
>> Pope, *Donne's Sat.* IV, *Versified*, 236.

Alas! What boots it *with* incessant care.
>> Milton, *Lycidas*, 64.

And her eyes on all my motions *with* a mute observance hung.
>> Tennyson, *Locksley Hall*, 22.

Examples will now be given of some of the derivative and compound prepositions.

against

Donne:

> And *against* me all day, His hand doth fight.[1]
> Built up *against* me and hath shut me in.[2]
> Her anger on himself. Sins *against* kind.[3]

Others:

> I murmur *against* God, for having ta'en.
>> Jonson, *Elegie on My Muse*, 33.

> *Against* or faith, or honour's lawes.
>> Jonson, *An Elegie* [Though beautie be, etc.], 12.

> Pride, malice, folly, *against* Dryden rose.
>> Pope, *An Essay on Criticism*, 458.

> Weigh thy opinion *against* Providence.
>> Pope, *An Essay on Man*, 114.

> Those words, that would *against* them clear the doubt.
>> Pope, *Donne's Sat.* II, *Versified*, 104.

> As a despite done *against* the Most High.
>> Milton, *P. L.* VI, 906.

> *Against* God and Messiah, or to fall.
>> *Ibid.*, 796.

---

[1] *The Lamentations*, 180.
[2] *Ibid.*, 182.
[3] *The Progress of the Soul*, 468.

amongst

Donne:

> Is as an unclean woman ámongst them.[1]
> No hand amóngst them to vex them again.[2]

Jonson:

> Or like a ghost walk silent ámongst men.
> An Elegie [Since you must go, etc.], 21.
> Monarch in letters! 'móngst the titles showne.
> An Epistle to ... Selden, 65.

into

Donne:

> Intó the Virgin whose womb was a place.[3]
> Formed into words, so many sighs should meet.[4]
> And thrust intó straight corners of poor wit.[5]
> Lately launched into the vast sea of arts.[6]
> And then thyself intó our flames did'st turn.[7]
> The soils disease and into cockle strays.[8]
> Though it be changed and put intó a chain.[9]
> All the world's form being crumbled into sand.[10]

No line in Donne's verse ends with *into*, therefore, to complete the list a line is borrowed from Jonson:

> That all they do
> Though hid at home, abroad is searched intó.
> A Panagyre, 81.
> These trifles into serious mischiefes lead.
> Jonson, Horace. Of the Art of Poetrie, 654.

---

[1] *The Lamentations*, 68.
[2] *Ibid.*, 292.
[3] *A Litany*, 155.
[4] *Elegy* XVI. *The Expostulation*, 14.
[5] *Upon the Translation of the Psalms, &c.*, 3.
[6] *To M(r). Samuel Brooke*, 4.
[7] *Elegy* XI. *His Parting from Her*, 38.
[8] *To the Countess of Bedford* (3), 50.
[9] *Elegy* XI. *The Bracelet*, 70.
[10] *To the Countess of Salisbury, etc.*, 11.

Others:

> And think to burst out *into* sudden blaze.
> Creep and intrude and climb *intó* the fold.
>> Milton, *Lycidas*, 74, 115.
> Went down *intó* the sea.
> The upper air burst *into* life.
>> Coleridge, *Ancient Mariner* I, 24 and V, 22.
> I look *intó* her eyes and say.
>> Tennyson, *Mariana in the South*, 75.
> I bubble *into* eddying bays.
>> *The Brook*, 41.

unto

Donne:

> *Untó* the mill out young men carried are.[1]
> Be *únto* us because we've sinnèd so.[2]
> If thou *untó* thy Muse be marrièd.[3]
> At once fled *úntó* him and stayed with me.[4]
> But am betrothed *untó* your enemy.[5]
> Is turned, our houses *úntó* aliens gone.[6]
> And level Sion's walls *untó* the ground.[7]
> Name not these living death-heads *úntó* me.[8]
> Are mysteries which none have reached *untó* : do.[9]

Jonson:

> Care not what trials they are put *untó* : do.
>> *An Epistle. Answering to the One*, etc., 2.
> Than which there is not *únto* study a more
> Pernicious enemie.
>> *An Epistle, To . . . Selden*, 13.

---

[1] *The Lamentations*, 373.
[2] *Ibid.*, 378.
[3] *To M(r). B. B.*, 15.
[4] *Elegy* IV. *The Perfume*, 56.
[5] *Elegy* XIV, 10.
[6] *The Lamentations*, 352.
[7] *Ibid.*, 118.
[8] *The Autumnal*, 43.
[9] *An Anatomy. Second Anniv.*, 289.

The Rhetoric of John Donne's Verse.

upon

Donne:

Up*ón* the heavens and now they are his own.[1]
And *úpon* our own wood a price they lay.[2]
Poured out *upón* the ground for misery.[3]
Yet neither all nor *úpon* all alike.[4]
All this in women we might think *upón*.[5]

Milton:

Have set to wonder at and gaze *upón*.
Arcades, 43.

Others:

You show'd like Perseus *úpon* Pegasus.
Jonson, *An Epigram* [New Castle], 17.
Thou would'st have written, Fame, *upón* my breast.
Jonson, *An Elegie* [Pawlet], 14.
And I will comment *úpon* that offence.
And look *upón* myself, and curse my fate.
Shakespeare, *Sonnets* LXXXIX, 2, and XXIX, 4.
A faint blue ridge *upón* the right.
To what is loveliest *úpon* earth.
Tennyson, *Mariana in the South*, 5, 64.

without

Donne:

Withóut it there is no sense; only in this.[6]
And *without* such advantage kill me then.[7]
The sword *withóut*, as death within, doth waste.[8]
Swim in him swallow'd dolphins *without* fear.[9]

---

[1] *An Anatomy. First Anniv.*, 280.
[2] *The Lamentations*, 356.
[3] *Ibid*, 131.
[4] *Elegy ... Prince Henry*, 14.
[5] *Elegy* XIX, 17.
[6] *Satire* IV, 17.
[7] *The Damp*, 16.
[8] *The Lamentations*, 80.
[9] *The Progress of the Soul*, 316.

Jonson:

> Sleep in a virgin's bosome *withóut* feare.
> *Epistle to My Lady Covell*, 15.
> And valiant were, with or *withóut* their hands.
> *An Epigram* [New Castle], 24.

In the writings of Shakespeare and Donne are numerous examples of a similar treatment of 'thereby,' 'therefore,' 'whereof,' 'thereof,' 'therein,' 'within,' 'wherefore,' etc.[1]

A few of these will suffice here:

Donne:

> By all desires which *théreóf* did ensue.[2]
> At end *thereóf* one of th' antipodes.[3]

Shakespeare:

> And in the praise *thereóf* spends all his might.
> *Sonnet* LXXX, 3.
> And all those beauties *whéreof* now he's king.
> *Sonnet* LXIII, 6.

Donne:

> Those thousand ghosts *whereóf* myself made one.[4]
> All those things *whéreof* I consist hereby.[5]

Shakespeare:

> Gentle thou art, and *thérefore* to be won,
> Beauteous thou art, *therefóre* to be assailed.
> *Sonnet* XLI, 5, 6.
> That *théreby* beauty's rose might never die.
> *Sonnet* I, 2.

---

[1] George H. Browne, *Notes on Shakespeare's Versification*, Boston, 1901, p. 8: '*Thérefóre* and *whérefóre* sometimes have two accents; never *whérefore*.' See *Sonnet* CXXXVIII, 9:
> 'But *whérefore* says she not, she is unjust?'

[2] *Elegy* XVII. *Elegy on His Mistress*, 2.
[3] *An Anatomy. First Anniv.*, 294.
[4] *Elegy* XII, 68.
[5] *The Dissolution*, 6.

She carved thee for her seal and meant *thereby* : die.
Sonnet XI, 13.

'The poets have always exercised the right,—and their art has always demanded that they should,—to place the ictus upon the second member of substantive compounds, and in like manner to call forth the suppressed note of such derivative syllables as *-lic (ly)*, *-ness*, *-ig (y)*, *-er*, *-en*, *-el*, *-or*, *-est*, *-ing*, etc.'[1]

'Nouns of agency in *-er* have been studied with regard to rhythmic value in the early periods of the language by ten Brink (*Anglia* v. 1 f.), and the poets of to-day are aware of the old value. The extension of this capability of ictus for nouns of relationship (*father, mother, brother, sister*) and formations like *after, never*, until even *water* is overtaken. . .'[2]

'In accordance with the rules laid down by Sievers, *Metrik* § 78, and confirmed by Huguenin [pp. 3, 4 ff.], the use of secondary accent for ictus may be classed under two general heads: I, Compounds, and II, Derivatives. . . As Sweet [discussing compounds] has shown, *Grammar*, §§ 889 ff., there is a strong tendency to *even* stress. . . All compounds, however, whether they have even or uneven stress may readily bear the ictus on the second member. . . Compounds of which the second member has become a recognized suffix may be classed together with all derivative and formative elements. Of these are two classes:

'(*a*) Derivatives which, like the second member of a compound, may use the secondary accent for ictus; . . . (*b*) Derivatives which seem to have no accent unless inflected. . . For modern verse this distinction may be disregarded, since the loss of inflectional endings has put them upon the same level for metrical purposes. . .

'The expansion of the language through the assimilation of French and Latin words developed new possibilities for secondary accent. Analogous forms threw native and foreign derivatives into similar categories, and the same accentual laws became common to both. Of especial significance at this point are the prefixes. In Anglo-Saxon, prefixual stress was rare, nearly all nominal

---

[1] Professor Bright, *Proper Names*, etc., p. 357.
[2] *Ibid.*, p. 359.

prefixes having lost their accent through the influence of analogy with cognate verbal forms (Huguenin, p. 18). Under the influence of new metrical forms, however, the native prefixes, such as *a-, an-, on-, un-, be-, for-, off-, out-, up-, wið-*, fell into line with foreign prefixes in their power to bear the ictus.

'French and Latin prefixes receive a secondary accent which may serve for ictus whenever the verse requires it. Chief among these are, *a-, ab-, abs-, ad-, amb-, am-, an-, bi-, com-, con-, co-, de-, dis-, di-, em-, en-, ex-, e-, im-, in-, il-, mal-, ne-, ob-, obs-, o(b)s-, per-, pro-, post-, pur-, re-, se-, sub-, trans-*, etc.

'Foreign suffixes have extended the range of secondary accent beyond the possibility of exact classification. It is necessary to enumerate only the most important French and Latin endings, such as *-age, -al, -el, -il, -le, -an, -ain, -ian, -ance, -ence, -ant, -ent, -ard, -ass, -ace, -ble, -ple, -ar, -er, -ier, -ior, -or, -our, -ess, -ice, -ise, -et, -id, -iff, -ive, -in, -ist, -est, -ment, -on, -ion, -ory, -ous, -ose, -ure, -y, -ey, -cy, -ty*, etc.'[1]

In the authorities just quoted, full and satisfactory explanation is to be found not only for the secondary, or 'unusual' (?), accents employed by Donne, but also for the multitude of such accents that he might have made use of without transgressing a single tenet of poetics, and without disregarding the history of the English language. One may even dare to assert that Donne was a true artist and that he aimed towards perfect art. The fluctuating tides of criticism which have continued since Ben Jonson 'troubled the waters' are to be interpreted as meaning, to many, that Donne's 'discord is harmony not understood.'

Sidney Lanier (*Science of English Verse*, p. 213), discussing Shakespeare's plays, remarks that the rhythmic accent sometimes falls on 'the unaccented syllable of a two-sound word as *quickêns* instead of *qúickens*,' and that 'this apparent carelessness is really perfect art...'

Professor Bright (*Concerning Gram. Ictus*, p. 23) observes: 'The true artist finds inspiring strength in the study of the technicalities of his art.'

---

[1] *Miller, op. cit.*, pp. 20, 21, 22, 27, 28.

If Donne sinned it was rather in excess of care than in carelessness, as will be shown in Chapter III. A further comparison of his 'ruggedness' with the 'smoothness' of others, contemporaries and successors, may now conclude this chapter.

Miller (pp. 22-27) gives a full exposition of secondary accent in its relation to 'Substantival, Adjectival, and Verbal Forms, and Grammatical Groups.' For our purpose the examples to follow may be grouped under his general heads: 'Compounds; Proper Names; Prefixes; Suffixes; and Miscellaneous.'

Compounds.[1]

Donne:
>Sómething did say, and sómething did bestow.
>>*The Legacy*, 6.

Shakespeare:
>As signal that thou hear'st *something* approach.
>>*R. and J.*, V, iii, 8.

Donne:
>"Tell her anon
>Thy mýself," that is you, not I.
>>*The Legacy*, 10.

Shakespeare:
>I mýself fight not once in forty year.
>>1 *H.⁶*, I, iii, 91.

Donne:
>Yet strive so, that before age, death's twílight.
>>*Satire* III, 83.

>Takes this advantage to sleep out daylíght.
>>*Elegy* IV, 15.

Shakespeare:
>That I may back to Athens by daylíght.
>>*M. N. D.*, III, ii, 433.

Donne:
>From the *rose-búd* which for my sake you wore.
>>*Elegy* XII, 58.

---

[1] These are in addition to those already given under *Prepositions*.

Giles Fletcher :
>   Onely a garland of *rose-búds* did play.
>   *Christ's Victorie on Earth*, 58, 3.

Donne :
>   Those great *grandfáthers* of Thy Church which saw.
>   *A Litany*, 56.

Shakespeare :
>   Conceit is still derived from some *foreváther's* grief.
>   *R.²*, II, ii, 25.

Donne :
>   There is not now that *mánkind* which was then.
>   *An Anatomy. First Anniv.*, 112.

Shakespeare :
>   As if a god, in hate of *mánkind*, had
>   Destroy'd in such a shape.
>   *A. and C.*, IV, viii, 25.

Donne :
>   The flail-finned thresher and *steel-béaked sword-fish*.
>   *The Progress of the Soul*, 351.

Shakespeare :
>   As the *death-béd* whereon it must expire.
>   *Sonnet* LXXIII, 11.

Milton :
>   So violence
>   Proceeded, and oppression, and *sword-láw*.
>   *P. L.*, XI, 672.

Donne :
>   To *oút-do* (Dildoes), and out-usure Jews.
>   *Satire* II, 32.

Shakespeare :
>   If thou wilt *oútstrip* death, go cross the seas.
>   *R.³*, IV, i, 42.

Proper Names.[1]

Donne:

> Though *Danubý* into the sea must flow,
> The sea receives the Rhine, *Volgá* and Po.
>
> *Elegy* III, 19-20.

Shakespeare:

> O, my good lords and virtuous *Henrý*.
>
> 1 *H.⁶*, III, i, 76.

Donne:

> And mangled seventeen-headed *Belgiá* : day.
>
> *Elegy* XI, 42.
>
> No poison's half so bad as *Juliá* : say.
>
> *Elegy* XIV, 32.
>
> Reclused at home, public at *Golgothá* : stay.
>
> *The Annunciation and Passion*, 12.

Milton :

> Here pilgrims roam, that stray'd so far to seek.
> In *Golgothá* him dead, who lives in heaven.
>
> *P. L.*, III, 477.

Donne:

> Now in these days of tears *Jerusalêm*.
>
> *The Lamentations*, 25.

Milton :

> Till underneath them fair *Jerusalêm*.
>
> *P. R.*, 544.

---

[1] '... The poets' use of foreign names, while its main features will reflect the current pronunciation, will occasionally make discernable possibilities of stress which are in part or altogether obscured in prose; besides other more or less artificial effects may be admitted which will remain inoperative in moulding the accepted form and pronunciation. A capricious accentuation of names by Chaucer and by Shakespeare, for example, has not disturbed the normal history of these words, but the average practice of these and of all the poets bears surest testimony to the validity of the laws of persistence and of change written in that history.' Professor Bright, *Proper Names, etc.*, p. 356.

Donne:

> Of France and fair *Itály's* faithlessness.
> > *To Sir Henry Wotton* (1), 66.

Shakespeare:

> Now in the fields of faithful *Italý* : chivalry.
> > *R. of L.*, 107.

Donne:

> As China when the sun at *Brázil* dines.
> > *To the Countess of Bedford* (2), 18.
>
> Twins, though their birth *Cuscó* and *Músco* take.
> > *To the Lady Bedford*, 7.
>
> In which *Nattá*, the new knight, seized on me.
> But as for *Nátta*, we have since fallen out.
>
> Writes thus and jests not. Good *Fidús* for this.
> His last; and, *Fídus*, you and I do know.
> > *Satire* VII, 22, 91, 89, 97.

Shakespeare:

> Tell me thy mind; for I have *Písa* left
> And am to *Pádua* come, as he that leaves
> A shallow plash. . .
> > *T. S.*, I, i, 21.
>
> And he shall be Vincentio of *Pisá*
> And make assurance here in *Páduá*.
> > *Ibid.*, III, ii, 135.

Donne:

> "'Tis sweet to talk of kings." "At *Wéstminstér*—
> > *Satire* IV, 74.

Shakespeare:

> And vows to crown himself in *Wéstminstér*.
> > 2 *H.*⁶, IV, iv, 31.

Donne:

> By silver-tongued *Ovíd* and many moe.
> > *Satire* VII, 8.

Shakespeare:

> Judas Maccabeus clipt is plain *Judás*.
> > *L. L. L.*, V, ii, 603.

Donne:

      O my America, my *Newfoundlánd*.
                                    Elegy XX, 27.

Shakespeare:

      Of you, my gentle cousin *Westmorelánd*.
                                    1 *H.*⁴, I, i, 31.

Donne:

      A thing which would have posed *Adám* to name.
                                    Satire IV, 20.

Jonson:

      Though you presume *Satán*, a subtle thing.
                                   Prologue, D. A., 5.

Milton:

      To whom, thus half abash'd *Adám* replied.
                                   P. L., VIII, 595.

Donne:

      Anyan, and Magellan, and Gibraltar.[1]
                            Hymn to God, My God, etc., 18.

---

[1]   Is the Pacific sea my home? Or are
      The eastern riches? Is Jerusalem?
  18 Anyan, and Magellan, and Gibraltar?
      All straits, and none but straits, are ways to them
      Whether where Japhet dwell, or Cham, or Shem.

It is very evident that line 18 is not the original. Were it a continuation of the interrogation we would have 'or' each time instead of 'and.'

Grosart prints the line: *Anyan and Magellan and Gibraltar are*, with a note which indicates that some edition, earlier than 1669, also omits the 'are'; but has a comma after 'Jerusalem.' This would permit the *ands* to follow in the interrogation, but for the fact that *are* instead of *is* would be required before Jerusalem; besides with *are*, and with the comma, the obscurity is sufficient to warrant a rejection of the line. It probably read, in the original: Anyan, Magellan and Gibraltar are All straits. . .

This line, like many others, illustrates the fact that Donne is not responsible for some of the 'ruggedness' which has been charged against him.

Prefixes.

a-

Donne :
    In length and ease are *álike* everywhere.
        To Sir Henry Wotton, etc., 40.

Milton :
    As a despite done *ágainst* the Most High.
        P. L., VI, 906.

ad-

Donne :
    Under the *ádverse* icy pole thou pine.
        To Sir Henry Wotton (1) 12.

Shakespeare :
    Thy *ádverse* party is thy advocate.
        Sonnet XXXV, 10.

be-

Donne :
    Grow your fit subject *bécause* you are true.
        The Indifferent, 18.

Donne :
    A better sun rose *béfore* thee to-day.
        Resurrection, 4.
    And so the heavens which *béget* all things here.
        To Mr. Tilman, etc., 51.

Shakespeare :
    As lightning *béfore* death : O ! how may I.
        R. and J., V, iii, 90.
    With plumèd helm thy slayer *bégins* threats.
        Lear IV, ii, 57.

cor-

Donne :
    But *córrupt* worms the worthiest men.
        A Fever, 12.

Shakespeare :
    Care is no cure, but rather *córosive*.
        1 *H.*[6], III, iii, 3.

con-

Donne :
  Making them cónfess not only mortal.
        Satire IV, 201.

Shakespeare :
  Good even to my ghostly cónfessor.
        R. and J., II, vi, 21.

Pope :
  And to be dull was cónstrued to be good.
        An Essay on Criticism, 690.

de-

Donne :
  These wits that say nothing, best déscribe it : wit.
        Satire VII, 16.

Donne :
  By which to you he dérives much of his.
        To Sir Henry Wotton, etc., 3.

Shakespeare :
  The pangs of déspis'd love, the law's delay.
        Hamlet III, i, 72.
  I dérived liberty. O ! by no means.
        Tim., I, ii, 8.

en-

Donne :
  Nor énjoy aught, do far more hate the great.
        The Progress of the Soul, 77.

Shakespeare :
  Where you shall host : of énjoin'd penitents.
        A. W., III, v, 97.

ex-

Donne :
  But, as from éxtreme heights who downward looks.
        To the Countess of Huntington (2), 11.
  Who in the other éxtreme only doth.
        Satire IV, 220.

Shakespeare :
>And *éxtreme* fear can neither fight nor fly.
>>*R. of L.*, 230.

Donne :
>This kind of beast, my thoughts shall *éxcept* thee.
>>*Elegy* XVI. *The Expostulation*, 24.

Milton :
>To tempt or punish mortals *éxcept* whom.
>>*P. L.*, II, 1032.

for-

Donne :
>Why should'st thou *fórget* us eternally ?
>>*The Lamentations*, 285.

Shakespeare :
>All *fórsworn*, all naught, all dissemblers.
>>*R. and J.*, III, ii, 87.

mis-

Donne :
>Keep midnight's promise ; *místake* by the way.
>>*Love's Usury*, 11.

Shakespeare :
>The *mísplac'd* John should entertain one hour.
>>*John* III, iv, 133.

pur-

Donne :
>To *púrsue* things which had endangered me.
>>*Farewell to Love*, 34.

Shakespeare :
>We trifle time ; I pray thee *púrsue* sentence.
>>*M. of V.*, IV, i, 298.

re-

Donne :
>As *réfuse* and off-scouring of the world.
>>*The Lamentations*, 242.

Shakespeare :
>This is the very *réfuse* of thy deeds.
>>*Sonnet* CL, 6.

The Rhetoric of John Donne's Verse. 95

un-

Donne:

After such pleasures, *únless* wise
Nature decreed...
Farewell to Love, 23.

That will consort, none *úntil* thou have known.
Satire I, 33.

Shakespeare:

And *úntil* then your entertain shall be.
Per., I, i, 119.

Milton:

And not molest us; *únless* we ourselves.
P. L., VIII, 186.

Suffixes[1]

-age

Donne:

When plenty, God's *imáge* and seal.
A Litany, 185.

Milton:

Created thee in the *imáge* of God.
P. L., VII, 527.

---

[1] That part of Mr. H. C. Beeching's criticism, in *The Atheneum*, June 1st, 1901, which relates to Professor Bright's scansion of lines containing such accents as *ámong* and *befóre*, is fully met by Brown, (p. 31), with examples from Wordsworth and Tennyson. On suffixes Mr. Beeching remarks (p. 21): 'The unphilological reader will probably retort upon the professor that nowhere in Shakespeare, Milton and Tennyson are *lover, rendered, doubtful,* and *going* accented on the final syllable, and the canons of practical scansion are made by the great poets.'

Let us re-read Mr. Beeching's remark on 'canons of poetical scansion' and 'great poets' with Dr. Miller's examples (pp. 57-59 and 68-9) before us. Here are four of them.

Shakespeare:

I pray you, uncle, give me this *daggér*.
R.[2], III, i, 110.

To see great Hercules *whippíng* a gig.
L. L. L., IV, iii, 167.

Milton:

Among *daughtérs* of men the fairest found.
P. R., II, 154.

As when two polar winds *blowíng* adverse.
P. L., X, 289.

-al

Donne:

For all our joys are but *fantastical*.
Elegy X, 14.

Shakespeare:

And so the *general* of hot desire.
Sonnet CLIV, 7.

Pope:

So man, who here seems *principál* alone.
An Essay on Man, I, 57.

-er, -or

Donne:

All news I think *soonér* reach thee than me.
To M(r). R(owland) W(oodward), 15.

Mine own *executór* and legacy.
The Legacy, 8.

Shakespeare:

My love shall make my verse *evér* live young.
Sonnet XIV, 14.

Thou hast done a deed whereat *valór* will weep.
Cor., V, v, 134.

Jonson:

To love not violence, here; I am no *ravishér*.
D. A., IV, iii, 2.

Or, with your Spaniard, your *provocadór*.
Ibid., III, i, 230.

Milton:

By the *watérs* of life where'er they sat.
P. L., XI, 77.

With lucky words *favór* my destin'd urn.
Lycidas, 20.

Coleridge:

And thus spake on that ancient man
The bright eyed *Marinér*: hear.
Ancient Mariner, 19-20.

Donne:
      -es
  Men are *spongés*, which, to pour out, receive.
      To Sir Henry Wotton (1), 37.

Shakespeare:
  Or Cytherea's breath ; pale *primrosés*.
      W. T., IV, iv, 122.

Milton:
  Unsung ; or to describe *racés* and games.
      P. L., IX, 33.

    -ness and *-ess*
Donne:
  To such *vastnéss*, as if unmanacled.
      The Progress of the Soul, 303.

Shakespeare:
  Fair sir, God save you ! Where is the *princéss*?
      L. L. L., V, ii, 310.

    -est
Donne:
For thou this day *couplést* two phoenixes.
 Epithalamion [Lady Elizabeth and Count Palatine], 18.

Milton:
  Tended the sick *busiést* from couch to couch.
      P. L., II, 490.

    -ing
Donne:
  And at Thy death *givíng* such liberal dole.
      La Corona. Crucifying, 13.

Shakespeare:
  And here ye lie *baitíng* of bombards when.
      H.⁸, V, i, 85.

Milton:
  Silence, and sleep *listeníng* to thee will watch.
      P. L., VII, 106.

    -ish
Donne:
  But these *puním* themselves. The insolence.
      Satire II, 39.

Shakespeare:
    Keep some state in thy exit, and *vanĭsh*.
                        L. L. L., V, ii, 598.

Milton:
    But to *vanquĭsh* by wisdom hellish wiles.
                        P. R., I, 175.

       -le, -el

Donne:
    In a *cradlé* free from dreams or thoughts there.
                        Satire VII, 5.

    Or as we paint *angéls* with wings, because.
                        To Mr. Tilman, etc., 19.

Shakespeare:
    How she came placèd here in the *templé*.
                        Per., V, iii, 67.

    I would keep from thee——For your sake, *jewél*.
                        O., I, iii, 195.

       -ow

Donne:
    If she be a *widów* I'll warrant her.
                        Satire VI, 25.

Shakespeare:
    The hope of comfort. But for the *fellów*.
                        Cym., IV, iii, 9.

Jonson:
    To practice there with any *play-fellów*.
                        D. A., I, i, 39.

    That was your *bedfellów*
The other month. . .
                        Ibid., II, iii, 31.

       -y, -ly

Donne:
    He faith in some, *envý* in some begot.
                        La Corona. Crucifying, 2.

    Jehovah here *fullý* accomplished ha^{ta}th.
                        The Lamentations, 305.

    Sweetness and wit they are, but *mummý* possess'd.
                        Love's Alchemy, 24.

Shakespeare:
> It is for him you do *envý* me so?
>> *Shrew*, II, i, 18.
> Leaves Love upon her back *deeplý* distress'd.
>> *Venus*, 814.
> It blows the wind that profits *nobodý*.
>> 3 *H.⁶*, II, v, 55.

For a further study of accented suffixes in Shakespeare, Jonson and Milton, and in which the accents employed by Donne are paralleled, the investigator is referred to the examples cited by van Dam and Stoffel,[1] Wilke,[2] Miller,[3] and Abbott.[4]

Miscellaneous.

Donne:
> I can convert *manná* to gall.
>> *Twickenham Garden*, 7.

Fraunce:[5]
Strengthened more than bread, and fed man more than a *Manná*:
> Iehoua.
>> *Emanuel*, p. 29, 3.

Donne:
> Are *únchangeable* firmament.
>> *A Fever*, 24.

Pope:
> And *charitábly* let the dull be vain.
>> *An Essay on Criticism*, 597.

Donne:
> Such is thy tan*g*'d skin's *lámentáble* state.
>> *Elegy* VIII, 32.

Pope:
> Fear most to tax an *Hónoráble* fool.
>> *An Essay on Criticism*, 588.

---

[1] *William Shakespeare, Prosody and Text.* Leyden, 1900, pp. 178-188.
[2] Wilhelm Wilke: *Metrische Untersuchungen zu Ben Jonson.* Halle, 1884, pp. 17-45.
[3] *Op. cit.*, pp. 57-60, 72.
[4] E. A. Abbott, *A Shakespearian Grammar*, n. e. London, 1884, pp. 388-96.
[5] Abraham Fraunce: 'The Countesse of Pembroke Emmanuel' *Miscellanies* III, *The Fuller Worthies' Library.*

Donne :
As *ignorántly* did I crave.
Farewell to Love, 6.

Pope :
The bookful blockhead, *ignorántly* read.
An Essay on Criticism, 612.

Donne :
For service paid *authórized* now begin.
Satire V, 33.

Shakespeare :
His rudeness so with his *authórized* youth.
Sonnet XXX, 6.

Donne :
Which are but *áccessóries* to this name.
A Valediction, etc., 14.

Shakespeare :
Then I an *áccessóry* needs must be.
Sonnet XXXV, 13.

Donne :
Which then comes *seasonáblest* when our taste.
Elegy IV, 27.

Shakespeare :
What *acceptáble* audit cans't thou have?
Sonnet I, 12.

Donne :
So we her airs *contémplate*, words and heart.
Elegy XIX, 35.

Shakespeare :
His goods *confiscate* to the duke's dispose.
C. of E., I, i, 21.

Donne :
As much *weariness* as perfection brings.
Epith. Lincoln's Inn, 66.

Shakespeare :
Robb'd others' beds *revénues* of their rents.
Sonnet CXLII, 8.

Donne :
Deliver us from the *siníster* way.
La Corona, 198.

Shakespeare:
   'Tis no *siníster* nor no awkward claim.
              H.⁵, II, iv, 85.

Donne:
   Deface *recórds* and histories.
              The Damp, 14.

Shakespeare:
   For thy *recórds* and what we see do lie.
              Sonnet CXXIII, 11.

Donne:
   Blasted with sighs and *súrroundéd* with tears.[1]
              Twickenham Garden, 1.

Shakespeare:
   A wise, stout captain, and soon *pérsuadéd*.
              3 *H.⁶*, IV, vii, 30.

   As great to me, as late; and, *súpportáble*
   To make the dear loss...
              Tp., V, i, 145.

Jonson:
   Blemish, or *sún-burnings*; and keeps the skin.
              D. A., IV, i.

   And for it lose his eyes with *gún-powdér*: quicksilver.
              An Execration upon Vulcan, 121.

These are not all the unusual accents to be found in the poetry of Donne; but they are fairly representative. In our next chapter other examples will appear; but it will not be necessary there to cite parallels. When one meets a 'harsh' or 'rugged' accent in Donne (barring misprints and transcribers' errors always) by turning to the tables of van Dam and Stoffel, Wilke, Miller, and Abbott,—already referred to,[2]—he will find there, that in so far

---

[1] Professor Norton (*Love Poems of John Donne* p. 81, note) states that 'surrounded' was still a rare word in Donne's time, and that Shakespeare does not use it. This line will be referred to again in the next chapter.

[2] A few of Shakespeare's accents, as recorded by Abbott, Miller, and van Dam and Stoffel. Abbott (pp. 388-96): *Charácters, confíscate, different, effígies, miséry, nothíng, oppórtune, sepúlchre, welcóme, cónfessór, délectáble, détestáble, fórlorn, máture, óbscure, óbservánts, Plébiáns, súccessive, púrveyór, rhéumatíc, útensíls*; Miller (pp. 56-

102 *The Rhetoric of John Donne's Verse.*

as word-accent, considering words taken singly, is concerned, Jonson and Shakespeare are quite as harsh as Donne. In subsequent pages it will be shown in what manner Donne differs from his contemporaries.

---

60) : *Sálisbúry, Edmúnd, Énglish, Richárd, Talbót, émpirics, ínterprèts, prótectór, séquestér'd, mád-womán, párk-cornér, murdér'd, sistérs, códpiecés, nouríshed, reasón'd, fortúne, authórized, mirácle, orísons, secrétly;* van Dam and Stoffel (178-184) ; *advérsary, álone, áppear, authórized, báboon, canónize, cáreer, certáin, charácter, Christópher, cóagúlate, cómmendáble, cónfessór, córrosíve, déclensión, démonstráble, dísordérly, flexíble, herétic, ídolátrous, intérruptér, ínvisíble, nóthing, oppórtune, purgátive, récéptácle, remédy, rhetóric, séquestér, subséquent, únauthórized, únhappý.*

A few of Jonson's accents, as recorded by Wilke (pp. 28-46) : *gránd-fathér, gránd-mothér, bónd-womán, lóve-lettér, nó-bodý, búll-rushés, bél-wethér, mílke-monéy, selfe-lóve, corke-shóes, nóthing, painefúll, envý, enviéd, recórds, honoúrs, pastór, natúre, satán, mistréss, góing, cóming, addéd, worthý, onelý, carrý, vanquísh, answére, hundréds, husbánds, undér, ovér, aftér, Engländ, massácre, siníster, miníster, infámous, meláncholý, ádvance, áffairs, búffon, cómpose, cónfer, cónfesse, décl)r'd, décay'd, díspatch, dívine, énjoy, éxtreme, néglect, óbscure, póssesse, prócure, prótect, réfuse, réturne, sécure, sérene, tráduce, ábout, ábove, ágainst, álike, ámongst, béfore, béyond, úpon, wíthout, bécome, bélieve, fórbid, úncleane, únrest, cóntribúte, prágmaticke, succéssórs, impórtune, ácceptáble, récéptácle, incómbustíble, ladý, Heidélberg, Rachél.*

CHAPTER III.

The Rhetoric of Verse in Donne.

I. *The Title Defined.*

Strictly speaking, 'The Rhetoric of Verse' is a large term including as its chiefest sub-division 'Secondary Word-accent.' The title is suggested by Professor Bright, who gives this definition:

'By the rhetoric of verse, or the rhetoric of poetry, is meant the emphasis elicited by verse-stress, when it is at variance with the usual (prose) emphasis. Thus, for example, the verse of Chaucer will teach how significant in "artistic expression" are the usually unemphatic members of compound words and many of the derivative and inflectional elements of the language. We are thus brought to see a new category of "meaning" and of "notional" suggestion. To this category an important contribution is made by the verse stress of particles, prepositions, etc. It is therefore necessary to recognize a verse-rhetorical counterpart to the accepted figurative use of language in verse.'[1]

'The rhetorical demands of emphasis, the rhetorical demands of the poetry (requiring an emphasis which is only exceptional in prose), the occasional ictus-use of subordinate accents, these are the principal means at hand for producing in the wave of measured and rhythmical utterance the desired variations in amplitude and curvature.'[2]

To quote again from Professor Bright:[3] 'Bysshe in his *Art of English Poetry* (London, 1714, p. 6) illustrates the poet's lack of rhythmic tact in the following lines from Davenant:

---

[1] 'The Rhetoric of Verse in Chaucer.' *Pub. Mod. Lang. Assoc. of America*, 16, p. xlii.
[2] *Concerning Gram. Ictus*, etc., p. 27.
[3] *Proper Names*, etc., p. 358.

"None thínk Rewárds rénder'd wórthy their Wórth.
And bóth Lóvers, bóth thy Discíples wére."

'... Bysshe proceeds to obviate "the undue seat of the accent," and presents the lines in "smooth and easy form":

"None thínk Rewárds are équal tó their Wórth.
And lóvers bóth, both thý Discíples wére."'

On Bysshe's effort to 'smooth' Davenant, Professor Bright comments: 'Surely the poet must be allowed to have his own way,' and scans the lines correctly,—

None think | Rewards | rendér'd | worthý | their Wórth
And both | Lovérs | both thy | Discip | les were.

'... Watts had also cited these two lines (*Works*, 1812-13, vol. IX, 442 f.) and declared that "worthy" and "Lovers," placed as they are, "turn the line into perfect prose."'

Professor Bright quotes these two lines as showing in *lovérs* and *rendér* 'the two principal classes of secondary word-accent (native and foreign), which have been at all times and are still available for ictus.'

To this I wish to add that it is important to notice the repeated and varying syllables *wórthy ... Wórth*, and *bóth ... bŏth*. If we are to attend to the artistic monotone of verse, then the appearance of the same word or sound, now in arsis and now in thesis, or *vice versa*, is quite as essential to the music or rhythm of the line as is secondary word-accent, the observance of which, in the first line above, makes such a variation possible.

The frontier singing-master long ago caught this idea and built up tunes with 'do re mi fa sol la si do.' Each of these senseless syllables stood for a given tone or pitch, and when an even, unvarying sound was desired, it was produced by the repetition of the same sound-representing syllable, as: Tra-la-la-la-la-la.'

Tennyson, wishing to represent the placid and ceaseless flow of the brook, writes,

For *mén máy* come and *mén máy gó*;
But I *gŏ* on forever.

Even the unpoetic Dr. Johnson recognized this principle. Having quoted (Chalmers, *Eng. Poets*, vii, 39) Cowley's defence of his representative, resembling, or imitative lines, Johnson adds, 'But, not to defraud him of his due praise, he has given one example of representative versification, which perhaps no other English line can equal:

> Begin, be bold, and venture to be wise:
> He, who defers this work from day to day,
> Does on a river's bank expecting stay
> Till the whole stream that stopp'd him shall be gone,
> Which *rúns*, and, as it *rúns*, forever shall *rŭn* on.

Professor Bright (*Concerning Gram. Ictus*, etc., pp. 26-27) speaking of 'the notion of musical or artistic monotone of verse,' refers to 'the several types of oral English as ... set forth by Professor Lloyd:[1] the formal type, appropriate to solemn occasions, as in the reading of the liturgy; the careful type, of the best conversation and of public speakers; the careless type which is tolerated "as containing no very disagreeable errors;" and the vulgar type containing inadmissable errors. It is important also to note that these types are described as differing chiefly in the matter of syllabic stress. "The first," says Professor Lloyd, "contains few syllables which are quite stressless;" the second has none of them; the third "exaggerates weakness of stress;" and in the fourth "it often happens that the fully stressed syllables alone preserve their formal quality." It is obvious enough,' concludes Professsor Bright, 'that in formal utterances the language has qualities (which may be described as musical) which are available for artistic use, and that these qualities are bound up with the careful observance of not only the principal but also the subordinate stresses of the syllables.'

By '*formal* utterances' Professor Bright does not mean to limit himself to the first, or '*formal* type' of Professor Lloyd, for, in the next sentence, he says, 'Much may be learned, therefore, ... from what the treatises say of the formal utterance of the stage

---

[1] R. J. Lloyd, *Northern English: Phonetics, Grammar, Texts*, London, 1899, p. 30.

and the pulpit, and the best manner of reading sometimes practiced by the poets.'

It appears, then, that Professor Bright has in mind both the 'formal' and 'careful' types of Professor Lloyd; but it is evident that the third type, regarded by the latter as 'careless' in 'oral English,' may become *careful* in rhythmically recited poems. Especially is this true if the reader subdues strength of stress, while exaggerating weakness of stress, so as to give arses and theses as nearly as possible the same pitch or duration. To accomplish this, it is the poet's prerogative to vary the same word or words even at the expense of having his lines bear the stamp of studied carefulness and purposed effect.

Observation of this arsis-thesis variation of the same word or words in the same line, or in close proximity, is the 'practically untouched aspect of the criticism of English verse' referred to in our introduction. Abbott approaches one side of the subject:

'A word repeated twice in a verse often receives two accents the first time, and one accent the second, when it is less emphatic the second time than the first. Or the word may occupy the whole of a foot the first time, and only part of a foot the second.'[1]

'On the other hand,' continues Abbott (p. 362), 'when the word increases in emphasis the converse takes place.' Thus, we see, he makes no provision for any repeated word or syllable which is not available for ictus; that is to say, he is concerned primarily and always with stressed syllables.

Browne paraphrases Abbott, citing five of his twenty-two examples, but getting no nearer to our subject than did his forerunner. He says: 'A word repeated in the same verse often has two accents the first time, and one the second; or occupies the whole bar the first time, and only part of a bar the second; and *vice versa*, according to emphasis.'[2]

Another side of the subject is approached by Hubbard:[3] 'By repetition is meant the use of the same word or words in the same

---

[1] E. A. Abbott, *A Shakespearian Grammar*, London, 1884, p. 361.
[2] George H. Browne, *Notes on Shakespeare's Versification*, Boston, 1901, p. 8.
[3] F. G. Hubbard, 'Repetition and Parallelism in the Early Elizabethan Drama,' *Pubs. Mod. Lang. Asso. of America*, n. s., vol. xiii, no. 2, pp. 360, 361.

line, or in succeeding lines of verse; where there is more than one word in the unit repeated, the term repetition implies the word in the same order.

> Locrine, draw near, draw near unto thy sire."
> *Locrine*, I, i, 146.

'By parallelism is meant the use of the same *form* of expression in the same line, or in succeeding lines of verse, the parallel expressions occupying the same relative place in the structure of the verse.

> " O life, the harbor of calamities !
> O death, the heaven of all miseries !"
> *Locrine*, IV, i, 5/6-7.

Professor Brumbaugh comes thrillingly near to our subject: 'The frequent repetition of the same monosyllable, generally at the caesural pause, the repeated word having often a different meaning, and giving his verse by this change of accent a peculiar "swing" that is at the same time characteristic and melodious, is very common in Donne's verse. It is indeed so frequent (I have noted about fifty instances) that illustration is necessary.'

Seventeen examples are cited of which these three are representative :

> *Up, up,* my drowsy soul, where th*ey.* . .
> *An Anatomy. Second Anniv.*, 339.
> Carrying his own house *still, still* is at home.
> *To Sir Henry Wotton* (1) 50.
> *She, she* is dead, she's dead; when thou know'st this.
> *An Anatomy. First Anniv.*, 183, 237, 325, 369, 427.

When, in person, I called Professor Brumbaugh's attention to the fact that Donne, some four thousand times makes use of this arsisthesis variation of the same syllable or syllables, word or words in the same line, or group of lines, and when I had read to him more than a hundred of the most striking examples, he replied, 'I am prepared to believe it;' and showed me the MS. page from which the above quotation is taken. Had he gone one step further he would have discovered the peculiar characteristic, which, as unmistakable as the red strand of the rope of the English Navy, runs through the entire body of Donne's verse. For example, had he considered the very next line he would have found this variation, not only at 'the caesural pause,' but every where else in the couplet, on similar words as: shĕ, shé; thóu, thŏu; and on similar sounds as: ĭs, thís, thĭs, ĭs; and knŏw'st, knów'st, ghóst.

> Shĕ, shé ĭs dead; shé's dead; when thóu knŏw'st thís
> Thŏu knów'st how wan a ghóst thĭs our world ĭs.

II. *The Mystery of Donne's Art.*

That there is something peculiar or mysterious, about Donne's method of expression, even more than about the matter expressed, has always been recognized as a fact. This statement is amply warranted by a large majority of the criticisms recorded in Chapter I. It will be remembered that Hazlitt spoke of his lines as 'riddles that the sphinx could not unravel;' Gosse, 'the riddle is soon read;' Theobald, 'a heap of riddles,' etc.

'Henry King speaks of the art of Donne as a mystery...'[1]

'One is tempted to wonder whether Donne did not leave his own character as one of the riddles which he wished posterity to solve.'[2]

Beers says all Donne's poetry is 'distinguished by such subtle obscurity, and far-fetched ingenuities, that they read like a series of puzzles... [His] verse is usually as uncouth as his thought. But there is a real passion slumbering under these ashy heaps of conceit, and occasionally a pure flame shoots up...'[3]

Elsewhere Beers says 'Donne [is] ... willfully quaint, subtle, and paradoxical.'[4]

Belden: '... Donne is never, I think, difficult through care-

---

[1] Gosse, *op. cit.*, ii, 346.
[2] *Quarterly Review*, vol. CXCII, ('John Donne and His Contemporaries,' pp. 217-240), p. 231.
[3] Henry A. Beers, *From Chaucer to Tennyson*, New York, 1890, pp. 106-7.
[4] *A History of Romanticism in the Eighteenth Century*, New York, 1899, p. 28.

lessness or obscure through vagueness or indefiniteness of thought. What he thinks is concrete; and the reader who will follow him in his wrestlings with the language will generally be rewarded, as even Dr. Johnson acknowledged, by "genuine wit and useful knowledge..."'

'True to his own nature, as to the inevitable secrecy of his youth, Donne drew around him a cloudy something which keeps him forever to himself. And whoever may have penetrated within has been unable, on coming forth, to render a good account of what he has experienced... Whoever can write anything which shall give a true and sufficient idea of John Donne, such an idea as will make the general reader of poetry understand why he is regarded as a poet of surpassing genius, may deem himself no longer an apprentice in the art of criticism ... Those who know the poet still remain an elect number.'[1]

'[Readers of Donne's poetry may find] paradoxical plays of words, antithesis of thought and expression, and purposed involution of phrase, that nothing but the most painful attention can untwist. All this they may find and more. But in the midst of it all, they not only may, but must find an unceasing activity and an overflowing fullness of mind, which seem never to fail or flag, and which would more than half redeem the worst faults (of mere style) that could be allied to them.'[2]

'Donne is a thoroughly original spirit and a great innovator; he is thoughtful, indirect, and strange; he nurses his fancies, lives with them, and broods over them so much that they are still modern in all their distinction and ardour, in spite of the strangeness of their apparel—strangeness no greater perhaps than that of modern poets, like Browning, as the apparel of their verse will appear two hundred years hence.'[3]

'Donne is full of salient verses that would take the rudest March winds of criticism with their beauty, of thoughts that first tease us like charades, and then delight us with the felicity of

---

[1] *The Dial*, Chicago, vol. xx, no. 237, p. 280.
[2] *Retrospective Review*, vol. viii, p. 55.
[3] Carpenter, *op. cit.*, p. lviii.

their solution; but those have not saved him. He is exiled to the limbo of the formless and fragmentary.'[1]

Opinions may differ as to whether this arsis-thesis variation was deliberately resorted to by Donne, or whether it was an unconscious exposition of his peculiar mental operations. This question is not germane to the present investigation; but it may be said that it seems almost certain that it was deliberately planned and executed with the greatest care, patience, and ingenuity.

Gosse has already been quoted as saying (ii, 334); '... It is evident that he [Donne] intentionally essayed to introduce a revolution into English versification.'

Saintsbury occupies a middle ground: 'The form of Donne is indeed the most puzzling thing about him... [His] roughness was undoubtedly to some extent deliberate. That Donne had any intention of attempting a new prosody there is not the least reason for believing.'[2]

The opinion of Symonds is also interesting: 'Donne's mind, ... if I may make my own attempt to understand him, was the mind of a dialectician, of the intellectual adventurer; he is a poet almost by accident, or at least for reasons with which art in the abstract has little to do... He began with metre and invented a system of prosody which has many merits, and would have had more in less arbitrary hands... If one will but read him always for the sense, for the natural emphasis of what he has to say, there are few lines which will not come out at all events in the way he meant them to be delivered. The way he meant them to be delivered is not always as beautiful as it is expressive. Donne would be original at all costs, preferring himself to his art. He treated poetry as Æsop's master treated his slave, and broke what he could not bend.'[3]

---

[1] James Russell Lowell: *Works*, iii, 35. This is quoted by Norton (Grolier ed., i, xxiv.) who adds: 'And yet, if he is to be adjudged to this limbo, he is one "of the people of great worth" who are suspended there.'

[2] George Saintsbury, *A Short History of English Literature*, New York, 1898, p. 366.

[3] Arthur Symonds, *Fortnightly Review*, vol. lxvi, n. s. ('John Donne,' pp. 734-45), pp. 735, 740.

This 'revolution,' or invention, could not have been in the matter of word-accent, for we have seen that Donne does not go beyond the 'poetic license' of his day, in this particular, unless it be that he resorts to secondary word-stress more frequently than his contemporaries.

To say that Donne's so called 'ruggedness' is due to this peculiarity would be a great mistake, for it is to be found in his daintiest song as well as in his sharpest satire.

If *théy* be [1] *twó, théy áre twŏ só*
As stiff twin compasses *áre twó*.
A Valediction Forbidding Mourning, 25-6.

In addition to the variation of *they, are, two* and *so* (which were both pronounced with long *o*), there is variation also in the similar sounds *Ĭf* and *stiff*, and *Äs-* and *compŭssés*.

Móre, móre thăn tén Sclavonians scolding, *móre*
Thăn whén wĭnds ĭn our *ruĭn'd* abbeys *róar*.
Satire, II, 59-60.

At that time *than* was spelled and pronounced *then*. Furthermore, we have here the *a*-sound in *Sclăv-*, and possibly in *-bĕys*, varying with the similar sound in *ăb-*; and the *o*-sound in Sclavón-, *scóld* and *óur* varying with the similar sound in *more* and *roar*, while *ru-* is sufficiently near to be classed with these; and a sound in *-ĭans* and *-ĭng* varying with a similar sound in *than, ten, when, winds, in,* and *-in'd*, leaving, in twenty syllables, only two sounds *ru-* and *-beys*, without decided variants; and yet, with all this, the lines possess a rhythm that is absolutely bewitching.

If John Donne followed the advice of John Done, his first concern, either in reading or in writing, was with method of expression: 'A good book should be read three times; first, to see his method; secondly, his matter; thirdly, to gather his instruction.' [2]

---

[1] Donne probably wrote *are* instead of *be*, giving the variation: *théy áre twó* ... *théy áre twŏ*.
[2] *Polydoron*, 1631, p. 90.

That he did exercise the greatest care needs no argument beyond what is to be seen in such lines as the four discussed above; but one of Donne's own serious statements is worthy of consideration at this point.

'About 1624, [?] when Donne was temporarily in disfavor with Charles, because of one of his sermons about which there was some misunderstanding, he wrote to Sir Robert Carr, "... The king who hath let fall his eye upon some of my poems, never saw, of mine, a hand, or an eye, or an affection, set down with so much study, and diligence, and labour of syllables, as in this sermon..."'[1]

It would be difficult to conceive of anything, short of amazing and brain-racking 'labour of syllables,' that would enable one to produce, with some three sounds, a couplet of twenty syllables, and approximately to adhere to this method throughout a life-time.

Donne designates his verse as 'syllables,' as others have done:

> Hear this, and *ménd* thyself, and thou *ménd'st mé*
> By making *mé*, being dead, do good for thee;
> And think *mé* well composed, that I could now
> A last sick hour to syllables allow.
>
> *On Himself*, 15-18.

III. *The Ends to be Attained by this Peculiarity.*

1. '*Artistic Monotone.*'

The question naturally arises: If this *was* a studied practice, what end had Donne in view? In addition to a possible attempt at 'innovation,' other reasons present themselves; first, as has already been intimated, he sought 'artistic monotone.' For example, if the reader will guard against undue stress in the following lines, he may congratulate himself upon having read them as Donne intended them to be read:

> *Lét mé pré*pare towards *hér, ánd lét mé* call
> *Thís* hour *hér* vigil, *ánd hér éve*, since *thís*

---

[1] Jessopp, *op. cit.*, p. 190.

Both *thĕ* years *ánd thĕ* day's *deĕp* midnight *ĭs*.
A Nocturnal, etc., 43-45.

In addition to the decided variable words and sounds marked in these lines, the ear catches other variations, such as *-páre* and *hĕr*; *towărds*, *hóur* and *Bŏth*; *cáll* and *-ĭl*; *víg-*, *sĭnce* and *mĭd-*, etc.

In reply to the possible question: How can such an arrangement of sounds and syllables be conducive to monotone? the reader is referred to the anticipatory statement on page 104.

One prefers the risk of being tedious to being misunderstood; therefore, it may be said, by way of further elucidation of this idea of 'artistic monotone,' that under normal conditions a given word or sound has an inherent quality of pitch or tone in the speech-organs of each individual. Outside of verse one would repeat 'let, let, let,' or 'me, me, me,' or 'her, her, her,'—provided other sounds intervene,—till the voice breaks down from sheer exhaustion, without varying this inherent pitch, or tone-quality.

Why must other sounds intervene? Because the normal, or average, ear prefers variety to monotony. Were 'me, me, me' repeated to any considerable extent there would soon be heard 'mĕ, mé, mĕ, mé, etc.' We hear the clock say 'tíck-tŏck, tíck-tŏck,' while, as a fact, it no more says 'tíck-tŏck' than 'tíck-tíck.' This difference of 'tíck' and 'tŏck' may stand for variation in pitch, or it may stand for inequality of duration. That there exists a psychological reason for preference of variety to monotony there can be no doubt.

'When we listen to . . . a rapid series, say of clicks that are of equal strength, if they come neither too fast nor too slow, most persons cannot actually hear them as equal. Certain regularly recurring numbers seem slightly more emphatic than the rest, and the whole series falls into objective rhythm. . .'[1]

A common device of the poets is to repeat the same word in ictus, in a given line, thereby calling forth the decided accent which the movement of the verse demands.

Longfellow writes:

[1] George Malcolm Stratton, *Experimental Psychology*, New York, 1903, p. 99.

> *Life ĭs* real, *life ĭs* earnest,

but Donne, in more than nine hundred lines, subdues arsis and elevates thesis in this fashion :

> Kiss *Hĭm,* and with *Hĭm* into Egypt go.
> *Nativity,* 13.
> No hand amongst *thĕm* to vex *thĕm* again.
> *The Lamentations,* 292.
> Shall *shĭne* as He *shĭnes* now, and heretofore.
> *A Hymn to God the Father,* 16.
> Our *stŏrm* is past, and that *stŏrm's* tyrannous rage.
> *The Calm,* 1.

Donne's poems, exclusive of the *Satires,* might be classed under the two general heads *Love* and *Grief.* He did not believe rollicking measures suitable for such themes :

> I am two fools, I know,
>   For loving, and for saying so
>   In whining poetry;
>   . . .
> I thought, if I could draw my pains
>   Through rhyme's vexation, I should them allay.
> Grief brought to numbers cannot be so fierce,
> For he tames it, that fetters it in verse.
>
> But when I have done so,
> Some man, his art and voice to show,
>   Doth set and sing my pain ;
> And by delighting many frees again
>   *Griĕf,* which *vĕrse* did restrain.
> *Tŏ* love and *griĕf* tribute of *vĕrse* belongs,
>   But not of such as pleases *whĕn* 'tis *rĕad.*
> *Bŏth arĕ ĭncreasĕd* by such songs,
>   For *bŏth* their triumphs *só ăre* publish*ĕd,*
> And I, which was *twŏ foŏls,* do *só* grow three.
> Who *arĕ* a little wise, the best *foŏls* be.
> *The Tripple Fool.*

The Rhetoric of John Donne's Verse. 115

In his 'whining poetry' we observe his apparently purposed lack of variation:

> Í am two fools Í know,
> Fŏr loving and fŏr saying so.
> . . . . .
> For he tames ĭt, that fetters ĭt in verse.

The moment he would baffle the singers, and at the same time give his opinion of the appropriate themes for verse, and of the appropriate verse for such themes, we find variations in *grief, verse, both, are, when* and *in-, -ĕd* and *read, tŏ, twó* and *só,* and *fools.*

We have just seen, in *A Nocturnal,* how he arranges his words in a love-theme, so as to secure monotone. In grief he cries,

> Hĕ háth fill'd mĕ wĭth bĭtterness and Hĕ
> Háth made mĕ drunk wĭth wormwood.[1]
> *The Lamentations,* 196-7.

In the *Divine Poems,* Donne seems to have been moved by both *love* and *grief,*—love for God and the saints, and grief on account of the sins of his youth and of the weaknesses of his middle life. It is in these poems, therefore, that we may expect to find, unmistakably, what he means by saying,

> To love and grief tribute of verse belongs,
> But not of such as pleases when 'tis read.

Gosse (*Jacobean Poets,* p. 59) speaks of 'that very curious piece called *The Cross,*' and well he may have done so,

> Fŏr thĕ lóss
> Of thĭs crŏss wĕre tŏ mĕ anothĕr cróss.
> Bettĕr wĕre worse fŏr nó affliction,
> Nŏ crŏss ĭs só extreme as tó have none.

Here we see *Fŏr* and *fŏr; thĕ* and *mĕ; lóss, crŏss* and *cróss; thĭs* and *ĭs; wĕre -ĕr, -ĕr,* and *wĕre; tŏ, nó, nŏ,* and *só.*

[1] Observe the variation of *fill'd* and *wĭth* with *bĭt-.*

The poet and the philosopher agree as to the movement of serious verse:

'It is because of this general law [subordination either of meaning or of movement], it seems to me, that all poetry as it becomes more serious, suppresses, in some degree, the sensuous auditory element. Rhyme or recurrent alliteration are felt to obtrude themselves and hinder the higher functions of mind, as do also too obvious metrical effects. Children's verses can stand all this; it is suited to the lyric temper. But in general the more thoughtful,—the more spiritual,—the mood, the less it can tolerate of mere sensation.'[1]

Should one's ear be incapable of appreciating the beauty of monotone, probably a straight or unwavering line would appeal to the eye. When Donne pictures a tropical circle around the earth, he describes it as having

> Ăll thĕ same roundnĕss, evennĕss and ăll
> Thĕ endlĕssnĕss of the ĕquinoctiăl.
> *Obsequies* ... *Lord Harrington, etc.*, 113-14.

In addition to the marked variations, we observe here -vĕn, ănd and ĕnd-; and -qŭi- and ĭt- varying with thĕ and ĕ-.

Curiously enough, Donne has left us, in black and white, a picture of monotone:

> Ănd smŏoth as ă vĕrse, ănd like that smŏoth vĕrse.[2]
> *Love and Wit*, 10.

2. *Lipogrammatic Verse.*

Occasionally Donne's lines are suggestive of the lipogrammatic. The following is written in the key of ō, with the variation *ou*:

---

[1] Stratton, *op. cit.*, p. 255.
[2] Chambers includes this among 'Doubtful Poems;' but Donne's unmistakable stamp is upon it. The Haslewood Kingsborough MS. has the line as here; Stephens MS., *Smooth as a verse*; but this leaves the line a syllable short, and also robs it of its distinguishing characteristic.

Poor *sóul*, in this thy flesh what *dóst thŏu knŏw ?*
Thŏu knŏw'st thyself *sŏ* little as *thóu knŏw'st* not
Hŏw thóu didst die, nor *hŏw thŏu* wast begot.
Thŏu neither *knŏw'st hŏw thóu* at first camest in,
Nor *hŏw thŏu* took'st the poison of man's sin ;
Nor *dóst thŏu- thóugh thŏu knŏw'st* that *thóu* art *só-*
By what way *thóu* art made immortal *knów*.
An Anatomy. Second Anniv., 254-260.

There is in this something that reminds one of Lord Holland's 'Eve's Legend:' 'Men were never perfect; yet the three brethren Veres were ever esteemed, respected, revered, even when the rest, whether the select few, whether the mere herd, were left neglected. . .'

> Where, whenever, when, 'twere well
> Eve be wedded? Eld seer, tell!'[1]

Saintsbury catches this *sound* which Donne's verse means to impart : 'The Songs are, of course, in different lyrical forms, and the Anniversaries are in couplets. But both agree in the unique *clangour* of their poetic sound . . . now exquisitely melodious, now complicated and contorted almost beyond ready comprehension in rhyme or sense, but never really harsh, and always possessing, in actual presence or near suggestion, a poetical quality which no English poet has ever surpassed.'[2]

3. *Special Stress.*

Another object Donne had in view was to secure a stress for his words which would fill his lines with meaning, and give them a strength above anything attainable in unitalicised prose.

To illustrate: the reviewer of Miles Franklin's *A Bashkirtseff of the Bush* quotes Sybylla's note of despair,

---

[1] William T. Dobson, *Poetical Ingenuities, etc.*, London, 1882, p. 220. 'The reading of Lope de Vega's five novels, in each of which a different vowel is omitted, led to Lord Holland writing . .˙. [this] curious production.'

[2] *A Short History of Eng. Lit.*, p. 367.

' " I love you, I love you," she cries to the working men and women of Australia.' [1]

The readers of this quotation will invariably accent it : 'I lóve you, I lóve you,' and some may even doubt that the poet has power to make the declaration more emphatic and at the same time fuller of meaning and sentiment,—and to do this he needs no display type, but may conform to his plain verse-pattern. The prose writer would say : 'So, if I dream I háve you, I háve you, and that is all there is to it.'

Donne writes :

> So, if I dream Ĭ háve yŏu, Ĭ háve yŏu.
> Elegy X. The Dream, 13.

Likewise he would have written :

> My commonérs, Ĭ lóve yŏu, Ĭ lŏve yŏu !

To re-quote Professor Bright, 'We are thus brought to see a new category of "meaning" and of "intentional" suggestion. . . By the rhetoric of verse, or the rhetoric of poetry, is meant the emphasis elicited by verse-stress when it is at variance with the usual prose emphasis.'

4. Obscurity.

It seems, also, that Donne resorted to this peculiarity, in a playful attempt at obscurity,—the obscurity being in so arranging his words that one in trying to find or follow his verse-pattern would lose the thought; or, on the other hand, if grasping the thought, would lose the measure.

Donne said to Jonson that he 'wrote that epitaph on Prince Henry, Look to me, Faith, to match Sir Ed. Herbert in obscureness.' [2]

If one, whose ear is vexed with any verse except the sing-song, galloping kind, will forget the rime and read this epitaph as if it were plain prose, *thinking* as he reads, he will be ready to say with

---

[1] *The Literary Era*, vol. 8, no. 9, pp. 574-5, copied from *The Speaker* (London).
[2] *Conversations*, p. 8.

Grosart, (ii. 113, note): 'I confess I find nothing unusually obscure, and some of Donne's other poems are far more difficult.' The poem begins:

> Lŏok tó mĕ, fáith, and lóok tŏ mў fáith, God;
> For both mў centers féel this pérĭod.

and ends

> So, much as yóu twŏ mútŭal heavens wĕre hére,[1]
> I wĕre ăn ángel singing what yŏu wĕre.

In the body of the poem (79-88) we find simple but quaint thoughts so expressed that if we attempt to follow the scansion we shall come to the end wondering what we have read:

> . Thérefore wĕ
> Mǎy sáfelĭer sáy, that wĕ ăre déad, thăn hé;
> Sŏ, if oŭr grĭefs wĕ do nŏt well dĕcláre,
> Wĕ've double excuse; hē is nŏt dĕad, ănd wĕ áre.
> Yĕt Í would nŏt die yĕt; fŏr thóugh Ĭ bé
> Tŏo nárrŏw tó think hĭm, ăs hĕ ĭs hé
> —Oŭr sóul's best baiting ănd mĭd-pérĭod
> In hĕr lŏng journĕy of cŏnsĭdering God—
> Yĕt, no dishónour, Ĭ can réach hĭm thus,
> As hĕ ĕmbraced the fĭres of love, with ŭs.

Tabulating the similar words and sounds which vary in these lines we have: Thére, -lĭer, ăre, -oŭr, -cláre, áre, fŏr, nár-, Oŭr, hĕr fĭres; wĕ, wĕ, hĕ, grĭefs, wĕ, dĕ-, Wĕ've, hĕ is, wĕ, bĕ, hĕ, pĕ-, -rĭ-, -nĕy, rĕach, hĕ; Mǎy, sáfe-, sáy; déad, dĕad; Sŏ, Tŏo, tŏ; nŏt, nŏt, nŏt; thăn, ănd, ănd, căn; Yĕt, yĕt, Yĕt; Í, Ĭ, Ĭ; thóugh, -rŏw, sŏuls; hĭm, hĭm, ĕm-; ăs ĭs, ŭs; mĭd-, -sĭd-; lŏng, cŏn- -hŏn-, and one may well add 'and so forth;' for, while there is also variation in wĕll and the second syllable of doublĕ, in spite of the elision 'double excuse,' and in jóurney and dishonŏur, as well as in some of the other few unmarked syllables, surely enough, and

---

[1] At that time were and here were pronounced more alike than at present.

more than enough, variations have been noted to convince the most skeptical of what Donne meant, in part at least, by 'obscurity' in this poem.

Where Grosart finds 'nothing unusually obscure' in the sense or meaning of this poem, Courthope would find what obscurity there is in it, in the method of expression: 'Eagerness for novelty and paradox leads him [Donne] to obscurity of expression; and the reader is justly incensed when he finds the labour required to arrive at the meaning, hidden behind involved syntax and unmeasured verse, has been expended in vain. Ben Jonson does not express it too strongly when he says, "That Done for not keeeping of accent deserved hanging." It is superfluous to justify this verdict by examples. The reader will have observed how deliberately he seeks to attract attention to the extravagances of his thought, by the difficulty of his grammatical constructions, and by the dislocation of his accents.'[1]

'It was . . . of deliberate endeavor that Donne darkened his language and knotted his versification. The point is valuable, for these characters clung to Donne ever afterwards. [After the Satires.] . . . The unusual accentuation is sometimes found to be highly expressive, when you consider it; sometimes it is purely wanton and defiant.'[2]

Sanders recognizes Donne's 'technical habit' as conducive to obscurity for the 'modern reader': 'That it is not this technical habit only which obscures Donne from the modern reader is emphasised by the statement of a far-sighted contemporary critic—that Donne for not being understood would be forgotten.'[3] This 'technical habit' may have been the very thing Jonson had in mind.

Since Donne claimed to be matching obscurity, with obscurity, it seems necessary, at this point, to turn to Sir Ed. Herbert's *Elegy*, also on Prince Henry, and see what peculiarities, if any, it has. The poem begins:

---

[1] *History of English Poetry*, iii, 167.

[2] *The Academy*, vol. lvii, pp. 505-6. (The same article in *Living Age*, vol. ccxxiii, p. 762 ff.)

[3] *Temple Bar*, vol. 121, p. 626.

> Must he be ever dead? Cannot we add
> Another life unto that Prince that had
> Our souls laid up in him? Could not our love
> Now when he left us, make the body move
> After his death one Age? And keep unite
> That frame wherein our souls did so delight?
> For what are souls but love? Since they do know
> Only for it, and can no further go.
> Sense is the soul of Beasts because none can
> Proceed so far as t' understand like man.

And so the lines run on, easy enough to scan, without attending to the metre; but, notwithstanding this, the thought is more obscure than in Donne's *Elegy*. Primarily, Herbert was a philosopher and Donne a word-manipulator. We have no record of a challenge 'to match Sir Ed. Herbert in obscureness.' The fact that Donne confessed to writing, not to the honor of a dead Prince, but to match a fellow-poet in obscurity, leaves us free to believe that he resorted to the thing in which he was most skilful, word-play.

Further along in Herbert's *Elegy* we find:

> Nor shall we question more
> Whether the soul of man be memory
> As Plato thought.

with reference to which, his editor states, ' It would be interesting to know where Plato has made this singular assertion.[1] I fear it is more easy to account for Herbert's remark than to corroborate it.'[2]

The fact that a modern, with no excuse, finds obscurity in the *thought* of Herbert, may allow the supposition that he was

---

[1] B. Jowett, *The Dialogues of Plato*, (4 vols.) New York, 1885, i, 261. In 'Meno,' Plato has Socrates to say, 'If the truth of all things always existed in the soul, then the soul is immortal—Wherefore be of good cheer, and try to recollect what you do not know, or rather what you do not remember.'

[2] John Churton Collins, *The Poems of Lord Herbert of Cherbury*, London, 1881, p. 34, note.

similarly obscure to his contemporaries. That his senior, Donne, was, is, and always will be regarded as obscure in his manipulation of the vehicle of all thought is self-evident.

5. *Affinity to Prose.*

We have suggested that one, who cannot grasp Donne's thought and at the same time measure his lines, resort to the expedient of reading them as if they were prose. Happily, this suggestion is made by Donne himself, and leaves, apparently, no room to doubt that whatever of obscurity, or other peculiarity, there is to be found in his lines is there because he put it there deliberately and for effect. He says,

'Now, if this song be too harsh for rhyme, yet, as the painters' bad God made a good devil, 'twill be good prose, although the verse be evil, if thou forget the rhyme as thou dost past.'[1]

This is purposely printed in the form of prose although it is taken from his poem *To M(r) I. W.* (25-28), beginning:

> *Ăll* hail, sweet poet, *mŏre fŭll* of *mŏre* strong fire,
> Than hath or *shăll* enkindle my *dŭll* spirit.

Chambers puts a period after 'evil' and a comma after 'pass,' giving the lines a kind of obscurity that can never be chargeable to Donne. Grosart punctuates the lines correctly.

To illustrate further, Donne describes *The Storm* (65-72), as follows: 'Compared to these storms, death is but a qualm, hell somewhat lightsome, the Bermudas calm. Darkness, light's eldest brother, his birthright claims o'er the world, and to heaven hath chased light. All things are one, and that one none can be, since all forms uniform deformity doth cover; so that we, except God say another *Fiat*, shall have no more day.'

This seems simple enough, but on putting it back into verse,

---

[1] H. M. Sanders (*Temple Bar*, vol. 121, p. 624) notices Donne's suggestion to 'I. W.', to read the poem as prose, if too harsh for rime; and on the preceding page (623) expresses the belief that according to Coleridge's notion some of Donne's poetry would be but 'disguised prose.'

and looking out for the scansion, one who has the lines committed to memory finds himself going back to grasp the meaning.

> Cŏmpared tŏ these storms, death ĭs but a qualm,
> Hĕll sŏmewhat lightsŏme, thĕ Bermudas calm.
> Darknĕss light's ĕldĕst brother, his birthright
> Claims o'ĕr thĕ world and tŏ heaven hăth chased light [1]
> Ăll things ărĕ óne, and thăt ŏne nŏne can be,
> Since áll fŏrms unifórm defórmity
> Dŏth cóver; só thăt we, except God say
> Anóther Fĭat, shăll hăve nó mŏre day.

Here we observe the following varying syllables and sounds: Cŏm-, sóme, sŏme; tŏ, tó; ĭs, his; Hĕll, ĕld-; light-, light's, -right; thĕ, thĕ; -nĕss, -ĕst; o'ĕr, ăre; hăth, thăt, thăt, hăve; Ăll, áll, shăll; óne, ŏne, nŏne; fŏrms, -fórm, -fórm-; Dŏth, -óth- (of another), cóv; só, nó, mŏre.

This is enough; but there are also other variations which are more delicate, e. g., the ĭ in *uniform* and *deformity*, varies with -tý and hĕ. One can scarcely escape noticing that of repeated similar sounds, syllables and words in this group of lines, *and*, in lines 68 and 69, is the only one that does not vary; but line 63 preceding those given here, is as follows:

> Hearing hath deaf'd our sailors, ănd if they.

This space of five lines between variable words is rather unusual in Donne, but occasionally he seems to look back over his work and put down something he had forgot.

---

[1] Professor Norton's three Donne MSS. have 'world' in this line; but, aside from the fact that 'heaven and earth' are more commonly paired than 'heaven and the world,' it is impossible to think of Donne,—seeing his arsis-thesis variation of all other sounds and syllables convenient,—as writing this line otherwise than:
> Darkness light's eldest brother, his *birth*right
> Claims o'er the *earth* and to heaven hath chased light.

IV. *Monosyllabic Diction not Conducive to Harshness when the Verse-Pattern is Known.*

Professor Belden presents a very interesting table comparing the monosyllabic diction of Jonson, Donne, Hall, Shakespeare, Drayton, Marlowe, Denham, Waller, Dryden, Milton, and Pope. He finds the percentage higher in Donne than in any of the others; and then shows how monosyllables may contribute to condensation (economy in space); evenness of stress between successive words; and to the opportunity to stress, rhetorically, almost every syllable in a line. He quotes Waller's anonymous editor (1690), who 'praises him especially for having taught how to avoid monosyllables, "which, when they come together in any cluster, are certainly the most harsh, untunable things in the world. If any man doubt this, let him read ten lines in Donne, and he will be convinced".'[1]

Professor Belden finds that 'Donne uses only about six more monosyllables to the hundred words than Waller does;' and shows that Pope, 'the master of "correct" versification, uses many lines entirely monosyllabic; and not dull lines, either.'

It can readily be understood why words of more than one syllable were and are regarded as more 'tunable' than monosyllables: in poetry the position of the monosyllable determines whether or not it is to receive the ictus. For example, take the opening line of Lovelace's *To Althea from Prison*:

> When Lóve with únconfinèd wíngs.

Now, by a simple change in the sense of the line, we have:

> Whén Love wíth confinèd wíngs.

In polysyllables accent becomes crystalized, and the measure of a line, standing alone, can be determined by the word-accents. Milton (*P. L.*, X, 228) illustrates the point:

> Recounted, mixing intercessions sweet.

---

[1] See Chalmers, *English Poets*, viii, 33.

While it was an easy matter to change 'When Lóve with' to 'Whén Love wíth,' it would be a great transgression, at this day, to write :
    And récountéd, mixíng intércessión.

Dr. Johnson believed 'that the great pleasure of verse arises from the known measure of the lines . . . by which the voice is regulated, and the memory is relieved.'[1]

Professor Belden has already been quoted as saying that 'Donne leaves you line after line and phrase after phrase in doubt of the pattern, or how the line is to be fitted to the pattern, producing thereby a searching pause on almost every syllable.' It may have been this feature, of the verse of Donne, which caused Sprat, one of his followers, to believe that the highest kind of writing 'is chiefly to be preferred for its near affinity to prose.'[2]

It is evident, however, that Donne's supposed roughness is not due to monosyllabic diction. If we undertake to write prose as iambic verse, we find it running smoothly enough till we encounter crystalized accent in some word of more than one syllable :

    I do not make account that I am come
    To London when I get within the wall ;
    That which makes it *Lòndón.* . .
      Donne's Letter to Gerrard, *Gosse,* ii, 172.

V. *Donne's Ear for Rhythm.*

The point seems to have been reached at which it is necessary to determine whether or not Donne had an ear for rhythm. That he appreciated the harmony of music is known from his own words. Walton quotes *A Hymn to God the Father,* with this comment : 'I have the rather mentioned this hymn for that he caused it to be set to a most grave and solemn tune, and to be often sung to the organ by the choristers of St. Paul's Church, in his own hearing, especially at the evening service ; and at his re-

---

[1] 'Life of Cowley,' Chalmers, *English Poets,* vii, 30.
[2] *Ibid.,* (Quoted by Johnson.)

turn from his customary devotions in that place, did occasionally say to a friend, "The words of this hymn have restored to me the same thoughts of joy that possessed my soul in my sickness, when I composed it. And, O the power of church-music! That harmony added to this hymn has raised the affections of my heart, and quickened my graces of zeal and gratitude; and I observe that I always return from paying this public duty of prayer and praise to God, with an unexpressible tranquility of mind, and a willingness to leave the world.'[1]

In the sermon preached at St. Paul's, Christmas Day, 1622, (Alford, i, 11.) Donne quotes '*Pax non promissa, sed missa; non dilata, sed data; non prophetata, sed praesentata*' adding '[so] says St. Bernard in his musical and harmonious cadences.'

It is not necessary to requote opinions as to Donne's 'knowing how to scan,' possessing a 'fine musical ear,' etc. Nor does it seem best to look to his 'smooth' poems, on which these critics base their opinions, to decide on the quality of his ear. The rather let us turn to imitative, or representative passages in his poems:

> He, like to a high-stretched lute-string, squeaked, "*O, sir,*
> '*Tis sweet to talk of kings.*"
> Satire IV, 73-4.

> Though I can pity those sigh twice a day,
> I hate that thing *whispers* itself away.
> To the Countess of Huntingdon, 29-30.

Listen:

> *Than when winds in our ruin'd abbeys roar!*
> Satire II, 60.

One instinctively shudders and listens for something to fall.

> When I behold a stream, which from the spring
> *Doth with doubtful melodious murmuring,*

---

[1] Izaak Walton, *The Life of Dr. John Donne*, London, 1899, (Camelot Series), ed. by Charles Hill Dick, pp. 43-4.

*Or in a speechless slumber, calmly ride
Her wedded channels bosom...*[1]

Elegy VI, 21.

*Nor in bed fright thy nurse
With midnight startings, crying out, O! O!
Nurse O! my love is slain; I saw him go
O'er the white Alps alone; I saw him, I,*[2]
Assailed, fight, taken, stabb'd, bleed, fall and die.

Elegy XVI, 50-54.

If Whitefield, by pronouncing 'Mesopotamia,' could make an audience weep, it would have been positively hazardous for him to have recited these lines.

Why present other examples? It would be more difficult to prove that Donne was not *all* ear, than that he had *no* ear. The curious variations which we have been considering are unsurpassable for beauty and delicacy.

VI. *Donne's 'Secret.'*

The examples of arsis-thesis variation on similar syllables, words, and sounds, which, of necessity, have been presented in preceding pages, would seem to render supererogatory a statement of Donne's *Secret*.

Professor Belden, discussing the statement of Gosse to the effect that Donne purposed innovation, believes 'the verse-rhythm of Donne's poetry is the natural outward and visible form of his mental temper. He writes so because he can best express his thoughts and his feelings.'

Professor Norton (Grolier ed., i, xxiii) agrees with Gosse, in this particular: 'Putting Shakespeare out of the question, as form-

---

[1] Of these lines the *Retrospective Review* (vol. vii, p. 49) says, 'The admirer of Wordsworth's style of language and versification will see, at once, that it is, at his best, nothing more than a return to this.'

[2] MS. authority may yet be found for the supposition that Donne wrote this line:

Over the white Alps all alone; I (aye), I (aye).

ing a class by himself, there is no poet of the time who surpasses Donne in the occasional power of his imagination, in easy flights of fancy, in sincerity of passionate utterance, in sweetness and purity of sentiment, in depth and substance of reflection, in terse expression of thought. But, on the other hand, his poems equally reflect the poetic age in its gross sensuality and coarse obscenity; *in studied obscurity*,[1] fantasticality of conceit, exaggeration of affected feeling, harshness of diction, and cumbrousness of construction.'

Chadwick[2] quotes *Satire* III, 79-84, saying:

'Certainly the metre does not necessitate the proper reading in such lines as these, and if Donne, knowing what he meant, and preferring quantity to accent, could read them musically, the *secret*[3] of his art is hidden from us, and Mr. Gosse has done little to make it opener than it was heretofore. But, as in Emerson, there are passages of perfect music to make us wonder that he could ever be willingly harsh. And, as in Emerson, we frequently condone the metrical offence through gratitude for the informing thought.'

Between these extremes of opinion, stands Gifford:

'It would require a subtle critic to distinguish between Donne's natural and simulated obscureness.'[4]

According to DeQuincy, 'The first very eminent rhetorician in English literature is Donne. Dr. Johnson inconsiderately classes him in company with Cowley, &c., under the title of *Metaphysical* Poets; but Rhetorical would be a more accurate designation. In saying that, however, we must remind our readers that we revert to the original use of the word *rhetoric*, as laying the principal stress upon the management of the thoughts, [the *dispositio*], and only a secondary one upon the ornaments of style, [the *elocutio*].'[5]

That critics have not been able to understand Donne's pecu-

---

[1] The Italics are mine.
[2] *The New World, etc.*, vol. ix, no. 33, p. 37.
[3] The Italics are mine.
[4] Cunningham's *Works of Ben Jonson*, i, 474.
[5] *Blackwood's Magazine*, vol. xxiv, p. 892.

liarity is evidenced by the fact that Johnson describes him as 'Metaphysical;' DeQuincy, as 'Rhetorical;' Masson, as 'Metrical.' The last of these expresses himself as follows:

'... Collectively the ... [Metaphysical poets] might be described as *the Poets of Metrical Exposition and Metrical Intellection.* ... It was mainly for poets practicing this process of metrical intellection, though with some inclusion, also, the poets of metrical exposition, that Dr. Johnson invented or adopted from Dryden, the designation Metaphysical poets.'[1]

Observing how haltingly these great critics walk around the poetry of Donne, one cannot get away from the impression that he eluded their grasp. Some of them will not venture to view him singly, but place him in a class to which he does not belong; and, then, with one omniscient sweep of the hand, leave us in the dark.

Professor Brumbaugh, who prefers to think of the poet as standing alone,—belonging to no class,—sees him as he is:

'Donne ... is ... unlike all others in the range and limitations of his thinking, and in the marvellous power of condensation; ... contrary to most of his critics ... he has ... a very narrow range of thought. But in this limited field he holds absolute sway.'

Notice in these lines this 'marvellous power of condensation:'

> Tŏ have wrĭttĕn thĕ́n, whĕn yŏ́u wrĭ́t, seĕ́m'd tŏ mĕ́
> Wŏ́rst ŏ́f spĭ́rĭ́tŭăl vĭ́cĕs, sĭ́mŏny;
> Ănd nŏ́t tŏ have wrĭttĕn thĕ́n seĕ́ms lĭ́ttlĕ lĕ́ss
> Thăn wŏ́rst ŏ́f cĭ́vĭ́l vĭ́cĕs, thănklĕ́ssnĕ́ss.
> Ĭn thĭ́s, mў̆ dĕ́bt Ĭ́ seĕ́m'd lŏ́th tŏ́ confĕ́ss;
> Ĭn thắt, Ĭ́ seĕ́m'd tŏ shŭ́n bĕ̆hŏ́ldĭngnĕ́ss.
> But 'tĭs nŏ̆t sŏ́; nŏ̆thĭ́ngs, ă̆s Ĭ́ ăm mắy
> Pă̆y ắll thĕ̆́y hắve, ă̆nd yĕ̆t hắve ắll tŏ́ pắy.
> Such bŏ́rrŏw ĭ̆n thĕ̆́ir pắymĕ̆nts, ă̆nd ŏ̆we mŏ́re
> Bў̆ hắvĭng leắve tŏ́ wrĭte sŏ́, thắn bĕ̆́fŏ́re.
>   *To the Countess of Bedford* (3), 1-10.

In these ten lines, by using *to* seven times; *have* and *having*,

---

[1] *Life of Milton*, London, 1881, p. 484.

five times; *writ* and *written*, four times; *then* and *than* (then), four times; *seem'd* and *seems*, four times; *worst*, twice; *of*, twice; *vices*, twice; *and*, three times; *not*, twice; *in*, three times; *I*, three times; *so*, twice; *pay* and *payments*, three times; and *all*, twice; Donne makes forty-seven words do the service of eighty.

The greatest marvel of condensation, however, is not in *thought*, or *words*, but in *sounds*. We have here the following variations: *Tŏ, yóu, tŏ, tŏ, lŏth, tó, tŏ, -hóld-, sŏ, nŏ-, tŏ, -rŏw, ŏwe, móre, sŏ, -fóre; hăve, hăve, thănk-, thăt, háve, hăve; wrít-, wrĭt, spĭrĭtual, sĭm-, wrít-, lĭt-, cív; -tĕn, thĕn, whĕn,* simŏny, *-tĕn, thĕn, Thăn,* (then) *thán, -mĕnts; seém'd, seĕms, seĕm'd, seĕm'd; mĕ́, -ý, bĕ-, léave, bĕ; Wŏrst, wórst; óf, ŏf; -ăl, -tlĕ, -ĭl, áll, áll; Ánd, ăm, ănd,* and *ánd; nót, nŏt; lĕ́ss, -lĕ́ssnĕss, débt, -fĕ́ss, -nĕ́ss, yĕt;* vic-, *vĭc-, mӯ, Ĭ, Ĭ, bӯ,* and *Í; Ĭn, ĭn, ĭn; -ĕs, thĭs, 'tĭs, ăs; bár-, thĕir; -ĭng, -ĭngs, -ĭng;* and *máy, Păy, thĕy, páy, páy-*. Probably Donne's pronunciation of *Bŭt,* line 7, was close enough to vary also with *débt; shún* can vary with the middle syllable of *simŏny*. This leaves the lone word *Sŭch* line 9, without a variant; but line 11 begins 'Yĕt, *sínce,* which would indicate that Donne said '*Sĭch.*'

What a 'marvelous condensation!' What an extraordinary 'labor of syllables!' Not only are eighty words condensed, or compressed, into forty-seven, but these forty-seven words represent only about nineteen sounds.

This condensation may be seen in Donne's prose, but not so much as in his poetry. Jessopp (*John Donne*, p. 159), speaking of his *Devotions,* says, 'The thoughts are packed and crowded into sentences sometimes so confused and entangled that they seem to be staggering under the weight they have to carry; or, to change the metaphor, it is as if some craftsman were weaving a hundred threads at once, some fine as gossamer, some coarse as vulgarest tow.'

A better example of an 'entangled' or 'condensed,' sentence may be found in *Sermon* XIII (Alford i, 269):

'That world, which finds itself truly in an autumn, in itself, finds itself in a spring in our imagination.'[1]

---

[1] Coleridge comments on this sentence (*Notes on English Divines,* London, 1853, i, 103): 'Worthy almost of Shakespeare.'

Here we see thirteen words taking the place of twenty; and it is no extravagance to fancy the Dean of St. Paul's delivering his thought in this fashion:

> That wórld which *finds itsélf*
> Trúly *in* an autumn *in itsélf,*
> *Finds itsélf in* a spring
> *In* our imagination.

Do we write compact prose without close attention to words, phrases, clauses, sentences, and paragraphs? The original draft and finished poem of any great writer will show words changed, and verses,—and even stanzas,—altered. Why? Was Donne ignorant of what he was doing?

Jessopp's comparison of Donne to a craftsman weaving, applies quite as well to his words as to his thoughts. Certain similar words or sounds form the warp of his fabric, and sections of each strand in the warp are elevated (arses) or pressed down (theses) when his shuttle of other similar words or sound flies back and forth; and with each movement of the craftsman the strands of the woof like those of the warp, rise (arses) and fall (theses).

Carpenter (*Eng. Lyr. Poetry*, lvi) says, 'The lyric manner of Donne is in marked contrast with that of all preceding poets and of most of his early contemporaries, and the note of reaction in it is unmistakable. It was immediately recognized as a novelty, and, in that age of catholic tastes, it was very generally admired.' Note: 'What Donne's reform was, in the eyes of his contemporaries, is fully explained in this piece [Thomas Carew's *Elegy upon the Death of Dr. Donne.*']

Earlier in this study, when discussing critics, only Jonson and Drummond, of Donne's contemporaries, were quoted; but now the suggestion of Carpenter may be followed, as showing contemporary opinion of Donne's 'innovation,' or 'reaction.' In Carew it is partially but not 'fully explained.'

> Can we not force from widow'd Poetry
> Now thou art dead, great Donne, one elegy
> To crown thy hearse!
>
> . . . .

Have we no tune, nor voice? Dids't thou dispense
Through all our language both the word and sense?
Tis a sad truth.

   . . .

The muses' garden, with pedantic weeds
O'erspread, was purged by thee; the lazy seeds
Of servile imitation thrown away;
And fresh invention planted.

   . . .

Thou shalt yield no precédence, but of time,
And the blind fate of language, whose tun'd chime
More charms the outward sense: yet thou may'st claim
From so great disadvantage greater fame,
Since to the awe of thy imperious wit
Our troublesome language bends, made only fit
With her tough thick-ribbed hoops to gird about
Thy giant fancy, which had proved too stout
For their soft melting phrases.

   . . .

But thou art gone, and thy strict laws will be
Too hard for libertines in poetry.
They will recall the goodly, exil'd train
Of gods and goddesses, which in thy just reign
Was banished noble poems. Now, with these,
The silenc'd tales i' th' Metomorphoses
Shall stuff their lines, and swell the windy page;
Till verse, refin'd by thee, in this last age
Turn ballad-rime, or those old idols be
Ador'd again with new apostacy.
Oh pardon me! that break with untun'd verse
The reverend silence that attends thy hearse;
Whose solemn, awful murmurs were to thee,
More than these rude lines, a loud elegy;
That did proclaim in a dumb eloquence
The death of all the arts, whose influence
Grown feeble, in these panting numbers lies

Gasping short-winded accents, and so dies.

. . .

Here lies a king that ruled as he saw fit
The universal monarchy of wit.

Carew's lines show no more than that he 'recognized a novelty' without recognizing it. Had he known all that 'fresh invention planted' means, he would not have been willing to write 'soft melting phrases,' or 'untun'd verse,' or to acknowledge himself a 'libertine in poetry;' but he would have tried to 'bend,' as this 'king' had done, 'Our troublesome language.'

Gosse (ii, 336) corroborates this view: '... It would not be true, perhaps to say that ... Donne now or ever became Carew's model, but ... [Donne's poems] excited his amazement and curiosity.'

Even Donne's warm personal friend, Izaak Walton, seems not to have understood his 'innovation.' Discussing *The Bait*, (*Complete Angler*, Chap. IX) he says, '*Doctor Donne* made ... [this] to show the world that he could make soft and smooth Verses, when he thought them fit and worth his labor.'

> Thére wĭll the river whisp'ring run
> Warm'd bý thў eyĕs more than the sun;
> And thére th' enamour'd fish wĭll stáy,
> Begging themselves thĕy máy betráy.
>   *The Bait*, 5-8.

Walton's opinion that this is 'smooth' and cost 'labor,' would imply the contrary opinion that most of Donne's poetry is rugged and was composed without effort. But the fact that Donne's characteristic peculiarity crops out in this imitation lyric shows that Walton was the inventor of his statement, and that he was more conversant with angling than with his friend's secret.

VII. *Donne's Verse-References to Poetry.*

1. *Poeticness.*

In the lines of Donne, there are some fifty references to poetry, many of them to his own verse.

> *Thy̆* eagle-*sigh̆t*ed prophets too,
> —*Whĭch* were *thy̆* Church's organs *ănd dĭd* sound
> That harmony wh͡ich made of two
> One law, and *dĭd* unite, but *nŏt* confound;
> Those heavenly po*ĕts whĭch dĭd* see
> *Thy̆* will, *ănd ĭt* express
> IN RHYTHMIC FEET—in common pray for me,
> That *Ĭ by̆* them excuse *nŏt mý* excess
> IN SEEKING SECRETS, OR POETICNESS.
> A Litany, 64-72.

It seems almost sacrilegious to present a stanza of so beautiful a Litany in this mechanical garb; but if Donne could afford so to make a confession, the investigator may be pardoned for trying to find out what he is confessing.

2. *The Measure Changed.*

> No more dŏ Í wrong any, if Í adore
> *Thĕ sáme thĭngs* now which Í adored before,
> The subject changed and measure : *thĕ sắme thĭng*
> Ĭn á low constable, and ĭn ă king
> Ĭ réverencé his power to work on me.
> So dó Ĭ humbly réverĕnce each degree
> Of fair, great good. ⌣.
> To the Countess of Salisbury, 57-63.

Those familiar with Donne's fondness for play upon words, even upon his own name, will not find it difficult to believe that he is here playing upon 'measure;' else why 'Thĕ sáme thĭngs ... thĕ săme thĭng ?'

3. *Donne Imitates Abraham Fraunce.*

> Ŏ díre mischance
> And Ó víle verse! And yet our Abraham Fraunce
> Writes thus and jests not...
> *Satire* VII, 87-89.

'Writes thus!' How? Let us examine some lines of this *Satire* and see.

21. Fighting and untrussed *gál*lants company,
In which *Nát*ta, the new knight, siezed on me.
90. Must pardon me; *Sát*ires bite when they kiss.
But as for *Nát*ta we have since fallen out.
89. Writes *thús*, and jests not. Good Fid*ús* for this
M*ŭst* pardon me; satires bite when they kiss.
97. His last; and Fid*ŭs*, you and I do know
I was his friend and d*úrst* have been his foe.
33. Wh*ăt* fits summ*ér*, *wh*ăt* wint*ĕr*, *wh*át* the spring.
35.   Whére his whore now dw*élls*
And hath dw*ĕlt* since his father's death, h*ĕ* t*élls*,
Yea, h*ĕ* t*ĕlls*...
39. He knows of the du*él*, and touch his skill
The least jot in that or these he quarr*ĕl* will.
50. Áre órdinariés, where civil men áre fools,
Ŏr áre for being there...
116. Not true tr*ĕ*as*ón*, but tr*é*as*ŏn* handled ill.

Having seen how Donne 'writes *thus*,' the next step is to see how 'our Abraham Fraunce writes *thus*.'

Gosse (ii, 44) quotes,

> 'O vile verse! and yet our Abraham Fraunce
> Writes thus and jests not.'

with the comment, 'A curious reference to Abraham Fraunce, with his full name, has baffled the commentators; but it is surely an allusion to that popular and sentimental work in English hexameters, *The Countess of Pembroke's Ivychurch*, completed in 1592. In the *Ivychurch*, and still more in his version of the Psalms called *The Countess of Pembroke's Emanuel* (1591), Fraunce showed himself a belated and peculiarly unskilful hanger-on of the school of Gabriel Hervey and the other patrons of rhymeless, accentuated verse.'[1]

It seems very strange that Donne's reference to Fraunce should have 'baffled the commentators;' especially so, when he states so plainly that 'Abraham Fraunce writes *thus*.' For such commentators Donne should have provided a key, after this fashion: '*Thus* in *Satire* VII, 89, means that Abraham Fraunce writes as I am writing now, or, in other words, I am now writing as Abraham Fraunce writes.'[2]

It matters not that Fraunce called his lines 'hexameters';[3] Donne could scan them as he pleased, and this is what he saw, in the *Emanuell*:[4]

Làst wóork, and *lóst wóork*, Adam was filthily fowlĕd: defacĕd.
Page 14, 5.
Jesus thy son shall *bé ă* King, *bĕ ă* Lord, *bé ă* ruler: mother.
16, 3.

---

[1] The movement of Harvey's unrimed verse is very different from that of Fraunce; and the style of his rimed verse finds no echo in the poetry of either Fraunce or Donne. (See Alexander Grosart, *The Words of Gabriel Harvey*, 1884, i, 79 and 96.)

[2] Rudolph Richter, with all his blunders, seems almost to have grasped Donne's meaning here. It did not occur to him, however, to compare the verse of Donne and of Fraunce, for he is only quoting the lines as evidence that the former depreciates his work, and attempts no innovation. Richter says (p. 414) 'In der 6. Satire [VII, in Chambers] vergleicht er seinen Vers mit denen von Abraham France, fügt aber als Entschuldigung für sich hinzu, dass er ein Scherzbeziehungsweise Rüggedicht schreibe: *O dire mischance, etc.*'

[3] William Webb (*A Discourse of English Poetry*, Arber's Reprint, p. 71) describes the hexameter as a 'verse... which consisteth of sixe feete, whereof the first foure are indefferently either *Spondæi* or *Dactyli*, the first is euermore a *dactyl*, and the sixt a *Spondæ*.' An effort to make Fraunce's verse conform to this or to any other definition of a hexameter, will convince one that Donne,—who, as we shall see later, employed no measure but the iambic,—did actually so scan these lines.

[4] Alexander B. Grosart, *Miscellanies of The Fuller Worthies' Library*, iii, 11-71.

Husband iust *Jósĕph*, good-man, whoe thought it a wonder: mother.
17, 11.

And *gĕt áwáy, Jŏsĕph, gĕt áwáy*, and haste thee to Egypt: worshipt.
25, 9.

A balme box brooken brake *Júdás* hart ful of enuy: enuy.
35, 1.

The fore-man *Júdǎs* for a guyde went iollyly marching: apoynting.
43, 5.

Sought, found, and tooke vs from *sŏe mánў, sŏe máný* thousánds. Us ragged fishers, from *sŏe mánў, sŏe máný* thousands.
55, 1, 2.

We recall, at once, Ben Jonson's remark to Drummond 'That Abram Francis, in his English Hexameters was a foole'; and, while we may agree with him, we also see what he meant by saying 'That Donne for not *keeping* of accent [*i. e.*, varying the accent in words of more than one syllable coming close together, and excess in arsis-thesis variation of monosyllables in close proximity] deserved hanging.'

VIII. *What Jonson Meant by 'Keeping of Accent.'*

Gifford (Cunningham's *Jonson* i, 471, note) says, 'It is impossible to read Donne's *Anatomie of the World. The First Anniversary* and *The Progress of the Soul. The Second Anniversary* without admitting the truth of Jonson's criticism.'

Let us see:

<blockquote>
So mankind, feeling now a generál thaw,
A strong example gone, equál to law.
And wé
Dŏ what wĕ can to dó't so soon as He.
Wíth nĕw diseases on ourselves wĕ war,
And wíth nĕw physic, á worse engine far.
</blockquote>

. . .

<blockquote>
Loth tó gŏ up the hill, or labour thus
Tŏ gó tŏ héaven, we make héaven come tŏ us.
</blockquote>

. . .

> Would work more *fúllў*, and power*fúllў* on us.
> *An Anatomy. First Anniv.*, 47-8, 157-160, 281-2, 402.

> *Thŏu knŏw'st* thyself so little, as *thóu knŏw'st* not,
> How *thŏu* did'st die, nor *hŏw thŏu* wast begot.
> *Thŏu* neither *knŏw'st hŏw thŏu* at first camest in,
> Nor *hŏw thŏu* took'st the poison of man's sin;
> Nor *dŏst thŏu—though thŏu knŏw'st* that *thŏu ărt* so—
> By what way *thŏu ărt* made immortal, *knŏw*.
> *Thŏu ărt* too narrow, wretch, to comprehend
> Even thyself, yea *though thŏu* wouldst but bend
> To *knŏw* thy body...
> *The Second Anniversary*, 255-263.

> The *pŏisŏn's* gone through all; *pŏisŏns* affect
> *Chiĕfly* the *chiĕf*est part...
> *Ibid* 335-6.

In the same note, Gifford remarks, 'With regard to "not keeping of accent," read, or try to read, Donne's *Lines to Ben Jonson,-6 Jan., 1603.*'

Surely nothing is more pleasant than to *read* some of these lines:

1. If great men wrong me, *Ĭ will spáre* myself;
   If mean *Ĭ will spăre* them...

8. I had rathĕr suffĕrĕr than doĕr be.

23. He cánnot; thĕy căn theirs, and break them too;
    How un*lĭke* thĕy ăre that thĕy're *lĭke*n'd to.
    Yet I conclude, thĕy aré amidst my evils.

Yes, there is one thing more pleasant than reading these lines, and that is to realize that Ben Jonson knew Donne's secret, and to understand exactly what he meant by his censure (?). He writes:

> Who shall doubt, Donne, where[1] I a poet be,
> When I dare send my Epigrams to thee,
> That *só ălóne* canst judge, *só ălóne* make?
>   . . .
> Read all I send; and, if I find but one

---

[1] Whether.

> Mark'd by thy hand, and with the better stone,
> My title's seal'd...
>
> *To John Donne*, 1-3, 8-10.

While Jonson would not have hesitated to vary the accentuation of *alone*, and of many other dissyllables and polysyllables, it is so unlike him to allow such variants to appear in close proximity that we can be positive enough as to his purpose here. And, see, he is giving Donne a description of himself to himself:

> That só alóne can'st judge, sŏ alŏne make.

It may be a mere coincidence,—but if so it is rather striking,—that the 'passage of the Calme *That dust and feathers doe not stirr, all was so quiet,*' which Drummond (*Conversations*, p. 8) says Jonson 'heth by heart,' and in connection with which he quotes Jonson as esteeming 'John Done the first poet in the world in some things,' is the only line in Donne in which 'to-day' and 'yesterday' occur with 'day' both times accented:

> From owing thee yestérdăy's tears to-dáy.
>
> *A Litany*, 137.

> Yestérdăy's watĕrs and to-dáy's the same.
>
> *An Anatomy. First Anniv.*, 396.

Even when 'day' is repeated, both times under the ictus, Donne contrives to bring in a thesis-variant with a similar sound:

> But O, what áils the sun, that here hĕ stáys,
> Longér tŏ-dáy than othĕr dáys?
> Stăys hé new light from these to get?
>
> *Epithalamion ... Lady Elizabeth, etc.*, 57-9.

In the passage which Jonson 'heth by heart' there is arsis-thesis variation of the ā-, and of other sounds:

> Nŏ use of lánthorns; ánd in one plăce láy
> Feathĕrs ănd dust, tŏ-dáy ănd yestĕrdáy,
> Ĕarth's hollŏwnĕssĕs, which thĕ world's lungs are,[1]

---

[1] But for the *l*-sound, twice accented and twice unaccented, in this line, and the accented *ē*-sound, in close proximity, to accompany 'Ĕarth's' one would be tempted to think Donne wrote (and he may have done so):

> Ĕarth's hollownesses, which the éarth's lungs are.

> Have *nó móre wínd thăn*[1] *th'* uppĕr vault of air.
> We can *nŏr* lost friends *nór* sought friends recovĕr.[2]
> *The Calm*, 17-21.

Since Jonson 'esteemed' the conceits in this passage, regardless of the accents, it may be that Drummond was right, both in his quotation from Jonson and in his own addition (*Conversations*, p. 26): 'That verses stood by sense without either coulors or accent; *which yett other tymes he denied.*'

Proceeding with Donne's lines on poetry, we notice that very unique verse-letter *To M(r). R(owland) W(oodward).*

> 5. As this my letter is like me, for it
>   Hath my name, words, hand, feet, heart, mind and wit.

Taking these in their order we look, first, for his *name*. It is to be presumed that the original bore his signature; in addition to this, we have (line 23):

> Perchance, these Spanish businesses being *done*.

The *words*, in the poem, are all his (while he is using them), except such as have crept in through carelessness or smartness of transcriber and printer. The line just quoted has 'business' for 'businesses' in the 1633 edition; and 'this business' for 'these businesses' in the 'N' MS. now in the possession of Professor Charles Eliot Norton.

The consecutive lines (22-3) in 'N' MS. are:

> Our slown*ĕss ĭs* our punishment and sin.[3]
> Perchance, *thĭs* Spanish búsinĕss being *done.*

and thus we are forced to anticipate a subsequent statement as to the value of knowing Donne's *Secret*,—or *characteristic peculiarity.*

It was his *hand* that wrote the poem, and the poem reached W(oodward) in the *hand*-writing of Donne.

---

[1] Donne wrote, '*nó more wínd then.*'
[2] 1633, and Stephens MS. :
> We can nŏr lóst friends nór lóst foes recover.

'Vaúlt' and 'soŭght,' however, may have satisfied Donne's ear.
[3] *Bárr'd* (21) is the variant for *Oŭr* and *oŭrs* in 22.

Passing over *feet*, for the moment, we look for *heart*. In addition to the notion that his *heart* may have indited the poem, we find his *heart* in line 12:

> Though *Ĭ* stay here, *Ĭ* thus can send my *heart*.

His *mind*: the poem has the general appearance of *mental* gymnastics, rather than heart-throbs; besides, we have the lines (8-9):

> It is *mў* WILL, *mў*self the legacŷ.
> So *thŷ* retĭrings *Ĭ* love, yea envŷ.

The poem bears the stamp of his *wit* as unmistakably as the individuality of his *hand*-writing.

Returning now to his *feet*, a curious little riddle must be solved. Of course he means primarily his metrical feet; witness the following:

16.   *Hăvĕns* are *hĕávĕns*, and ships wing'd angels be.
18.   *Guĭánă's* harvest is nipp'd *ĭn* the spring.
25.   Eclipse the light which *Guĭănă* would give.
27.   But *ĭf*—as *ăll* th' *Ăll* must—*hŏpes smŏke ăwáy*,
         Ĭs not *ălmighty vĭrtŭe an Ĭndia?*
         Ĭf mĕn be *wŏrlds*, there *ĭs ĭn* every one
         *Sŏ*mething to *ănswer ĭn sŏme* propŏrtion
         Ăll thĕ wŏrld's richĕs; and *ĭn* good *mĕn thĭs*,
         Vĭrtŭe, oŭr fŏrms fŏrm, and *oŭr sŏul's sŏul, ĭs.*

We observe in these last six lines: *ĭf* and *Ĭf*; *ăll*, th' *Ăll*, and *ăl-*; *hŏpes* and *smŏkes*; *ă-* and *-wăy* (away); *Ĭs*, *ĭs*, *-ĕs*, *thĭs* and *ĭs*; *vĭrtŭe an* and *Vĭrtŭe*; *virtue ăn* and *ănswer*; *Ĭndia*, *mĕn*, *ĭn*, *ĭn*, *ĭn*, and *mĕn*; *wŏrlds* and *wŏrlds*; *Sŏ*mething and *sŏme*; *-pŏr-*, *oŭr* and *oŭr*; *fŏrms* and *fŏrm*; and *sŏul's* and *sŏul*.

The riddle is this: in addition to his characteristic metrical *feet*, in the body of the poem, the last line,—the *foot* of the page,—shows his *two feet*:

> Virtue our *fŏrms fŏrm*, and our *sŏul's sŏul* is.[1]

---

[1] Possibly Donne scanned this line:
     Vĭrtue óur fŏrm's fórm, and *óŭr sŏul's sŏul is.*

IX. *Arsis-Thesis Variation of Repeated Sounds, Syllables, and Words.*

Going on with Donne's verse-references to poetry we have:

And *thĭs* I *múrmŭr ĭn mў* sleep;
*Ĭ*mpute *thĭs* idle *tálk, tŏ* that *Ĭ gó,*
  For *dýĭng mĕn tălk* often *só.*
      A Valediction to My Name, etc., 64-66.

My sick*nĕss tŏ* physicians, or ex*céss*;
Tŏ nature all that I in rhyme have writ.
      The Will, 31-2.

  In me your father*lў* yet lust*ў* rhyme.
        . . .
  Be strong enough, and Nature *dŏth* admit.
        . . .
I choose *yŏur* judgment, which the same degree
Dŏth with her sister, *yŏur* invention, hold,
  Ăs fire these drossy rhymes *tŏ* purify,
  Or *ăs* elixer, *tŏ* change them *tŏ* gold.
      To the E(arl) of D(oncaster) etc., 3, 6, 9-12.

Deign at my hands this *crówn* of prayer and praise,
        . . .
All *chánging unchángĕd* Ancient *ŏf* days.
But do not with a vile *crówn ŏf* frail bays
Reward my Muse's white sincerity;
        . . .
The *ĕnds crówn oŭr* works, but Thou *crówn'st oŭr ĕnds.*[1]
      La Corona, 1, 4-6, 9.

The spheres *hăve* music, but they *háve* no tongue,
Their harmony is rather danced than sung;
        . . .
—*Thŏugh sŏme hăve* other authors—David's all,
So *thŏugh sŏme háve, sŏme* may *sŏme* Psalms translate.
      Upon the Translation of the Psalms, etc., 25-6, 48-9.

---

[1] Or, less probably: The ends *crówn oŭr* works, but Thou *crówn'st oŭr* ends.

Like one who in her third widówhood doth profess[1]
Herself a nun, tíed to retíredness,
So affects my Muse now, a chaste fallŏwness

. . .

Seek me then oúrselvĕs in oúrselvĕs; for as.
To Mr. Rowland Woodward, 1-3, 19.

Só these lines áre due.
If you can think these *flátteriĕs*, they áre,
If they were so, oft, *flátteriĕs* work as far.
To the Countess of Huntingdon (1), 48-9, 51.

And bégin soon, lest my *gríef gríeve* thee too,
Which is *thát thát*, which I should have bĕgun
In my youth's morning. . .

. . .

My Muse—for I had one—becaúse I'm cold
Divorcèd herself, the *caŭse* being in me.
To M(r) B. B., 9-10, 19-20.

Mad paper, stay, and grudge not here to burn
With all those sons whom my brain did create.

. . .

Tŏ come intó great place as others dó.

. . .

Yet *thóu wilt gó*; gŏ since *thŏu góest tŏ* her.

. . .

Thŏu wilt not long dispute it, *thóu wilt* die.

. . .

When thou art there, *ĭf* any whom we know.

. . .

Márk *ĭf*, to get them, *shé* o'erskip the rest.

. . .

---

[1] This poem contains 36 lines, all with five accents except the first: Donne was looking after the variations, *widówhood* and *fallŏwness*. We may feel pretty sure of this, for the reason that only once in all his some seven thousand heroic lines appears an Alexandrine couplet:

And sáys, 'Sĭr cán yŏu spáre mĕ'—I said 'Willinglý':
'Náy, sĭr, căn yŏu spáre mĕ a crown? Thankfullý, I.
Satire IV, 143-4.

Mărk ĭf shĕ márk whethĕr hĕr woman came.

⋅ ⋅ ⋅

Reserved, and thăt shĕ grĭeve¹ shĕ's not hĕr own.

⋅ ⋅ ⋅

Ĭ bid the nŏt dŏ this tŏ bĕ mў spў,
Nŏr tŏ make mўself hĕr familiar;
But sŏ much Ĭ dŏ lŏve hĕr choice thăt Ĭ
Would fain lŏve him thăt shall bĕ lŏved of hĕr.
        To M(rs). M(agdalen) (Herbert), 1-2, 6, 10, 15,
                          37, 41, 44, 47, 49-52.

Care not then, madam, how lŏw yŏur praises lie;
Ĭn lăbourers' băllăds oft mŏre piety
God finds thăn² ĭn Tĕ Dĕum's melŏdy.
             To the Countess of Bedford (5), 13-15.

Thĕse verses bud, so thĕse confĕssions grow.

⋅ ⋅ ⋅

Next I confĕss mў ĭmpĕnitence, for I
Can scarce repĕnt mў first fault since therebў.

⋅ ⋅ ⋅

May in lĕss lĕssons find enough to do.
           To the Countess of Bedford (6), 10, 21-2, 24.

Ĭf ĭn this sacrifice ŏf mine bĕ shown
Ănў smăll spark ŏf thĕse, căll it your own.
And ĭf things like thĕse hăve been said by mĕ
Ŏf others, căll not that idŏlatry;
For hăd God made măn first, and măn hăd seen
The third day's fruits and flowers...

⋅ ⋅ ⋅

Thĕ săme thĭngs now which Ĭ adored before,
Thĕ subject changed, and measure; thĕ săme thĭng
Ĭn ă low constable, and ĭn ă king
Ĭ rĕverĕnce, his power to work on me.
So did I humbly rĕverĕnce, each degree
Of fair, great, good...

⋅ ⋅ ⋅

---

¹ So 1635, Norton and Grosart; Chambers: 'grieves.'
² Donne wrote 'then.'

For as your fellow-*ángĕls, só yŏu dó*
Illustrate them who *cóme tŏ* study *yoú*
The first *whŏm* we in histories *dŏ* find.

. . .

Not those by which *ăngĕls* are seen and see.
   To the Countess of Salisbury, etc., 35-40, 58-63, 73-5, 78.

Whĕre[1] *is thăt* holy fire, which *vérse is* said
To have? *Is thát* enchanting force decay'd?
Vĕrse thát drăws nature's *wórks* from nature's law,
Thee, *hér* best *wórk*, to *hér wŏrk* cannot *dráw*.
Have *mў* tears quench'd *mў* old poetic fire?
                      Sappho to Philœnis, 1-5.

Sickly, alas! short-lived, abortive *bĕ*
Those carcase verses, whose soul is not *shĕ*;
And can *shĕ*, who no longer would *bĕ shĕ*,
Bĕing such a tabernacle stoop to *bĕ*
In paper wrapp'd...

. . .

The offic*ĕr's* for *hánds, mĕrchănts* for feet,
By which remote *ănd distănt* countries meet.

. . .

Clothed *in* her virg*in* white *ĭntegrity*.

. . .

For though she *cŏuld nŏt, nŏr cŏuld* choose *tŏ* die,
Shĕ hath *yĭelded tó tŏo* long an ecstasy.
          A Funeral Elegy, 13-17, 25-6, 75, 81-2.

Immortal maid, who though thou wouldst refuse
The name of mother, be unto my Muse
A father, since her chaste ambition is
Yearly to bring forth such a child as this.

. . .

But pause, my soul, and study, ere thou *fáll*
On accident*ăl* joys, th' essenti*ál*.

---

[1] *Where* was then spelled and pronounced *wher*, giving a variant with *her* and *her*, line 4; and with *verse* in line 1.

Still be*fóre* access*óries* do abide
A tri*ăl,* must the princip*ál* be tried.

   .   .   .

The ancient Church *knĕw nót,* Heaven *knŏws nŏt* yet;
And where what *láws ŏf* poetry admit,
Lăws óf religion have at least the same.

   .   .   .

But *thóu wŏuld'st* not, *nŏr wŏuld'st thŏu* be content,
Tŏ take *thĭs, fór* my second year's true rent,
Did *thĭs* coin bear any other stamp than His,
That gave thee power *tŏ* do, me *tó* say this.
  An Anatomy. *Second Anniv.,* 33–36, 383–5,
           513–15, 519–22.

As in some organ, puppets dance above
And *béllŏws* pant *bĕlów,* which do them *móve,*
One would *mŏve* love by rhythms; but witchcraft's charms.
           Satire II, 15–17.

     But till that I can write
Thĭngs worth their tenth read*íng* (dear Nick, good-night).
           Satire VII, 132–4.

And by these meditations refined,
Can unapparel and enlarge my mind.

   .   .   .

For as he that should say *spĭrĭts* are framed
Of all the purest parts that can be named,
Honours not *spĭrĭts* half so much as he.

   .   .   .

It would *hăve* let him live *tŏ háve bĕen* [1] old;
So *thén thăt vĭrtŭe* in season, *ánd thĕn* this,
Wĕ might *hăve sĕen, ănd* said, that *nŏw hĕ* is
Witt*ý nŏw* wise, *nŏw* temper*áte nŏw* just.
In good short lives, *vĭrtúes* are fain *tŏ* trust,
Ănd tó bĕ sure *bĕ*times *tŏ* get a place.

   .   .   .

---

[1] It is scarcely necessary to call attention to the sameness of the pronunciation of *been* and *seen,* in England.

Ăll thĕ same roundnĕss evennĕss ănd áll
Thĕ éndlĕssnĕss of th' équĭnoctiál.

　　．　　．　　．

There is the best cŏncourse ănd cónfluence,

　　．　　．　　．

Which doth extend her utmost gátes to them.
Ăt thát gáte, then, triúmphant soul, dost thóu
Begin thў triúmph. But since laws allow,
Thăt ăt thĕ triumph dáy the people máy
All thăt thĕy will 'gainst thĕ triúmpher sáy.

　　．　　．　　．

And though ĭn no degree I can express
Grief ĭn greăt Alexander's greát excess.
　　Obsequies of the Lord Harrington, etc., 11-12,
　　　　63-65, 70-75, 113-114, 173, 176–180, 251-2.

Having seen how he can 'unapparal and enlarge' his mind, the last line of this poem, considering the content, is very striking:

Do not, fair soul, this sacrifice refuse,
That ĭn thў grave I do ĭnter mў Muse,
Which, bў mў grief, great as thў worth, being cast
Behindhand, yet hath SPÓKE and SPÓKE her last.

Noticeable also, in this connection, are the opening lines of *Death*.

Language, thou art TŎO narrow and TŎO weak
Tŏ ease us now; great sorrows cannot speak.

and *Eclogue*, 92-6,

　　　　　　　　　Ĭ KNÉW
ĂLL THÍS, and only therefore Ĭ withdrew.
Tŏ KNÓW and feel ĂLL THÍS, and not tŏ have
Words tŏ express it, makes ă man ă grave
Of his own thoughts;

immediately, however, he 'utter'd some' words:

　　　　I would not therefore stay
At á great feast, havĭng no grace to say.
And yet I 'scaped not here; for beĭng come,
Full of the common joy, I utter'd some.

X. *Donne's Rule.*

Enough of Donne's characteristic peculiarity has appeared in his verse-references to poetry, and in the other examples quoted, to make a statement of his 'secret' seem more believable now than it would have been in the beginning of this chapter; furthermore, it can better be understood, now, what he means, in part at least, by 'excuse not my *excess*,' in *A Litany*.

The 'rule' by which Donne seems to have worked, was: When a word, a syllable, or a sound, appears in arsis, get it into thesis as quickly as possible, and *vice versa;* having twisted, pressed, or screwed (Coleridge uses all three of these words in his quatrain) all the meaning out of that word, take up another and carry it through the same process. Better still, instead of pressing one word at a time, whenever convenient, take a whole handful of words and twist them so that men will not find out for centuries what it all means.

1. *A Line Begins and Ends with the Same Word.*

Readers of Donne's verse have probably noticed the number of lines beginning and ending with the same word. This is to be met, sporadically, in other poets, as also is a further arsis-thesis variation of the same word. A line from Shakespeare has both these features:

> Kắte of Kắte-Hall, my super-dainty Kắte.
> *The Shrew*, II, i, 286.

other lines show the same word only twice:

> Ănd to be short, for not appearance ănd.
> H^8., IV, i, 30.

> Kĭnd is my love to-day, to-morrow kĭnd.
> *Sonnet*, CV, 5.

Once in a great while the *searcher* finds such a line in Shakespeare, and others, but in Donne they are so numerous as to attract attention of the *reader*.

Browning:

    Ŏn doth she march and ŏn.
                              Mesmerism, XXV, 1.

    Sŏ did *Ĭ* leave you, *Ĭ* have found you sŏ.
                                Mumpholeptos, 53.

Donne:

    Ĭ sing not *s*íren-like to tempt for *Ĭ*
    Am harsh...[1]
    Ĭ wonder *bý mý* troth what thou and *Ĭ*
    Did, till we loved?...[2]
    Ĭ will renounce *thý* dalĭance when *Ĭ*
    Am the recusant...[3]
    Ăll the same round*nĕss* even*nĕss* and *ăll*.[4]
    Bĕ so as every several angel bĕ.[5]
    Căn dung or garlic be perfume? Or căn.[6]
    Ĕnds of much wonder; and be thou those ĕnds.[7]
    Gŏ then, and as to thee, when thou didst gŏ.[8]
    Grĕw frŏm thĕir reason; mine *frŏm fáir* faith *grĕw*.[9]
    Hĕ hath fill'd mĕ with bitterness and Hĕ.[10]
    Hĕre are God's conduits, grave divines, and hĕre.[11]
    Ĭt leans, and hearkens after ĭt.[12]
    Mŏre, mŏre thăn tĕn Sclavonians scolding mŏre.[13]
    Păy all thĕy hăve, and yet hăve all to páy.[14]

---

[1] *To M(r) S(amuel) B(rooke)*, 9.
[2] *The Good Morrow*, 1.
[3] *Elegy*, VI, 44.
[4] *Obsequies . . . . Lord Harrington, etc.*, 113.
[5] *A Hymn to the Saints, etc.*, 6.
[6] *To Sir Henry Wotton* (1), 17.
[7] *Epithalamion (Lady Elizabeth, etc.)*, 40.
[8] *Upon Mr. Thomas Coryat's Crudities*, 21.
[9] *To the Countess of Bedford* (1), 4.
[10] *The Lamentations*, 196.
[11] *Satire*, I, 5.
[12] *A Valediction Forbidding Mourning*, 31.
[13] *Satire* II, 59.
[14] *To the Countess of Bedford* (3), 8. Variants for *all*, twice in thesis in this line, have been given.

> Shĕ who left such a body as even shé.[1]
> Sŏ may all thy sheep bring forth twins and só.[2]
> Tĕn is the farthest number; if half tén.[3]
> Tĕll you Călais or Saĭnt Michaels tales as téll.[4]
> Thĕse things are beauty's elements; where thése.[5]
> Thĭnk further on thyself, my soul, and thínk.[6]
> Thŏu, Lord, my soul's cause handled hast, and Thóu.[7]
> Thŭs solitary and like a widow thús.[8]
> { And knĕw'st my thoughts beyond ăn ángel's art,
> { Whĕn thóu knĕw'st what I dreamt, whĕn thóu knĕw'st whĕn.[9]
> Yĕt such are these laws that men argue yét.[10]

Other such lines might be given, but these are enough to illustrate both the frequency of their occurrence and the wide range of subjects in which they appear. It remains for the dissenters from the opinion that Donne purposed innovation, was conscious of his art, or had a metrical secret, to show why, in all his lines, beginning and ending with the same word, only in one instance is this word in arsis both times.

Lover's Infiniteness, 23-4 :

> Yĕt I would not háve áll yét.
> He that háth áll can háve no more;

This is the first line of a stanza; and, comparing it with the other first lines in the poem, there is room to doubt that Donne so wrote it. Having observed how frequently he places *and* in arsis when *can* appears, near by in thesis, and *vice versa*, I am inclined to believe that Donne wrote the lines,

---

[1] *An Anatomy. Second Anniv.*, 501.
[2] *To M(r). I. P.*, 15.
[3] *The Primrose, etc.*, 25.
[4] *To Sir Henry Wotton* (2), 2.
[5] *Elegy* II, 9.
[6] *An Anatomy. Second Anniv.*, 157.
[7] *The Lamentations*, 58.
[8] *Ibid.*, 2.
[9] *The Dream*, 16-17. *Thou* is in thesis in line 15.
[10] *Holy Sonnets*, XVI, 10.

The Rhetoric of John Donne's Verse.

Yĕt,—ănd I would not háve ăll yĕt,—
He that hăth ăll căn háve no more.

To put the matter in prose, 'Yet ... he that hath all can have no more, and [for that reason] I would not have all yet,' expresses the thought quite as well, and holds it together better.

2. A Line Begins and Ends with the Same Sound or Syllable.

Having seen that the only difference between Donne and other poets, in the matter of lines beginning and ending with the same word, is his 'excess,' it is interesting to see him go beyond them and begin and end lines with the same sound:

Ălmighty chemics from each minerăl.[1]
Hŏw could I think thee nothing that see nŏw.[2]
Ĭn paradise would seek the cherubĭn.[3]
Ĭndeed is great, but yet I have been ĭn.[4]
Măn is the world, ănd death the ŏceăn.[5]
Strănger than strángers; one who for a Dăne.[6]
{ Life-keeping moisture untŏ every părt;
{ Părt hardened itself tŏ a thicker heărt.[7]
Tŏ make us like and love, must I change tŏo.[8]
Tŏ come untŏ great place as others dŏ.[9]
Tŏ this wŏrld, ere this wŏrld dŏ bid us gŏ.[10]
Yĕt let not this deep bitterness begĕt.[11]

There are other such lines, but they need not be given; suffice it to say, there are about half as many lines beginning and ending with the same syllable or sound as there are beginning and ending with the same word.

---

[1] *Elegy* XI, 44.
[2] *Elegy on Mistress Boulstred*, 25.
[3] *To the Countess of Bedford* (2), 72.
[4] *Satire* IV, 2.
[5] *Elegy on the Lady Markham*, 1.
[6] *Satire* IV, 23.
[7] *The Progress of the Soul*, 498-9.
[8] *Elegy* III, 24.
[9] *To M(rs). M(agdalen) (Herbert)*, 6.
[10] *A Litany*, 180.
[11] *Elegy* VI, 35.

3. *Arsis-Thesis Variation of Repeated Sounds and Syllables in the Interior of the Line.*

The next thing, in Donne's verse, to attract attention, is arsis-thesis variation of the same sound or syllable in the interior of the line. In this, also, he differs from other poets only in 'excess,' and very marvellous excess it is,—both as to multiplicity of appearance, and indications of purpose.

In the poetry of Chaucer, there are many lines in which a repeated word appears once in arsis and once in thesis; sometimes two words, and even three, are thus varied; but it does not seem that he purposed the effect, unless it be in such lines as the last here given:

{ O verray cause ŏf hele and óf gladness,
Y-heried be thў might and thý goodness!
T. and C., III, 6, 7.

But what is thăt thăt love kannat espye?
The Legend of Good Women, 742.

Ŭp rŏos the sonne and úp róos Emelye.
Knight's Tale, 2273.

Hĕ mŏot ŭs clothe and hé mŏot ús arraye
Shipman's Tale, 1202.

Of Cowley's seven examples illustrating his method of painting 'in the number the nature of the thing which it describes,' one shows this variation:

Brăss was hĭs helmet hĭs boots brăss, and o'er
Hĭs breast a thick plate of strong brăss he wore.[1]

At the time Pope wrote,

The proper study of mănkind is măn,[2]

and

---

[1] Johnson, *Life of Cowley*, Chalmers' *English Poets*, vii, 39.
[2] *An Essay on Man*, II, 2.

Nor is Pău̇l's Chu̇́rch more safe than Páu̇l's chŭrchyard,[1]

he may have been unconscious of the varying pitch of his words.

It is easy to understand how the poet's mind, especially in 'imitative' verse, becomes so atuned to what he is describing; that he writes musically without special effort. Spenser writes:

> Soon as the chaff should in the fan be fined,
> All was blown áwȧy of the wávering wind.[2]

and to say that he 'figured' this out, before putting it down, would be unwarranted. This effect, however, may have been brought about by after-polishing. Aside from imitative verse, possibly,—and especially when words are 'twisted, pressed, and screwed' for effect,—purpose becomes apparent.

Donne writes:

> Seek we then oúrselves in oursélves; F Ŏ R A S
> Men F Ó R C E the sun wĭth much more F Ó R C E to pass,
> By gathering his beams wĭth a crystal glass.[3]

> 'From kíng to kíng, and all their kín căn walk.
> Yŏur ears shall hear naught but kĭngs; yóur eyes meet
> Kĭngs only; the way to it is Kĭng's street.'
> He smack'd and cried, 'He's base, mechanic, C Ó A R S E,
> Sŏ A R E all yŏur Englishmĕn in their disc Ó U R S E.
> Are not yŏur Frenchmĕn neat?...'[4]

---

[1] *An Essay on Criticism*, 623.
[2] *The Shepherd's Calendar, December*, 125-6.
[3] *To Mr. Rowland Woodward*, 19-21. Elsewhere Donne has a similar variation of *for* and *force*, which would indicate that he pronounced *for* with ŏ; or *force* with ŏ; or both with ŏ; or, if he pronounced them as we do now,—*force* with ō, and *for* with ŏ,—the difference was not great enough to restrain him from the variation. One other example will suffice:

> Sŏ doth hĕr face guard hér; and só fŏr thee
> Which fórced by business, absent oft must be.
>   *Elegy II. The Anagram*, 43-4.

[4] *Satire IV*, 78-83.

Here's no more news than virtue; I mÁy as well
Tell you cÁlaÍs, or saÍnt michaÉl's tÁles, as tell
That vice doth here hÁbituÁlly dwell.[1]

As in plain maps, the furthĔst wĔst is east—
Of th' angels *Ave,* and *Consummatum* Ĕst.[2]

But though bĔsides thyself I leave bĔhind
Heavens' libĔral, and the thrice fair sun.[3]

The difference between these examples and those found in other poets, is both seen and felt.

Browning:
He looks out o'er yon sea which sunbeams crŏss
And rĕcrŏss till they weave a spider's web.[4]

Milton:
But sŏmetĭmes in the air as we sŏmetĭmes
Ascend to heaven. . .
P. L., V, 79.

In Elegiac movement such variation is expected as a natural expression of the poet's emotions:

Wĕep nŏ mŏre, woful shepherds, wĕep nŏ mŏre.
Milton, *Lycidas,* 165.

Such variation as, for example, a couplet already quoted from Donne,

Shĕ, shĕ ĭs dead; shĕ's dead; when thŏu knŏw'st thĭs,
Thŏu knŏw'st how wan a ghŏst thĭs our world ĭs;[5]

would probably attract no attention; but when the same variation is found in bewildering excess in *Sonnet, Satire, Verse-Letter,* and *Divine Poem,* the 'purposed innovation' cannot be overlooked.
Even in *Satire* 'Versified' slight variations are scarcely notice-

---
[1] *To Sir Henry Wotton* (2), 1-3.
[2] *The Annunciation and Passion,* 21-2.
[3] *To M(r). C(hristopher) B(rooke),* 9, 10.
[4] *Caliban upon Setabos,* 12-13.
[5] *An Anatomy. Second Anniv.,* 369-70.

able; probably because there are other words always either in in arsis or in thesis to swing the lines along :

> He gránts salvation cénters *in hĭs* own,
> And gránts it cénters but *ĭn hĭs* alone.
>
> . . .
>
> Tŏ will alone, *ĭs* but tŏ mean delay,
> Tŏ work at present *ĭs* the use of day.[1]

One of Shakespeare's lines at once presents itself:

> Lĭght, seeking lĭght, doth lĭght of lĭght beguile.[2]

and in his *Sonnets* are examples even more noticeable :

> Or tĕn tĭmes happier, be it tĕn for one :
> Tĕn tĭmes thyself were happier than thou art,
> If tĕn of thine tĕn tĭmes refigured thee.
> VI, 8-10.
>
> So thou, being rich in *Will*, add tŏ thy *Will*
> Ŏne *will* of mine, to make thy large *Will* more;
> Let nŏ unkind, nŏ fair beseechers kill;
> Think all but ŏne, and me in that ŏne *Will.*
> CXXXV, 11-14.

Whether these variations be studied or not, they convey a different impression from those single lines in which one such variation occurs, while an equal or larger number of other repeated words or syllables are invariable. As, for example, in other of Shakespeare's *Sonnets*:

> Thou of thўsĕlf thў sweet sĕlf doth deceive.   IV, 10.
>
> Be, as thў presence is, gracious and *kĭnd*
> Or, to thўself at least, *kĭnd*-hearted prove.   X, 11-12.

Here is a line from Swinburne which would seem to indicate purposed shifting of accent :

> Fair fŏrtrĕss and fŏstrĕss of sons born free.
> *Erectheus*, 139.

---

[1] Parnell, *Dr. Donne's III. Satire Versified*, 73–4, 115–116.
[2] *L. L. L.*, I, i, 77.

while a more extended variation in *monosyllables* may have been unstudied:

> What power is in them all to *práise* the sun?
> His *práise* is this—he can be *práised* of none.
> Man, woman, child, *prăise* God for him; *bŭt* he
> Exults not *tó bĕ* worshipped, *bŭt tŏ bé*.
> <div align="right">Swinburne, <i>William Shakespeare</i>, 4–7.</div>

From a collection of nearly 500 examples of arsis-thesis variation in sounds and syllables, found in single lines, or in two or three consecutive lines, a few may now be given.[1]

ă-sound.

> She hath yet *ăn ănăgrăm* of *ă* sweet face.[2]
> Of elements *ănd ăn ăngelic* sprite.[3]
> *Ănd* as this *ăngel* in *ăn instănt* knows.[4]
> Be more *thăn măn*, or thou'rt less *thăn ăn ănt*.[5]
> My kingdom safest when with one *măn mănn'd*.[6]
> He's *ăn* infernal God *ănd* underground.[7]
> Utopi*ăn* youth grown old Itali*ăn*.[8]
> My picture *vănishĕd vănish* all fears.[9]
> { *Ănd* wilt *ănŏn* in thy loose-rein'd career
> { At Tagus, Po, Seine, Thames, *ănd Dănŏw* dine.[10]
> For *măn căn* add weight to heaven's heaviest curse.[11]

---

[1] These variations, to the similar variations in words, stand, approximately, in the ratio of 1:8. It is well to call attention to the fact that these tables of sounds are arranged according to present-day pronunciation; but this is immaterial as the conditions are usually favorable for uniformity of sound-shift.

[2] *Elegy*, II. *The Anagram*, 16.
[3] *Holy Sonnets*, V, 2.
[4] *Obsequies of Lord Harrington, etc.*, 87.
[5] *An Anatomy. First Anniv.*, 190.
[6] *Elegy*, XX, 28.
[7] *Elegy*, XIX, 29.
[8] *To Sir Henry Wotton* (1), 46.
[9] *Witchcraft by a Picture*, 10.
[10] *Progress of the Soul*, 15, 16.
[11] *To Sir Edward Herbert, etc.*, 18.

{ Reason is oúr soul's léft hănd, faith her right.
{ But as, although a squint lĕft hándedness.¹

ā-sound.

Yestérdăy's waters and to-dáy's the same.²
From owing thee yestérdăy's tears to-dáy.³
All chănging unchăngĕd Ăncient of dáys.⁴
{ Whether it táke ă náme námed there before,
{ Or be ă náme itself and order more.⁵
Our práise nor other's dispráise so unite.⁶
And you, and it, too much grăce might disgráce.⁷

ạ-sound.

True virtue's soul, ălways in áll deeds áll.⁸
That áll, which álways was ăll, everywhere.⁹
Áll the same roundness, evenness, and áll.¹⁰
{ But if—as áll th' Áll must—hopes smoke away,
{ Is not ălmighty virtue an Índiá?¹¹

a, as in final.

{ So mankind, feeling now a generăl thaw,
{ A strong exam*plĕ* gone, equál to law.¹²
On accidentăl joys, th' essentiál.¹³

---

¹ *To the Countess of Bedford* (1), 1, 5.
² *An Anatomy. Second Anniv.*, 396.
³ *A Litany*, 137.
⁴ *La Corona*, 4.
⁵ *A Hymn to the Saints, etc.*, 3, 4.
⁶ *A Litany*, 220.
⁷ *To the Countess of Bedford. On New Year's Day*, 25.
⁸ *A Letter to the Lady Carey, etc.*, 36.
⁹ *The Progress of the Soul*, 74.
¹⁰ *Obsequies... Lord Harrington, etc.*, 113.
¹¹ *To M(r) R(owland) W(oodward)*, 27-8.
¹² *An Anatomy. First Anniv.*, 47-8.
¹³ *An Anatomy. Second Anniv.*, 384.

á-sound.

As, water being intó áir rárified.¹
{ That néither would, nŏr needs fŏrbeár, nŏr stay;
{ Neithér desires to be spáred nór to spáre.²

ä-sound.

Of which she was pä̀rtaker and a pä́rt.³

é-sound.

That béfore thée one day bĕgan to bé.⁴
{ Men say, and truly, that they better bé
{ Which bé enviĕd than pitiĕd; therefore I,
{ Bĕcause I wish thée best, do thée envy.⁵
{ Was not his pitў towards thée wondrous high,
{ That would have need to bé pitiĕd by thée.⁶
{ And bégin soon, lest my griĕf griéve thée too,
{ Which is, that that, which I should have bĕgun.⁷

ĕ-sound.

Then solidnĕ́ss and roundnĕ́ss have no place.⁸
In drĕ́ssĭng mĭstrĕ́ssĭng and compliment.⁹

---

¹ *To the Countess of Huntingdon* (1), 34.
² *Epithalamion, Lady Elizabeth, etc.*, 91-2.
³ *An Anatomy. First Anniv.*, 434.
⁴ *The Progress of the Soul*, 19.
⁵ *To M(r). I. W.*, 9-11.
⁶ *Nativity*, 11.
⁷ *To M(r). B. B.*, 9-10. I have no authority for the suggestion, but seeing *which* twice in thesis, in line 10, and observing the 'twists' Donne is giving his other words, I doubt not that he wrote:

        Which is, *that that, that* I should have begun.

or,

        That is, *that that,* which I should have begun.

or, if he wrote it as it stands, he read it with initial inversion:

        Whĭch is, that that, *whĭch* I should have begun.

⁸ *An Anatomy. First Anniv.*, 299.
⁹ *To Mr. Tilman, etc.*, 30.

The Rhetoric of John Donne's Verse.

{ Sún, or stars are fitlĭĕst view'd
At their brightĕst, but to conclude.¹
All wŏmĕn shall adore us and some mĕn.²
Can mĕn more injure wŏmĕn than to say.³
Who strives through wŏmăn's scorns wŏmĕn to know.⁴
{ —Whose soul is sĕnse—cannot admit
Of absĕnce, 'cause it doth remove.⁵
Lĕt me think any rivals lĕtter mine,⁶
For armlĕts of that thou may'st lĕt me wear.⁷
May in lĕss lĕssons find enough to do.⁸
So may a sĕlf-despising get sĕlf-love.⁹
From tĕmpting Satan to tĕmpt us.¹⁰
{ Angels did hand her up, who next Gŏd dwell,
For from lĕss virtue, and lĕss beauteousnĕss,
The Gentiles framed them gŏds and gŏddĕssĕs.¹¹
Durst look in thĕmselves, and thĕmselves retrieve.¹²

ē-sound.

To make hĕr lovable, and I avĕr.¹³
What walls of tendĕr crystal hĕr enfold.¹⁴
Hĕr ĕarly child misspeak half uttĕred words.¹⁵

ī-sound.

Nor thy̆ lĭfe, ever lĭvely, know gray hairs.¹⁶
The world by̆ dy̆ing, bĕcause love dĭes too.¹⁷

---

¹ *Valediction to His Book*, 60–1.
² *The Relic*, 19.   ³ *Elegy* XIX, 19.
⁴ *To the Countess of Huntingdon* (2), 65. Query? wŏmăn's scorn wŏmăn to know.
⁵ *A Valediction Forbidding Mourning*, 14–15.
⁶ *Love's Usury*, 9.   ⁷ *Elegy* XI, 2.
⁸ *To the Countess of Bedford* (6), 24.
⁹ *The Cross*, 58.   ¹⁰ *A Litany*, 145.   ¹¹ *Death*, 51, 55–6.
¹² *To Sir Henry Wotton* (1), 44.   ¹³ *Elegy* XVIII, 19.
¹⁴ *To the Countess of Bedford* (2), 45.
¹⁵ *To M(rs). M(agdalen) (Herbert)*, 22.
¹⁶ *Translated out of Gazaeus, etc.*, 4.
¹⁷ *The Will*, 47.

With thee *mў kĭnd* and un*kĭnd* heart is run.[1]
Yet them all these un*kĭnd kĭnds* feed upon.[2]
Now *lĭke* an owl-*lĭke* watchman, he must walk.[3]

ĭ-sound.

{ Death gets '*twĭxt* souls and bodies such a place
{ As *sĭn ĭnsĭ*nuates '*twĭxt* just men and grace.[4]
{ As, '*twĭxt* two equal armies, Fate.
{ Were gone out—hung '*twĭxt* her and me.[5]
Love these *mĭx'd* souls doth *mĭx* again.[6]
*Ĭn*herit nothing but his *ĭn*famy.[7]
Clothed *ĭn* her virg*ĭn* white *ĭn*tegrity.[8]
They re*ĭn*vest thee *ĭn* white *ĭn*nocence.[9]
Which learn vice there and come *ĭn ĭn*nocent.[10]
Purpled thy nail *ĭn* blood of *ĭn*nocence[11]
Some coff*ĭn'*d *ĭn* their cab*ĭn*s lie equally.[12]
{ Was not His *pĭty* towards the wondrous high,
{ That would have need to be *pĭtĭ*ed by thee?[13]
Be thirsty *stĭll*, and drink *stĭll tĭll* thou go.[14]
But these as nice *thĭn* school div*ĭn*ity.[15]

ō-sound.

And bel*lŏws* pant be*lŏw*, which them do move.[16]
{ At court your fel*lŏws* every day.
{ But am, alas! by being *lŏ*wly, *lŏ*wer.[17]
Twins, *thŏugh* their birth Cuscŏ and Muscŏ take.[18]

---

[1] *To M(r). I. P.*, 9.
[2] *The Progress of the Soul*, 288.
[3] *Satire* II, 65.
[4] *Elegy on Mistress Boulstred*, 43–4.
[5] *The Ecstacy*, 13, 16.
[6] *Ibid.*, 35.
[7] *The Curse*, 21.
[8] *An Anatomy. First Anniv.*, 75.
[9] *Ibid. Second Anniv.*, 113.
[10] *To the Countess of Bedford* (3), 60.
[11] *The Flea*, 20.
[12] *The Storm*, 45.
[13] *Nativity*, 11, 12.
[14] *An Anatomy. Second Anniv.*, 47.
[15] *To the Countess of Bedford*, 61.
[16] *Satire* II, 16.
[17] *Love's Exchange*, 3, 7.
[18] *To the Lady Bedford*, 7. (So Chambers, ii, 60; Index: *To the Countess Bedford*).

{ Which I dare *fóre*say, nothing cures but death,
{ Tell her all this, be*fóre* I am *fór*got.[1]
With care's harsh *hóa*riness *ó*'erspread.[2]
Still, be*fóre* accessó*ries* do abide.[3]

ŏ-sound.

The *plŏt* of all, that thĕ *plŏt*ters were two.[4]

ó-soŭnd.

Since all *fŏrms* uni*fórm* de*fór*mity.[5]
{ Sad that her sons did seek a *fór*eign grave
{ —*Fŏr* Fate's *ŏr Fŏr*tune's drifts none can soothsay.[6]
Debt*ór* to th' old *nŏr* credit*ŏr* to the new.[7]

ōō-sound.

Alas! *poŏr* joys, but *poŏr*er men whŏse trust.[8]

ŭ-sound.

Hell *sŏme*what lights*ŏme*, the Bermudas calm.[9]
Now drinks he *úp* seas, and he eats *ŭp* flocks.[10]
Open to all searchers, *ŭn*prized if *ŭn*known.[11]
{ Of formless curses, projects *ŭn*made *ŭp*,
{ Abuses yet *ŭn*fashiŏn'd, thoughts corr*úpt*,
{ Misshapen cavils, palpa*blĕ ŭn*truths.[12]

ū-sound.

And better thro*úgh*-pierced, than thro*ŭgh* penŭ*ry*.[13]
{ But I must end this letter; though it d*ó*
{ Stand on *twŏ trŭths*, neithĕr is *trŭe tŏ yŏu*.[14]

---

[1] *To Sir Thos. Rowe*, 1613, 28-9.
[2] *An Anatomy. Second Anniv.*, 385.
[3] *Elegy V. His Picture*, 8.
[4] *The Progress of the Soul*, 347.
[5] *The Storm*, 70.
[6] *The Storm*, 10, 11.
[7] *To the Countess of Bedford* (4), 7.
[8] *To Mr. Tilman, etc.*, 31.
[9] *The Storm*, 66.
[10] *The Progress of the Soul*, 331.
[11] *Elegy* III. *Change*, 6.
[12] *Elegy* XIV, 25-7.
[13] *The Lamentations*, 302.
[14] *To the Countess of Bedford* (3), 71-2.

ou-sound.

When I cry *oút* He *oút*shuts my prayer and hath.[1]
To *oút*do (Dildoes) and *oút*-usure Jews.[2]
*Oút*flatter favorites, or *oút*lie either.[3]

d-sound.

Like to a grave, the yielding *d*own *d*oth *d*int.[4]

f-sound.

Grew from their reason; mine *f*rom *f*air *f*aith grew.[5]

-ing-sound.

And spy*ing* heirs melt*ing* with luxury.
And barrell*ing* the dropp*ings*, and the stuff.[6]
In flatter*ing* eddies promis*ing* return.[7]

st-sound.

Pur*sue'st* ŭs, kill'*st* ŭs, cover'*st* ús with wrath.[8]

y-sound.

In me your father*lў* and lust*ў* rime.[9]

ĭ- and *ĕ*-sounds.

She was *ĭn* all m*ĕn* th*ĭn*ly scattered th*ĕn*.[10]
{ But if my days be long, and good *ĕ*nough,
{ In vain this sea shall *ĕ*nlarge or *ĕ*nrough.[11]
But says, I there*ĭn* no rev*ĕn*ge shall find.[12]
*Ĭnn ány*where; cont*ĭn*uance maketh hell.[13]
Worn by as m*án*y several m*ĕn ĭn* sin.[14]

---

[1] *The Lamentations*, 183.
[2] *Satire* II, 32.
[3] *Satire* IV, 47.
[4] *Epithalamion*, (*Lincoln's Inn*), 5.
[5] *To the Countess of Bedford* (1), 4.
[6] *Satire* II, 79, 82.
[7] *Elegy* VI, 32.
[8] *The Lamentations*, 239.
[9] *To the E(arl) of D(oncaster)*, 3.
[10] *To the Countess of Huntingdon*, 23.
[11] *The Progress of the Soul*, 51-2.
[12] *Elegy* XII, 37.
[13] *To Sir Henry Wotton* (1), 48.
[14] *Satire* I, 54.

ŏ-, a (as in final)*-, y-,* and *ĭ-* sounds.

Cŏnstánt, you're hour*lў ĭn ĭncŏnstăncў.*¹

ou-, ŏ-, and *ē-*sounds.

Whom *thóu cŏncéivĕst cóncĕived; yea, thŏu art nów.*²

ă- and *ō-*sounds.

So long he *háth flŏwn* and *hăth flówn* so *fast.*³

*á-, ā-, ĭ-, ă-*sounds, etc.

He *cánnot; thĕy căn* theirs, and *breák* them too;
How un*líke thĕy ăre* that *thĕy're líke*n'd to.
Yet *Í* conclude, *thĕy áre ăm*idst *mў* evils: devils.⁴

Need we remind ourselves that the last example,—which has been given elsewhere for a different purpose,—is from Donne's lines to Ben Jonson?

4. *Arsis-Thesis Variation of Repeated Words.*

To pass beyond single lines and couplets, and to cite examples of the same word,—as well as the same syllable, and similar sounds,—in arsis-thesis variation, would be to quote a 'knot' of verses from practically every poem Donne ever wrote. It would be almost to reprint, in italics, and with marks of arsis and thesis, all his poetry.

It was planned, originally, to present examples under the general heads, *One Line: One Word Twice: Once in arsis and Once in Thesis;* then, *One Line: Two Words,* etc.; then, *Two Lines, etc.;* and on to *Fifteen Lines: Twenty Words,* etc.; but, before half the verses were given in which Donne refers to poetry, the thing which these hundreds of examples were collected to prove became apparent. Only a few more examples, therefore, need to be given.

---

[1] *An Anatomy. Second Anniv.*, 400.
[2] *La Corona. The Annunciation*, 11.
[3] *The Progress of the Soul*, 255.
[4] *To Ben Jonson, 9 November, 1603*, 23–5.

That being *rĕd*, it dyes *rēd* souls to white.[1]
With hideous gázing to *fĕar* *áwăy* *fĕar*.[2]
In *th' hŏur ŏf* death, *th' ĕve ŏf* last Judgment-day.[3]
But when *Ĭ* waked, *Ĭ săw* that *Ĭ săw* not.[4]
Tŏ rage, *tŏ lŭst, tŏ* write *tŏ, tŏ* command.[5]
{ Profane, to think *thĕe* anything but *thĕe*.
{ Com*ĭng* and stay*ĭng*, show'd *thĕe, thĕe*.[6]
{ And Jacob came *clŏthed ĭn vĭle* harsh attire,
{ God *clŏthed* himself *ĭn vĭle* man's flesh, that so.[7]
If thou *stăy hĕre*. O *stăy hĕre, fŏr fŏr* thee.[8]
It, and *ŭs fŏr* it, *and* all else *fŏr ŭs*.[9]
{ *Lŏve măy măke mĕ* leave *lŏving* or might try
{ A *dĕeper* plague *tŏ măke mĕ lŏve* her *tŏo*.[10]

5. *Donne's 'Rule' Stated, and Its Operation Observed.*

Two more examples and we shall have done; to put it in his own language, we shall, in some degree, 'have Donne.' This expression is taken from his verse-letter *To Sir Henry Wotton* (1), 39-52, which closes with a statement that may refer to other matters, as well as to his metrics,—seeing the noun ('rules') is in the plural,—but which, in view of what he has just written, leaves one in open-mouthed amazement. Why has not some Englishman, in whose metropolis there yet linger traditions of the pronunciations in vogue in the days of Donne, long ago unraveled his riddle?

It seems that Donne purposely hinted at his peculiarity many times in his verse, as has been shown; and, while the single line already cited, from Jonson to Donne, indicates that the former grasped his secret as far as an arsis-thesis variation on three

---

[1] *Holy Sonnets*, IV, 14. [2] *The Storm*, 52.
[3] *A Litany*, 197. [4] *The Storm*, 37.
[5] *Love's Deity*, 17. [6] *The Dream*, 20-1.
[7] *Holy Sonnets* XI, 11, 13. [8] *Elegy* XVII. *Elegy on His Mistress*, 43.
[9] *A Litany*, 2. The indications are that Donne read this line with initial inversion.
[10] *Love's Deity*, 25.

syllables in the same line, he did not go beyond that, but gave it up with his famous dictum.

Later it will be shown that Coleridge possibly came a little nearer to an understanding of the matter, while Saintsbury, Craik, and others, with no 'deficiency' or 'obliquity' of ear,—to requote a part of Jessopp's confession,—recognize in Donne's Poetry 'deep and subtle music,' 'rich and pompous flow,' and the like, but cannot tell 'whence it cometh or whither it goeth.' As was said by Chadwick (p. 127), Donne's '*secret*' has been 'hidden from us.'

Ever grateful to Professor Bright for accurate instruction in regard to the scansion of verse, without which I might have 'hung' Donne, and passed on, I am humbly thankful to be able to open the way to a better knowledge of a partially neglected, poorly understood, but never-to-be-forgotten musician of syllables, magician of words, and potentate in the realm of thought.

This letter to Wotton, some parts of which have already been given, contains a criticism of country, court, and town. The statements are all plain enough, and yet Donne says (17–20):

> *Cán* dung *ŏr* garlic be perfume? *Ŏr cán*
> A *scórpion ŏr tŏrpedo* cure a man?
> Cities are *wórst ŏf áll thrĕe; ŏf áll thrĕe*?
> O KNOTTY̆ RIDDLE! *ĕach is wŏrst équallў*.

The absence of mystery or obscurity in the thought of this poem, and the very peculiar and original arsis-thesis variation in repeated sounds, syllables, and words, forces the conclusion that herein consists the 'knotty riddle.' The country, the court, and the town may 'each [be] worst equally;' but Donne, to arouse curiosity, takes up three words; 'of,' 'all,' and 'three,' in connection with, or in addition to the three objects he is describing, and makes them 'worst equally,' by making them unstable: '*ŏf áll thrĕe; ŏf áll thrĕe*.'

This poem closes:

> But if myself I've won
> To know my *rules*, I *hăve*, and you *hăve* DONNE!

Let us now witness the application of one of his *rules*,—and possibly of all of them so far as verse-construction is concerned,—noticing, the while, how the ĭ-sound holds the lines to the same key; and how other sounds, some full and round, some faint as remembered echoes, come and go. Notice, too, that as soon as some of the words have been employed in arsis and in thesis they do not appear again, but give place to others which behave in a similar manner.

39. Fŏr ĭn bĕst undĕrstándĭngs sín bĕgán,
40. Ángĕls sĭnn'd fĭrst, thĕn dévĭls, ánd thĕn mán.
    Ónlý pĕrchánce bĕasts sĭn not; wrĕ́tched wé
    Are bĕasts ĭn all but whĭ́te ĭntégrĭtý.
    Ĭ́ thĭ́nk ĭ́f mĕ́n, whĭ́ch ĭn thĕ́se pláces lĭve,
    Dŭrst look ĭn thĕmsĕ́lves, ánd thĕmsĕ́lves rĕtriĕ́ve,
45. Thĕ̆y would lĭke stránğĕrs grĕ́et thĕmsĕ́lves, seeĭng thĕ́n
    Ŭtópĭ̆ăn yóuth grŏ̆wn óld Ĭtálĭán.
    Bĕ́ thĕ́n thĭ́ne ŏ́wn hŏ́me, ánd ĭn thŷsĕ́lf dwĕ́ll;
    Ĭnn ánȳwhĕ́re; contĭnuănce mákĕ̆th hĕ́ll.
    Ánd seeing thĕ̆ snáil, whĭ́ch ĕverȳwhĕ́re dŏ̆th rŏ́am,
50. Carryĭ́ng hĭ́s ŏ́wn house[1] stĭll, stĭll ĭs ăt hŏ́me;
    Follŏ́w—fŏ́r hĕ́ ĭ̆s eas̆y̆ páced—thĭ́s snáil,
    Bĕ́ thíne ŏ́wn palăce, ŏr thĕ̆ world's thỹ gaol.

Grouping these several sounds we have: ĭn, -ĭngs, sĭ́n, sĭnn'd, sĭ́n, ĭn, ĭn-, thĭ́nk, ĭn, ĭn, ĭn, Ĭnn ány-, -tĭn-, -ĭng; bĕst, -gĕls, dĕvĭls, wrĕtch-, -tĕg-, -sĕlves, -sĕlves, -sĕlves, -sĕlf, dwĕll, -ĕth, hĕll, ĕv-; -dĕr-, fĭrst, pĕr-, Dŭrst, -ĕrs, -whĕre, whĕre, (spelled and pronounced then *wher*); -stánd-, -gán, Ăn-, ánd, mán, -chánce, ánd, -ĭăn, ánd, -ănce, Ánd, ăt; bĕ-, -lý, bĕasts, wé, bĕasts, -rĭtý, thĕse, rĕtriĕve, grĕet, seeĭng, Bĕ, seeĭng, -rȳ-, hĕ, ĕ-, Bĕ, thĕ; thĕn, thĕn, mĕn, thĕm-, thĕm-, thĕm-, thĕn, Itálĭán, thĕn; Ŏn-, -ó-, grŏwn ŏ́ld, ŏwn hŏme, dŏth rŏam, ŏwn, hŏme, -lŏw, ŏwn; whĭte, -ĭ-, Ĭ, lĭke, thĭne, thȳ́-, thĭne, thȳ; ĭf, whĭch, lĭve, hĭs, stĭll, stĭll ĭs, ĭs, thĭs; pláce-, Thĕy, stráng-, mák-, snáil, páced, snáil, -ăce; Ŭ-, yóuth; Fŏr, fŏr, ŏr.

---

[1] Query? Carrying hĭs own [hŏme] stĭll, stĭll ĭs at hŏme.

Glancing back over these lines the attention is attracted by several things: (1) The repetition of 14 words, in the 14 lines, causing 82 words to take the place of 107; (2) These 107 words, —comprising 140 syllables, in which are five elisions,—are represented by some twelve sounds; (3) The few sounds which have no arsis- or thesis-variant, judging by present day pronunciation; (4) How certain words,—*e. g., beasts,* and *themselves,*—disappear from the poem as soon as they have received arsis-thesis variation; (5) The sequence of sounds, the ī- sound beginning in 42; ă-, in 43; ō-, in 46, etc.; (6) How certain words, in pairs, give the arsis-thesis variation on the same sound: 'grŏwn ōld,' 'ōwn hŏme,' 'dŏth rōam,' 'stĭll, stĭll,' etc.; (7) How impossible it would be to tell just when Donne is working by *rule*, and when not: *seeĭng* and *seeĭng*; *thĕmselvĕs, thĕmselvĕs, thĕmselvĕs,* and *thўsĕlf* are no doubt purposed, as also probably is line 46. The same may be said of his general tone-scheme. To be sure, I do not believe he figured out all the variations here indicated: such a thing would have made him more mad than his verse has been said to be.

The next example is interesting, for the reason that Donne, in addition to allowing no repeated sound to appear always in arsis, or always in thesis, begins and ends the stanza with the same word.

> Gŏ; ănd ĭf that wŏrd have not quite kĭlled thee,
> Ease mĕ with death by bidding mĕ gŏ tōo.
> Or, ĭf it have, let my wŏrd wŏrk ŏn mĕ,
> Ănd ă just office ŏn ă murderĕr do.
> Except it bĕ tōo late, to kĭll mĕ so,
> Bĕing double dead, gŏing, ănd biddĭng, 'Gŏ.'[1]

Coupling Donne's frequent rather mysterious remarks on his verse,—in which he uses such terms as 'measure,' 'secret,' 'excess,' 'feet,' and 'rule,' and at the same time showing his characteristic accentuation in the most bewildering extravagance in some of the

---

[1] Purposely I have refrained from indicating the similar sounds which appear now in arsis and now in thesis, so as to bring out more noticeably the words and syllables so varying.

poems in which these references are made,—with the fact that whenever a word receives unusual accent, the same word, almost always, as has been seen from examples, stands near by accented as we expect it to be,—convinces me, unalterably, that his art was carefully mastered and executed with diligence and delight.

Fortunately the service to which a knowledge of Donne's peculiarity in verse may be put does not depend upon whether or not it was intentional. The field is inviting for psychological investigation.

Saintsbury and Richter and Trost will have to reconstruct their 'three-period' theories, leaving out of consideration Donne's metrical peculiarity, for in his earliest *Satire* he writes:

> Hĕre are God's conduits, grave divines, and hĕre.
> The nakednĕss and barenĕss to enjoy.
> Hate virtue, though she be năkĕd and bare?
> At birth, and death, our bodies năkĕd are.
> Th' ĭnfănt of London, heir to ăn Índiă.[1]

and near the close of his career, in not the 'last,' but in another 'seraphical hour in his bed-chamber' he sings:

> When Thŏu hăst done, Thŏu hăst not done
> For I hăve more.[2]

[1] *Satire* I, 5, 39, 41-2, 58.
[2] *A Hymn to God the Father*, 5, 6, 11, 12.

NOTE: For each time that I have quoted:

> 'To know how my *rules*, I hăve, and you hăve Donne.'

I have, with no thought of being sacrilegious, a hundred times, said to myself,

> 'When thŏu hăst DONNE, thŏu hăst not DONNE,'
> *For he has more.*

Nor was I thinking of George, or Anna, or Sir Thomas More. Borrowing a noun from Coleridge, and an adjective from Donne, one may well say of some of his 'love-knots,' they were not made to be 'un-Donne.'

One other possibly unscholarly digression,—for which, however, there is not the excuse of precedent,—and a practical application of Donne's 'measure,' 'secret,' 'excess,' or 'rule,' will be made.

Coleridge wrote,

> 'With Donne, whose Muse on dromedary trots,'

XI. Putting Donne's Metrical Peculiarity to the Test.

Applying the knowledge we have gained of Donne's metrical peculiarity, the following are some of the more important uses to which it can be put:

and seeing the numerous lines in which there is variation of three words or syllables, each once in arsis and once in thesis, I am willing to be laughed at,—by those who do not know how to scan English verse,—for presenting to the eye the mental picture which moved Coleridge to pen the line.

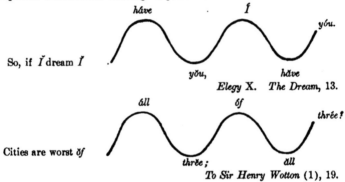

These humps are more suggestive of the Bactrian camel than of the dromedary. They are not given as representing the outline of a camel's back, but as illustrating the up-and-down swing of a swiftly moving camel.

May not there have been a somewhat similar picture in the mind of Macdonald when he lovingly regrets 'that Donne should have ridden his Pegasus over quarry and housetop, instead of teaching him his paces?'

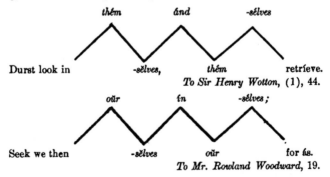

When Chadwick (quoted p. 51) speaks of 'how daintily the ponderous elephant [Donne's Muse] could dance,' he is only imitating Coleridge, without feeling what Coleridge felt, and as a result brings an unpicturable animal into Donne's poetical menagerie.

(1) We can determine what poems classified by Chambers (ii, 249–318) as 'Doubtful,' 'Hitherto Uncollected,' and 'Spurious' are Donne's; and what are not his. Furthermore, as anonymous poems of the late sixteenth and early seventeenth centuries come to light, those that are Donne's may be recognized; and we may yet find some of his poems among the works of his contemporaries and successors.

As it is not my purpose to attempt a restoration of Donne's poetry to the original, till I have seen all the other MSS. known to exist; and as space cannot here be given to a republishing of all poems about which there is question, a few examples, under each head, must suffice.

(a.) 'Doubtful Poems.'

Love's War (Chambers, ii, 250) is Donne's.

The evidence (1–3):

Till *I hăve peace* with *thĕe, wăr* other men,
And when *Ĭ hăve peăce,* can *Ĭ* leave *thĕe* then?
All other *wărs* are scrupulous.

Love Sonnet, I, II (Chambers, ii, 254) is Donne's.

The evidence (Sonnet I, 1–4):

O MADAM, *yŏu* are of all women true,
Nay virtue's self, *thăt's* more, for only *yŏu*
Are *thăt* which we imagine *tŏ bĕ shĕ*;
Yŏu, and but *yŏu*, make virtue here *tŏ bĕ*.[1]

(Sonnet II, 10–11):

Frŏm light, *frŏm* truth, and *frŏm* the sight of men
My guides should *tŏo* late and quickly know.[2]

Love and Wit (Chambers, ii, 272) is Donne's.

The Evidence (7, 10):

Doth measure *wĭn* wom*ĕn?* *Thĕn* I know why,
Ănd smŏoth as a *vĕrse, ănd,* like that *smŏoth vĕrse.*

---

[1] I have purposely abstained from indicating arsis-thesis variations, in sounds and syllables, in these lines, to bring out the varying words more plainly.

[2] It is necessary to apply our principle for the correction of this line:

My guides should *tŏo* late and [*tŏo*] quickly know.

Borrowing (Chambers, ii, 268) is Donne's.
   The evidence (the whole quatrain):
      One calls mĕ friend and urges mĕ to pay
      A debt Ĭ borrow'd, not ŭpón a day,
      But ŭpŏn terms of love; am Í his friend?
      Ĭ may then owe ăs freely ăs he lend.
On a Flea in His Mistress's Bosom (Chambers, ii, 252)
   is not Donne's.
   The evidence (The whole poem, especially lines 5 and 12):
      Hŏw it did suck, hŏw eager tickle you!
      Abŏút hĕr heart, abŏút hĕr anywhere.[1]
A Warning (Chambers, ii, 255) is not Donne's.
   The Evidence (the whole poem, especially lines 23-25):
      Though yŏu have stólen my heárt away,
      If all your servants prove not true,
      May stéal a heárt or two from yŏu.
Believe Your Glass (Chambers, ii, 257) is not Donne's.
   The Evidence (30, 45):
      Look to yoursélf, compare yoursélf with them
      So light regard wĕ what wĕ little love.
and more especially the fact that *bend* occurs three times; *tend*, once; and *end* once; and the sound is always in arsis.
Dr. Donne's Farewell to the World (Chambers, ii, 273) is not
   Donne's.
   The Evidence (17-20):
      Ĭ wóuld bĕ wise, bŭt that thĕ fox Ĭ sée
      Suspected guilty when thĕ áss ĭs free;
      Ĭ wóuld bĕ poor, bŭt sée thĕ humble grass
      Ĭs trampled on by each unworthy áss.

---

[1] Only the last line, of the 14, has the Donne-touch:
      If thou could'st suck from hĕr hĕr cruelty.

But the fact that the syllable 'suck' occurs three times in the 14 lines, and always in arsis, is evidence enough that Donne did not write it. On the other hand, see Donne's poem, *The Flea*, 1, 3 (Chambers, i, 1):
      Márk but thĭs flea and márk in thĭs.
      It sŭck'd me first and now sŭcks thee.

(b.) 'Poems Hitherto Uncollected.'

To My Lord of Pembroke (Chambers, ii, 285) is Donne's.

The Evidence (3-5, 14-16, 22):

For as love greater grŏws, so he grŏws less.
Hĕ thăt disdains, what honour wins thereby,
Thăt hĕ feels not . . .
By gentleness wĕ ăre betrayĕd thus.
Wĕ will not strive with love that's ă she beast;
But playing wĕ ăre bound and yield ĭn jest,
As ĭn ă cobweb toil ă fly hath been
Undone . . .
Heăt ŏr cŏld there, was hŏt ŏr cŏld before.

The Lie (Chambers, ii, 292) is not Donne's.

The Evidence (5-6):

Yŏu săy Ĭ lĭe, Ĭ săy yŏu lĭe, judge whether;
If we then both doe lĭe, let's lĭe together.

Among the 'list of pieces' which Chambers does not include (beyond introductory couplets) in 'Appendix B,' it would be interesting to see the complete poem beginning,

Lĭke to the damask rose you see,
Or lĭke the blossom on the tree.

The same may be said of the poems, in the O'Flahertie MS.[1] beginning:

Nature amaz'd saw măn without măn's ayde
Borne of a mother nursĕd by her mayd.

and,

To sue for all thy̆ Love, and thy̆ whole hart.

(c.) 'Spurious Poems.'

About all that can be done with the few complete poems accessible, under this head, is to show the divergence, of some of them, from Donne's method.

On the Blessed Virgin Mary, 1-2:

In thăt, O Quĕen of Quĕens, thy birth was free
From thăt which others doth of grace bereave.

---

[1] R. Warwick Bond, *Note on the Donne MS.*, (Ellis & Elvey's Catalogue, No. 93, 1899, pp. 1-9) pp. 8, 9.

My Heart (1-4):

> Thou sent'st to me a *heárt wăs* sound,
>   *Ĭ* took *ĭt* to be thine;
> But when *Ĭ* saw *ĭt* had a wound,
>   *Ĭ* knew that *heárt wăs* mine.[1]

(*d*). Poems Published as Certainly Donne's.

If *Farewell to Love* (Chambers, i, 76–7) is Donne's it has undergone great changes since it left his hand.

(2) Was Joseph Hall 'the harbenger to Donne's Anniversarie,' as Jonson said to Drummond?

The first ten lines of *To the Praise of the Dead, and the Anatomy* (Chambers, ii, 102) will convince one that Donne did not write it: *world*, for example, appears four times, always in arsis, and with no companion-sound in thesis. Two lines (21–2) both have and have not Donne's 'measure.'

> Enough is us to *práise* them *thát práise* thee,
> And say, *thát* but enough those *práises* be.

This arsis-thesis variation of *praise*, and *that*, is to be found in Donne, to be sure; but it is also in Shakespeare. The repeated word, *enough*, with the first syllable in thesis and the second in arsis, both times, is not in Donne's manner and therefore furnishes the solution.

Donne:

> Thou I be dead and buried, yet I have
> Living *ĭn* you—court *énough ĭn* my grave.
>   *To the Countess of Bedford* (6), 1, 2.

> But if my days be long, and good *ĕnough*,
> *Ĭn* vain this sea shall *énlarge* or *énrough*.
>   *The Progress of the Soul*, 51–2.

> 'If you'd liv'd, sir,
> Time *énough tó* have been *ĭnterpreter*
> *Tŏ* Babel's bricklayers, sure the tower had stood.
>   *Satire* IV, 63–5.

---

[1] It is noticeable that 'I' 'was' and 'it' are always in thesis, while 'heart' is both times in arsis; 'to' is the only repeated word that varies.

Donne has no line in which *enough* is repeated, and no two consecutive lines in which it appears; but if, occasionally, he could not, or would not, use the word *one* time without an arsis-thesis variant for the *en-* (*e-*), surely he would have shifted the accent on the repeated word.

Lines 17, 20, 21, 40–42 of *The Harbinger* (Chambers, ii, 125–6) show that the poem is not Donne's; and lines 1, 5, and 8 give one the impression that Donne, to satisfy his ear, may have transposed some of the words.

(3) The Missing Word can be Supplied.

Satire V, 9–16.

> If *áll thíngs bé ín áll*
> —As I *thínk*, since *áll whích* were, *áre*, *ǎnd sháll*
> *Bĕ, bé* made [*éach*] of *thé* same elements,
> *Ĕach thíng ĕach thíng* implies or represents—
> Then man is a world; *in whích* officers
> *Ăre thé* vast *rávishíng sĕas*, *ánd* suitors
> *Spríngs, nów* full, *nów shállow, nŏw* dry, *whích* to
> That *whích* drowns them run...

Observing, in these lines, the variations: *áll, áll, ăll*; *shăll, shăllow*; *thĭngs, thĭnk, thĭng, thĭng*; *bé, Bĕ, bé, thé, thé, sĕas*; *ĭn, ĭn*; *whĭch, whĭch, whĭch, whĭch*; *áre, Ăre*; *ănd, ánd*; *ravishíng, Spríngs*; *nów, nów, nŏw*; and seeing, furthermore, in 19–23, the variations: *mĕn, mĕn*; *dŭst, dŭst*; *wŏrms, wŏrms*; *ĕat, ĕat*; *yoú, yoŭ*; what are we to do but supply 'each' in arsis to vary with 'each' twice in thesis in the next line? It is true that there are numerous long *ē* variations, but the poet seems here to be shifting accent on words as well as on syllables and sounds.

Satire IV, 235–241.

> No tokĕn óf worth but 'Queen's man,' and fine
> Living, barréls ŏf beef, flagóns ŏf wine,
> I shook like a *spĭed spý*. Preachers, which are
> Seas óf [*ăll*] wits and arts, you can then dare
> Drown the sins of this place, [yĕt] fór, fŏr me.

Seeing here the variations: tokĕn, flagón; óf, ŏf, ŏf, óf; spĭed and spý; I accept Lowell's suggestion of *ăll*, in 38, as a variant-sound for the purposed wrenched accent in *barréls*. Instead of his suggestion 'for (as) for me,' I prefer ' [yet] for, for me,' because it preserves Donne's variation 'fór, fŏr';[1] and for the equally important reason that 'yet' appears in arsis in 241 and 242, without a thesis-variant.

Satire V, 72–3.

Grosart prints the lines, without variants:[2]

                              And she
Speaks Fate's words, and tells who must be
Rich, who poor, who in chairs, and who in jayles.

Chambers, also without variants, gives them:

                              And she
Speaks Fate's words, and but tells us who must be
Rich, who poor; who in chairs, who in gaols.

Whatever the source of Chambers' reading we can see that two syllables are wanting in 72; and that, while he restores the two last phrases, in 73, to Donne's measure, he leaves the line one syllable short.

I would suggest:

                              Ănd shé
Speaks Fate's words, ánd [shĕ] tells [mĕn] whó must bé
Rich, whó [bĕ] poor; whó ín chairs, whó ín gaols.

I reject *but* and *us*, because *but*, *us*, and *must*, all in thesis so near together, and without a similar sound in arsis, would not be like Donne.

My reason for suggesting *shĕ* and *bĕ* is apparent. The reason for suggesting *men* is that the *tone* of the poem seems headed in that direction,—*men* occurring in arsis in 76, and in thesis in 80.

An Anatomy of the World. The Second Anniversary, 290–2.
The Grosart and Norton editions give line 291:

    When wilt thou shake off this pedantery?

---

[1]   If thou stăy hére. O stăy hĕre, *fór fŏr* thee
      England is only a worthy gallery.
                                        Elegy XVII, 43–4.

[2] So Norton.

Chambers:
>   When wilt thou shake off this pedantry?

which leaves the line wanting a syllable. Evidently Donne wrote:

>   In this low form, poor soul, what *wĭlt thŏu* do?
>   [And] when *wĭlt thŏu* shake *óff* this pedantry,
>   *Óf* being taught by sense and fantasy?

The Lamentations of Jeremy, 280–4.

>   As *dó thĕ* owls in *thé* vast wilderness.
>   *Ănd whĕn thĕ* sucking child *dŏth* strive *tŏ* draw,
>   *Hĭs* tongue *fŏr* thirst cleaves *tó hĭs* upper jaw;
>   *Ănd whĕn fŏr* food *thĕ* children cry,
>   There *ĭs* no *mán* that *dóth* them satisfy.

Here we see every repeated word or sound in arsis-thesis variation except *whĕn* and *fŏr*; but line 283 has only four accents. Conforming to Donne's 'rule' it is easy to reconstruct the line.

>   And [*thĕn*] *whĕn fŏr* food *thé* childrĕn [*dŏ*] cry.[1]

Now we have the variations: *dó, dŏ; thĕ, thé, thĕ, thĕ; Ănd, Ănd, mán; whĕn, thĕn, whĕn,* childrĕn; *dŏth, dóth; tó, tŏ; Hĭs, hĭs, ĭs;* and *fŏr, fŏr*.

(4.) *The Superfluous Word may be Recognized.*[2]

---

[1] Compare accented *the* in line 280; and *chĭldrĕn* in the following:
>   Honest *chĭldrĕn*, let her dishonest be.
>   *Satire* VI, 24.
>   O, too bad
>   To be countéd *chĭldrĕn* of poetry,
>   Except confirmèd and bishop'd by thee.
>   *To M(r). B. B.*, 26-8.

In Chambers this last line is given:
>   Except confirm'd and bishoped by thee.

presumably meaning that the *-ed* of 'bishoped' is to be accented. In Norton it is the same, except that this *-ed* is accented. Grosart, thinking that Donne is always 'solemn,' renders the line unscansionable:
>   Except confirmèd and bishopèd by thee.

Donne purposely accented the *-ed* of 'counted' so as to have it vary with the *-ed*, in thesis, in 'confirmèd.'

[2] This is the only example that will be given under this head. There are several other lines, with one or two extra syllables, and in which elision seems impossible, but the surrounding text is also evidently corrupt, and I am unwilling to venture a conjecture till I have more light.

> Manure *thysélf* then, *tó thysélf* bĕ improved;
> And with vain outward things bĕ no more moved,
> But *tó* know that I *lóve* thee and would bĕ *lóved*.
>   *To Mr. Rowland Woodward*, 34-6.

Having seen, in previous examples, that Donne does not allow *be* to appear in thesis three times, in succession, without an arsis-variant,—here we have *thee* also in thesis,—and his fondness for shifting accent on *themselves* and *ourselves* when the word is repeated in a line, and, especially, noting line 19, of this poem,

> Seek we then *oúrselves* in *ourselvés* ; for as,

we can with confidence, restore the lines to their original 'roughness (?)':

> Manure *thýsélf, tŏ thýsĕlf bé* improved ;
> And with vain outward things bĕ no more moved,
> But *tó* know I *lŏve thée* and would bĕ *lóved*.

or, the last line may be (following a comma and a dash):

> But know that I *lŏve* thee and would be *lóved*.

If *then* is essential to the sense of the first line, which is improbable, it can be retained and scanned:

> Manure *thýsélf* then, to *thýsĕlf bé* improved.

(5) *The Correct Variant can be Selected.*[1]

To the Countess of Bedford (5), 23-5.

> You, *fór* whose body God made better clay,

---

[1] This statement needs only one modification ; to illustrate :
    If thou be'st born *tó* strange sights,
       Things invisible *tŏ* see.   *Song*, 10-11.

The 1669 variant of the second *to* is *go;* and as these words were pronounced almost alike, I could not, judging from sound alone, decide which is Donne's. If, however, the variants had been *to* and *come*, I could have said, at once, *to* is Donne's. This sort of conflict occurs in less than 10 per cent. of the variants, which is not strange, because Donne depended so largely upon arsis-thesis variation of sound, or tone, that any change in a line would, usually, take away from it the very thing he put into it.

Of the many variants, space can be afforded for only a few, which will be presented, first as they appear in Chambers, and then restored with no comment, save the marks of arsis and thesis.

>   Or took soul's stuff, such as shall late decay,
>   Or such as needs small change at the *làst* day.
>   You, *fór* whose body God made better clay,
>   *Ŏr* took soul's stuff, *sŭch ăs* shall *làst fŏr* aye,
>   *Ŏr sŭch ăs* needs small change at the *làst* day.
>   Haslewood-Kingsboro MS.[1]

Satire II, 1-4.

>   Sir, though—I thank God for it—I do hate
>   Perfectly *áll* this town, yet there's one state
>   In *áll* ill things so excellently best,
>   That hate towards them breeds pity towards the rest.
>
>   Sir, though—*Ĭ* thank God for *ĭt*—*Í* do hate
>   *Ăll* this town perfect*lý*, there is one state
>   In *áll* ill things so excellent*lý* best,
>   That hate *tòwards* [*ĭt*] breeds pity *tòwards* the rest.
>   Harleian MS. 4955.[2]

Love's Deity, 24-5.

>   Love *máy* make me leave loving, or might try
>   A deeper plague, to make her love me too.
>
>   *Lŏve might măke mé* leave *lóv*ing, or *mĭght* try
>   A deeper plague, *tŏ máke* her *lóve mĕ tóo.*
>   MS. 'N' 'Norton Collection,' Harvard Library.[3]

Eclogue, 1613, December 26, 56-9.

>   Dreamer, thou art:
>   Think'st thou, fantastic, that thou hast a part

---

[1] Grosart, ii, 48, note.

[2] Chambers, ii, 180, note. The Harl. MS. has a double version, one of which I accept. Both versions have *them* where I have inserted *it*. *Hate* occurs twice in arsis in these lines; sometimes Donne allows this to happen when he is *very busy* with other variations. A little more than a half century before Donne wrote this Satire, Lord Berners spelled 'p-e-r-f-e-y-g-h-t-l-y' (see N. E. D.); and if we may take this as an indication of the pronunciation of 'perfectly,' at the time of Donne, we have here the variations *háte, -fĕyght-, háte*. 'Perfitly' was the usual spelling at the time of Donne, and according to Skeat (*Principles of English Etymology*, 1887, p. 172, note) *ĭ* at that time is supposed to have had the sound of *a* in *name*.

[3] As this MS. bears no indication of its former ownership, and as Mr. Quaritch, from whom Professor Norton obtained it, 'as well as others,' could give no information as to its source (see *The Text of Donne's Poems*, p. 11), and, furthermore, in recognition of Professor Norton's devout study of Donne, I beg the privilege of hereafter designating this as the Norton MS.

> Ĭn the Ĭndian fleet, because thou hast
> A little spice or amber in thy taste?
>
>   Dreamer, thŏu art
> Thinkĕst thŏu, făntăstĭc, that thóu hăst part [1]
> Ĭn thĕ Ĕast Ĭndian flĕet, bĕcause thŏu hăst
> A little spice or amber in thy taste?
>   Norton MS.

Holy Sonnets, VIII, 12–14.

>   Then turn
> O pensive soul, to God, fŏr Hĕ knows best
> Thy grief, fŏr Hĕ put it into thy breast.
>
>   Then turn
> O pensive soul, to God, fŏr Hĕ knows best
> Thy true grief, fŏr Hĕ put it in thy breast.
>   Westmoreland MS.[2]

Elegy . . . *Prince Henry*, 32–4.

> Was his great father's greatest instrument,
> And activest spirit to convey and tie
> This soul of peace *through* Christianity.
>
> Was hĭs grĕat father's grĕatĕst instrument
> And activĕst spirit tŏ convey and tie
> Thĭs soul of peace tŏ Christianity.
>   Editions of 1635, '39, '49, '54, '69.[3]

Satire I, 47–8.

> And in this coarse attire which Ĭ now wear
> With God and with the Muses Ĭ confer.
>
> And in this coarse attire which now Ĭ wear
> Wĭth God and wĭth the Muses Ĭ confer.
>   Harl. MS.

The Legacy, 1, 2.

> When last Ĭ died, and dear, Ĭ die

---

[1] I have omitted the 'a' from line 57, because I do not believe it is Donne's. The reason is obvious.

[2] *Gosse*, ii, 368. There numbered 'X.'

[3] The pronunciation of *to* and *through* were and are so much alike that *sense* aids *sound* in restoring this line; whereas, in others, sense vindicates sound.

As often as from thee I go.
When Í díed last, and dear Ǐ die
Ǎs often ás from thee Ǐ go.

Edition of 1633.

To Sir Tho. Rowe, 1603, 23-32.

And all's well, for had she loved, I'd not had
All my friend's hate; for now departing sad
I feel not that; yet as the rack the gout
Cures, so hath this worse grief that quite put out.
My first disease naught but that worse cureth,
Which, I dare foresay, nothing cures but death.
Tell her all this, before I am forgot,
That not too late she grieve she loved me not.
  Burden'd with this, I was to depart less
  Willing than those which die, and not confess.

And *áll's* well, *fór hád shé lóved, Í'd nǒt had*
Ǎll my friend's hate *fǒr nót dĕpár*ting sad;[1]
Í feel *nǒt thát*; yet as the rack the gout
Cúres, só hath *thís wǒrse* grief *thát* quite put out.[2]
Mý first dis*éase naúght bút thát wórse cǔréth*,[3]
Which, *Í* dare *fóresěe, naúght* [will] *cúre bǔt* death.[4]
Tell her *áll thís*, be*fóre Í* am *fǒrgót*,
Thát nót tǒo late *shě griéve shě lóved mě nót.*
  Burden'd with *thís Í* was *tǒ dĕpárt* less
  Willing, than those which die, *nǒt tó* confess.[5]

Elegy XIII, 82.

We'll leave her ever, and love her alone.

Grosart:

We'll *lóve hěr* ev*ěr*, and *lǒve hér* alone.[6]

---

[1] Stephens MS. has 'not.'
[2] Stephens MS. has 'this this'; but omits 'quite.'
[3] Stephens MS., 'first cureth.'
[4] Stephens MS., 'foresee, naught,' which necessitates a change of tense, and the supplying of 'will.'
[5] A change without MS. authority.
[6] Chambers: 'Query? *love her ever.*'

Eclogue, etc., 149-52.

> Thus thou descend'st to our infirmity,
>   Who can the sun in water[1] see.
>   So dost thou, when in silk and gold
> Thou cloud'st thyself...

> Thus thóu descend'st to our ínfirmitý,
>   Who cán thĕ sun ĭn wínter sée.
>   Sŏ dŏst thŏu whén ĭn silk ănd góld
> Thŏu clóuld'st thyself...

Addl. MS. 18, 617.

(6) *Difficult Lines may be Scanned.*

To Sir Edward Herbert, etc., 31-2.

The average reader would scan these lines:

> Thus mán, that míght be His pléasure ís His ród,
> And is His devil, that might be his God.

Donne scanned them:

> Thus man, *thăt míght bĕ Hĭs* pleasuré is *Hĭs* rod,
> And *ĭs Hĭs* devil *thăt might bĕ hĭs* God.

Mr. Gosse should have selected *Satire* I, 77-8, as lines that 'may excusably defy a novice':

> And as fidlers stop lowest, at highest sound,
> So to the most brave, stoops he nighest the ground.

Before attempting to scan these lines, it is necessary to correct them: *stop* appears in Harl. MS. and in the editions of 1635, '39, '49, '54, '69; *stoopt*, in 1633; *stoop* in Norton's MS. 'C.' Aside from the fact that 'stop lowest at highest sound' is foolishness, and the further fact that 'fidlers' *do* 'stoop,' or lean forward, 'at highest sound,' we may be sure that Donne's purpose in repeating the word, is to give it arsis-thesis variation. The same may be said of *highest* and *nighest*, and of *lowest* and *most*. Beginning at the ends of the lines, and scanning backward, we are able to supply one missing word, and dispose of two words, 'And' and 'So,'

---

[1] So 1633, '35, '39, '49, '69; Stephens MS., *waters*.

that have been added, not 'lest some spark be lost,' but in a vain attempt to 'smooth' what was not understood.

> As fidlers stŏop [thĕ] lŏwest at hĭghĕst sound,
> To thĕ mŏst brave, stŏops hĕ nĭghĕst thĕ ground.

Saintsbury, discussing *Absence*, says, 'I would almost go to the stake on it that the piece is Donne's,'[1]—a question that I am not quite prepared to answer with so much confidence, although I should like to,—but, concerning the lines just scanned, I am ready to quote him, almost leaving out 'almost'; for this is Donne's: stŏop, stŏops; thĕ, thĕ, hĕ, thĕ; lŏwest, mŏst; hĭghĕst, nĭghĕst!

We come now to that troublesome line, *Twickenham Garden*, 1:

> Blasted with sighs, and súrroundéd with tears,
> Hither I come to seek the spring.

Professor Norton (*Donne's Love Poems*, p. 81, note) says, 'The stress on the first syllable of 'surrounded' calls attention to the fact that Donne uses the word here with the meaning suggested by its etymology,—a meaning which it soon lost under the compelling influence of the syllable "round." The word was derived from the French obsolete *suronder*, and this from the mediæval Latin *superundare*. It was still in Donne's time a rare word in either of its senses. Shakespeare does not use it. In Howell's edition of Cotgrave's French and English Dictionary, published in 1660, in the English vocabulary "surround" appears as follows: "To surround (or overflow), *oultre couler*," as if the word had no other meaning than "overflow." It was with this significance and with the pronunciation proper to it that Donne uses the word here.'

There can be no objection to the prefix 'sur' receiving the ictus. Donne's contemporaries, and all poets since his day, have reserved the right,—endorsed by the history of our language,—to accent prefix and suffix. However, there is something more peculiar than this about the line. Observe that 'with' stands twice in thesis, which is contrary to Donne's method. Possibly he read the line,

---

[1] Chambers, i, xxviii.

> Blastĕd with sighs, and surroundĕd with tears,

thereby securing enough variation to satisfy him; but accepting Professor Norton's explanation, I think it more likely that Donne wrote,

> Blastĕd wĭth sighs, and wĭth surroundĕd tears,
> Hither I come to seek the spring.

or,

> Blasted wĭth sighs, and wĭth surroundĭng tears,
> Hither I come to seek the sprĭng.

To express the matter in prose, giving the word its original meaning, we have, Blasted with sighs, and overflowed with tears; or, Blasted with sighs, and overflowing with tears. To transpose the 'with,' we have, Blasted with sighs, and with overflowing tears.

There are several reasons why a transcriber might have made the change: he might have objected to 'Blasted ... with tears'; it might have been made to suit the later meaning of the word 'surrounded'; he might have objected to accenting the preposition 'with'; he might have fancied that,

> Blásted with síghs, and surróunded with téars,

(four accents) is more rhythmic than,

> Blastéd with síghs, and wíth surróunding téars.

The only other instance I have recorded of 'with' occurring twice in the same line, or in successive lines, and both times unaccented, is in the fifth stanza of *The Bait;* and the ed. of 1633 has 'which' for the second 'with.' Grosart's note (ii, 207) on line 20, of this poem, indicates some alteration in the whole stanza.[1]

(7.) *In Dialogue Poems, Donne's Part may be Recognized.*

In a note (i, 232) on *A Dialogue Between Sir Henry Wotton and Mr. Donne*, Chambers says, 'No division of the verses between

---

[1] Confirmatory of this, see Coleridge's quotation from *Sermon* LXXI, *Notes on English Divines*, London, 1853, i, 118. See also *Sermons* LXXI and LXXII, Alford, vol. iii.

the two authors is given in any of the editions of Donne. I have attempted to supply one, conjecturally.' Of the six stanzas, he assigns to Wotton the first and third, and to Donne the others.

Chambers seems to have overlooked Grosart's note (ii, 245-6): 'The second stanza is in continuation of the first and by the same speaker, and so the third. These are answered by the second speaker in the last three stanzas, each of which is a reply in order, to each stanza of the preceding speaker. I have accordingly placed the word "Answer" between the third and fourth stanzas. Which are by Wotton and which by Donne is a more difficult question, but guessing by the middle of st. v. and the end of st. vi, I should be inclined to appropriate them in the order given in the heading.' He, as we see, agrees with Chambers in all but the second stanza.

In the first stanza, notwithstanding the conjectures of Grosart and Chambers, the evidence is against them; it is Donne's:

> If her disdain least change in *yoú* can move,
>   *Yoŭ* do not *lóve*,
> For when that hope *gíves fúĕl* to the fire
>   *Yoŭ séll* desire.
> *Lŏve ĭs* not *lóve*, but *gíven* free;
> And *só ĭs* mine; *sŏ* should yours be.

On stanza II. I agree with Grosart; it is Wotton's (1, 3):

> *Hĕr heárt, thăt wĕeps* to hear of others' moan,
> *Hĕr eýes, thăt wĕep* a stranger's *eýes* to see.

In stanza III. the only repeated words are *her*, both times in arsis; and *disdain* (*disdainings*), with the accent both times on the second syllable. The only repeated syllables, with a similar sound, are *just-* and *must*, both times in arsis. Considering only repeated words and their arsis-thesis variation, or lack of it, the evidence, in this stanza, is too slight to form the basis of an opinion; but the very fact that there are so few repeated words, indicates that it is not Donne's. The first line,

> Say her disdainings justly must be graced,

seems to take up and question the first line of stanza I.,

>   If her disdain least change in you can move,

which, according to our test, belongs to Donne. It seems pretty clear, therefore, that Grosart and Chambers are right: this stanza is Wotton's.

They are both right in assigning the fourth stanza to Donne (23–4):

> Who cán of lóve more rich gifts make,
> Thán to Lóve's self for lóve's own sake?[1]

At first sight there appears a contradiction in stanzas I. and IV., which would indicate difference in authorship, but Donne simply changes the application from 'her' to 'self.'

In stanza V., the only repeated words are *in* and *his* always in arsis. What has been said of stanza III., therefore, applies to this. With less confidence, than heretofore or hereafter, I would dissent from the conjecture of Grosart and Chambers and assign this stanza to Wotton.

All having agreed that the third stanza is Wotton's, all must likewise agree that the last stanza is Donne's; for it ends with a question about 'private ends,' on which Wotton had made a statement; besides, the variations are Donne's: fŏr, fŏr, fŏr, humoúr; and thére (ther) and gentlĕr.

In 'Poems Hitherto Uncollected,' (ii, 287–8) Chambers gives *A Letter Written by Sir H[enry] G[oodyere] and J[ohn] D[onne], Alternis Vicibus.* It being known, presumably, that all the stanzas with odd numbers are Goodyere's, a couple of examples from Donne may be given, as showing his *mark*.

Stanza VI.

> Admit our magic then by which we dó
> Make you appear tŏ ús, and ús tŏ yoú,
> Supplying all the Musĕs in yŏu twó.[2]

Stanza XII.

> For 'twere ĭn us ambition tŏ write

---

[1] This line has variants, but none of them take away the arsis-thesis variation of *love*.

[2] Besides the variations ús, ús, and -ĕs, *us* appears in thesis in Donne's next stanza.

Sŏ, that because we twó yoŭ twó ŭnite,
Our letter should, as yoú, be ínfĭnite.

XII. *The Way is opened for an Investigation of the Sources of Donne's Metrical Peculiarity.*

In the *Epistle* to *The Progress of the Soul*, Donne expresses himself on influence or borrowings: 'Now when I begin this book, I have no purpose to come into any man's debt; how my stock will hold out I know not; perchance waste, perchance increase in use. If I do borrow anything from antiquity, besides that I make account that I pay to posterity, with as much, and as good, you shall still find me to acknowledge it, and to thank not him only that hath digged out the treasures for me, but that hath lighted me a candle to the place.'

Since this poem contains no quotations, direct or indirect, we may take his statement to mean: (1) That, so far as he went, his 'stock' held out and there was no need of borrowing; (2) That, on general principles, he believed in 'paying.' Have we not seen his acknowledgment to Abraham Fraunce, who 'writes thus'; and his reference to 'The Prophets' 'which did . . . Thy will . . . express in rhythmic feet,' by whom he excuses not his 'excess in seeking secrets, or poeticness?' Both of these seem to be acknowledgments for mere manner of expression, without reference to matter or thought.

Professor Brumbaugh, before having learned fully the nature of Donne's metrical peculiarity, reviewed the opinions of Johnson, Gosse, Coleridge, and Saintsbury, as to the *Sources of Donne's Style*: 'Dr. Johnson finds it in Marino[1] . . . Gosse believes that the "fantastic Spanish school of conceits which takes its name from Gongora may have effected the style of Donne"[2] . . . Coleridge, forgetting that Donne had this style before he became a student of the Church Fathers, asserts that "Donne acquired from that too great partiality for the Fathers, from Irenæus to

---

[1] *Life of Cowley*, Cassell's Nat'l Lib., No. 18, pp. 47–52.
[2] *Encyc. Brit.*, vol. viii.

Bernard, the taste for these forced and fantastic analogies"[1] ... Saintsbury finds him closely in touch with the French Renaissance poets.'[2]

Elsewhere Dryden has been quoted as saying that Donne in his *Satires* 'followed Horace so closely that he must of necessity fall with him.'

Gray, in the sketch he sent to Warton, asserts that 'A third Italian school, full of conceit, began in Queen Elizabeth's reign, continued under James and Charles the first, by Donne, Crashaw, Cleveland; was carried to its height by Cowley, and ended perhaps in Sprat.'[3]

Professor Brumbaugh concludes: 'It is remarkable that these four eminent critics should find Donne imitating the writers of four different and widely divergent national types. Nobody would scorn such an imputation with greater vehemence than Donne himself. He did not imitate anybody.' (Here are quoted the four lines from Carew, in which he speaks of 'fresh invention' being planted in the 'Muses' garden'). 'Had his method been such as to allow of what he would call zany[4] efforts, he would in all probability have put himself in touch with some of the many poetic influences of his own times and of his own associates...'

Professor Schelling partially agrees with both Coleridge and Brumbaugh: 'Except for a certain rhetorical and dialectical address, which might be referred to a study of the ancients, the poetry of Donne is marked by its disregard of conventions, by its extraordinary originality of thought and expression, by that rare quality of poetic insight that justifies Jonson's enthusiastic claim that "John Donne [was] the first poet in the world in some things."'[5]

All this has reference, of course, to more than the construction of Donne's verse, but it must, in some measure, relate also to it.

---

[1] *Works*, N. Y., 1884, v. 73.
[2] *Eng. Lit.*, iv, 144 ff.
[3] Edmond Gosse, *The Works of Thomas Gray* (4 vols.), London, 1884, iii, 367.
[4] See *To M(r). I. W.*, 30.
[5] Felix E. Schelling, 'Ben Jonson and the Classical School,' *Pub. Mod. Lang. Asso. of America*, Vol. xii, No. 2, p. 227.

Inviting as the subject is, but little attention can now be given to a study of the sources of Donne's style. However, one of Professor Brumbaugh's suggestions must be considered; and that is with reference to the 'probability' of his having 'put himself in touch with some of the many poetic influences of his own times and of his own associates.'

It has been shown that he *jestingly* imitated the ruggedness of Fraunce: 'Abraham Fraunce writes thus and jests not.' Furthermore, considering the immense popularity of *Tottel's Miscellany*, which, in thirty years, had reached its eighth edition,—by the time Donne was fourteen years old,—it is very reasonable to class it under the head of any list of 'poetic influences of his own times' as a 'probable' source of his style.

Let a comparison now be made of some of the lines of Donne and of Wyatt,—not always as they appear in the Harrington MS., but as they appeared in the *Miscellany* where Donne would have been more likely to see them.

Wyatt:
    With *Venŭs*, and *Bacchŭs*, all their life long.
        Of the Courtier's life written to Iohn Poins, 23.

Donne:
    Twins, though their birth *Cŭsco* and *Mŭsco* take.
        To the Lady Bedford, 7.

Wyatt:
    Of hye *Caĕsár* and damne Catŏ tŏ die:
    That with his death did scape out of the gate,
    From *Caĕsăr's* handes, if Liuye doth not lye.
        Of the Courtier's life, etc., 38–40.

Donne:
    His own? 'No; *Fĭdŭs*, he is thy dear friend;
    That keeps him *ŭp*. . .'
        Góod *Fĭdŭs* for this
    Mŭst pardon me; *săt́ires* bite when they kiss.
    But as for *Nátta*, we have since fallen out.
    Within a pint at mósṭ; Yet for all̄ this

—Which is most strange—*Nátta* thinks no man is
More honest than himself...
Satire VII, 70–1, 89–91, 43–5.

Wyatt:
If wail*ýng* or sigh*ýng* contínually.
Charging of his loue, etc., 10.

Donne:
Of spy*íng* heirs melt*íng* with luxurý.
Satire II, 79.

Wyatt:
My foode noth*íng* my faint*íng* strength repairs: weares.
To his unkind loue, 7.

Donne:
And barrell*íng* the dropp*íngs*, ánd the stuff.
Satire II, 82.

Wyatt:
'*Twíxt* wo, and welth: be*twíxt* earnést and game.
Of douteous loue, 11.

Donne:
As '*twíxt* two equal armies, Fate
Were gone out,—hung '*twíxt* her and me.
The Ecstasy, 13, 16.

Wyatt:
L*ét* h*ím* thank God and l*ét* h*ím* not provoke.
The louer describeth his restless state, 27.

Donne:
L*ét* m*é* prepare towards her, and l*ét* m*é* call
This hour her vigil...
A Nocturnal, etc., 46.

Wyatt:
Call h*ím* p*ítýful*, ánd h*ím* true ánd plaine.
Of the Courtier's life, etc., 73.

Donne:
Was not H*ís* p*ítý* towards th*ée* wondrous high,
That would have need to be p*ítiéd* by th*ée*?

Kiss *Hĭm*, and *wĭth Hĭm* into Egypt go,
With *Hĭs* kind mother, who partakes thy woe.
                    La Corona. Nativity, 11-14.

Wyatt:
                Me list not to report
Blame by *hŏnóur*, and *hŏnóur* to desire;
But how may I this *hŏnóur* now attaine?
                    Of the Courtier's life, etc., 16, 17.

Donne:
Nor shall I then *hŏnóur* your fortune more
Than I have done your *hŏnóur*, wanting it.
                    To Sir Henry Wotton, etc., 23-4.

Wyatt:
Drownde in *reasón* that should be my comfort: port.
                    The louer compareth his State, etc., 13.

Donne:
Whăt *tréason* is, and whát did Essex kill,
Not true *treasón*, but *tréason* handled ill.
                    Satire VII, 115-16.

Wyatt:
My body in *témpest* her delight émbrace.
                    The louer . . . complaineth etc., 8.

Donne:
And better *through*-pierced than *through* penury.
                    The Lamentations, 302.

Wyatt:
O *mĭschiefe* by *mischiéfe* to be redressed.
                    Whether libertie . . . be preferred, 8.

Donne:
Durst look in *thémselves* and *themsélves* retrieve.
                    To Sir Henry Wotton (1), 44.

Wyatt:
Withóut eÿe *Í* se, wíthout tong *I* playne.
                    Description, etc., 9.

Donne:
With *hĭs tŏngue*, ĭn *hĭs tŏngue*, called compliment.
                    Satire IV, 44.

Donne:
> Like á kíng's favorite, or líke a kíng.
>
> *Satire* II, 70.

Surrey:
> Now hé comes, will he cóme? Alas, no, no.
>
> *Complaint of the absence, etc.*, 42.

Donne:
> To thís world, ére this wórld do bid us go.
>
> *A Litany*, 180.

It is possibly well enough to call attention to the fact that there could never be any danger of confusing Donne's verse with that of Fraunce, Wyatt, or anyone else who may or may not have influenced him, or been influenced by him, for the reason that he extends throughout a poem what is to be found in only one or two lines of a poem by another. 'What he [Donne] did was to unite the vicious peculiarities of others, to indulge habitually in what they indulged in only occasionally.'[1]

If Garnett and Gosse consider word-accent, or the measure of a verse, it is impossible to understand how they can say, 'These satires might almost be written by the same hand; it is difficult to distinguish a page of Marston from a page of Donne. . . .'[2]

It is necessary to cite only a single example, and that from Marston's First Satire, and first 'page,' to distinguish him from Donne:

> Lett'st thou a superscribèd letter fall?
> And from *thysélf* unto *thysélf* dost send,
> And in the same *thysélf*, *thysélf* commend?[3]

Alden finds 'In some of . . . [Marston's] satires,—notably the First of the *Scourge*,—[that] the rhythm is more impossible than anything in Donne's satires.'[4] In Marston, however, the rugged-

---

[1] Collins, *The Poems of Lord Herbert, etc.*, p. xxiii.
[2] *English Literature, an Illustrated Record, etc.*, London, 1904 (4 vols.), ii, 272.
[3] A. H. Bullen, *The Works of John Marston*, (3 vols.) London, 1887, iii, 263, 8-10.
[4] *Rise of Satire*, p. 131.

ness is caused by crowding unelidable syllables into the line; while in Donne, it is caused by accent-shifting.

Concerning the source of this special feature of Donne's style, it may yet be learned that Dryden, Gray, Johnson, Gosse, Coleridge, Saintsbury, Schelling, and Brumbaugh, all are correct in their suppositions, and that the range of 'originality' and 'four different and widely divergent national types' is not sufficiently broad. Walton tells us that '[Donne] left the resultance of 1400 authors, most of them abridged and analyzed with his own hand':[1] and that these included English, Latin, Greek, French, Italian, and Spanish, we have much reason to believe. It is safe, also, to suppose that many of these authors were poets and that no feature of their verse escaped his keen eye.

Donne was as familiar with Latin as with English, and one example will suffice to show how he subsequently may have carried over into the expression of original thought a movement first acquired in translation. Any example will do if it may be translated so as to give arsis-thesis variation of words, and more especially of syllables. Here is the best example I have been able to find:

Tibi aras, tibi occas, tibi seris, tibi idem metis.[2]

We can easily understand how Donne would have put this into English heroic lines, the first with a feminine ending:

För yoúrsĕlf yoú plow, for yoúrsĕlf yoú harrow,
Yoŭ sŏw fŏr yoúrsĕlf, yoú reap fŏr yoúrsĕlf.

Compare the translation from Plautus with some of Donne's lines, and the identical movement is at once recognized:

They *fĕlt themsĕlves* turn beasts, *fĕlt mysĕlf* then
Becoming traitor...
                           Satire IV, 130.

That they *thĕmsĕlves* break, and do *thĕmsĕlves* spill.
                      The Progress of the Soul, 117.

Lŏok tŏ mĕ fáith, and lŏok tŏ mý fáith, God.
                        Elegy ... Prince Henry, 1.

---
[1] *Life*, p. 48.
[2] Plautus, *Mercator*, I, i, 70.

That quaint prose which was presented on page 130, and which was there put in verse form, may here be repeated, together with the original, or rather with the Latin out of which Donne twists it:

> 'And yet *Qui in seipso aruit, in nobis floret,* says St. Gregory, as wittily as St. Augustine, ... that world which finds itself truly in an autumn, in itself, finds itself in a spring in our imagination.'

Or, again:

> That wórld which fínds itsélf
> Trúly ín an aútumn ín itsélf,
>   Finds ítself ín a spríng
>   In oúr imáginátion.

This very movement,—this arsis-thesis variation of words and syllables in the same line, or group of lines,—is *the* feature of Donne's verse that suggests a new term to poetics: Donne's Measure, or Rhythm.

   XIII. *It may be shown that Donne's Influence in the Matter of Rhythm did not Found a School.*

Having gone over the verse of the so-called Metaphysical School of poets, I find only sporadic instances of the thing which stands out boldly on every page of Donne. The most striking example is that from Crashaw, already quoted, in which 'his' and 'brass' appear in arsis-thesis variation.

Without attending so strictly to the metrical side of Donne's verse, Carpenter has reached the right conclusion:

'[Donne's] influence is widely diffused, but he does not form a school. Indeed, some of those who show the attraction of his genius most are themselves in partial reaction against what is bizarre and extravagant in the rhythms and in the art of Donne.[1]

Saintsbury partially corroborates this opinion: 'The influence of John Donne was even more potent [than that of Jonson],

---

[1] *Eng. Lyr. Poetry,* lviii.

though it is extremely difficult to understand the precise manner in which it was exercised.[1]

Collins undertakes to show in what manner Donne's influence may be detected: 'The style of Donne is ... marked by certain distinctive peculiarities which no intelligent critic would be likely to mistake, and his influence on contemporary poetry was unquestionably considerable ... Where Herbert most reminds us of Donne is not so much in his lyrics as in his poems written in the heroic measures ... the poem ... "The Idea" is very much in his friend's vein, as well as written in a measure which Donne perhaps invented, and which was certainly a favourite with him.'[2]

Collins suggests others, of Herbert's poems, as resembling those of Donne, but none come nearer than *The Idea*, of which the first three stanzas may now be given:

> All Beauties vulgar eyes on earth do see,
> At best but some imperfect copies be
> Of those the Heavens did at first decree;
>
> For though th' Ideas of each several kind
> Conceiv'd above by the Eternal Mind
> Are such, as none can error in them find,
>
> Since from his thoughts and presence he doth bar
> And shut out all deformity so far,
> That the least beauty near him is a star.[3]

The conceits in these lines *are* somewhat suggestive of Donne; and the strophic form was also employed by him; but the rhythm,—the word-accent,—shows that Herbert was not influenced by Donne in this particular.

'Donne's influence was no doubt great; that it was not irresistable we may conclude from the fact that when he set himself to break up smooth versification by new rules of accent, and to depart from the iambic of his predecessors,[4] he was not able to

---

[1] *A Short Hist. of Eng. Lit.*, p. 365.
[2] *The Poems of Lord Herbert, etc.*, pp. xxiii, xxiv.
[3] *Ibid.*, p. 109.
[4] Donne wrote only in the iambic measure.

effect a revolution; nor was he successful in using the instrument which he had invented. . .¹ It was an experiment; it was not copied by his admirers; perhaps we should never have heard of it if Milton had not admitted something of Donne's principles of rhythm into the structure of his unmatched blank verse, stateliest of all measures next to Virgil's. . . One may perhaps trace the influence of Donne, but the thought, not the expression is what attracts.' ²

'Something new in English literature begins in Donne, something which proceeded, under his potent influence, to colour poetry for nearly a hundred years. The exact mode in which that influence was immediately distributed is unknown to us, or very dimly perceived. To know more about it is one of the great disiderata of literary history.' ³

XIV. *A Group of Additional Points.*

(1.) In all his verse Donne employed only the iambic movement; and there are but few lines, mostly in the strophic poems, which require "direct attack"—(fehlender Auftackt).

(2.) Some light has been thrown upon Donne's 'excess,' 'secret,' 'measure,' and 'rule.'

(3.) A reasonable explanation has been offered of Jonson's saying, and of Coleridge's quatrain.

(4.) The slight intimation we have had, by way of examples, shows that the alterations in Donne's verse have been made in the effort to 'smooth' it; and that Donne *restored* will be even more 'rugged' than Donne *deformed,*—until one's ear is cultivated to the point of appreciating *Donne's Measure.*

(5.) Of more than minor importance is the fact that we can now determine the relative authenticity of the various MSS. of Donne.

---

[1] Ellis' remark in regard to whether or not Donne's Satires are more generally admired since Pope 'translated' them, may also be applied to this statement: 'Every reader is able to form his own judgment on the truth of this opinion.' (*Specimens of Early English Poets*, 4th ed., London, 1811, ii, 383.)

[2] *Quarterly Review*, vol. cxcii, pp. 226 and 235.

[3] *Gosse, Jacobean Poets*, p. 47.

XV. *A Further Application of Donne's Measure.*

Application of Donne's Measure to lines that are nonsensical or obscure,—and in which variants have not yet been found,—restores not only the characteristic movement but also the sense. To illustrate, let us take the last stanza of *The Primrose*:

>   Live, primrose, then, and thrive
>   With thy true number five;
>   And, woman, whom this flower doth represent,
>   With this mysterious number be content;
> 25   Ten is the farthest number; if half ten
>   Belongs unto each woman, then
>   Each woman may take half us men;
>   Or—if this will not serve their turn—since all
>   Numbers are odd, or even, and they fall
> 30   First into five, women may take us all.

In the first place, we may accept the 1635 variant of 29:

> Numbers are odd, or even, *since* they fall.

This gives *since* in arsis to accompany *since* in thesis in the preceding line.

In line 30, the edition of 1633 inserts 'this' between 'into' and 'five,' leaving the line with an extra syllable, and offering no opportunity of elision, while the editions of 1635, '39, '49, '54, and '69 give the line as it appears above. This leaves the line with the requisite ten syllables, but also leaves it too obscure, and takes from it Donne's characteristic touch. Noting the sounds in this stanza which have arsis-thesis variation,—not to repeat all the words and syllables, so varying,—we observe: númbĕr, Nŭmbérs; thĭs, thís; bĕ, Bĕ; Tĕn, tén; hălf, hálf; máy, măy; tăke, táke; wómăn, wŏmén; sĭnce, sínce. The other repeated words which do not vary are *all, all*, both of which occur in the rime, and Donne frequently allows a repeated sound to stand in this position without a thesis-variant. *If* appears in arsis in 25, but the nature of 28 seems to call for initial inversion which would place the second *if* in thesis. Of repeated words which do not vary, and for which there is no explanation, only three are left: *us, us; five, five;* and *each, each.* Putting lines 27 and 30 together, it is clear enough that Donne repeated *each* in the last line:

> Each wómăn máy tăke half us men;
> ... wŏmĕn măy táke us all.

Restoring lines 29 and 30, and substituting *they* for *this* in 28, we have:

> Live, primrose, thén, and thríve
> With thý true númbĕr fíve;
> And, wómăn, whom thĭs flower doth represent,
> With thĭs mў̆sterious númbĕr bĕ content;
> Tĕn ĭs the farthest númbĕr; ĭf hălf tén
> Bĕlongs unto ĕach wómăn, thén
> Ĕach wómăn máy tăke hálf ŭs mĕn;
> Ór,—ĭf [they] will not serve their turn sĭnce all
> Nŭmbĕrs are odd, or even,—sĭnce they fall
> Fĭve thŭs in eách, wŏmĕn măy tăke ŭs all.

Not only does this restore Donne's variations: *ŭs, ŭs, thŭs*,[1] *thríve, fíve, Fíve*; *ĕach, Ĕach, ĕach*; but it also explains Grosart's mystery (li, 225, note): 'In st. iii, 10 the conceit is obscure, unless the Poet be still referring to the theory that the five of one hand is the first unit in the calculations of primeval man, and the ten of both hands the duplicate unit of this first one.'

Chamber's note (i, 230) on 'they fall first into five' is unsatisfactory: 'That is, the first even number, two, added to the first odd number, three,—one, the unit, of course not counting—makes five.' Donne may or may not have regarded *one* as an odd number. (See N. E. D., 'odd.')

In the second stanza, the poet knows not which flower he wishes, 'a six, or four.' One of these numbers, 'four,' presumably, represents one 'less than woman' who is 'scarce anything;'

---

[1] Such a variation pleases Donne, for example:

> For oughtest Thou, O Lord, despise *ŭs thŭs*,
> And to be utterly enraged at *ŭs*.
> *The Lamentations*, 389-90.

and the other, 'six,' one 'more than woman' who 'would get above all thought of sex, and think to move my heart to study her, and not to love.' Both of these, the poet regards as 'monsters;' and 'since there must reside falsehood in woman, [he] could more abide' a woman falsified by art than by nature. The primrose with four or six petals would be a 'monster' falsified by art or nature: a woman with no thought of sex, and one 'above all thought of sex' would likewise be monsters falsified by art or nature. Here we have a 'six' and a 'four' making 'Ten [which] is the farthest number,'—the sum of six and four, and the extremes of womankind. This, however, is not the only 'ten' to which the poet has reference. In the next stanza he makes up his mind that he does not want a primrose with four petals, 'one less than woman;' nor a primrose with six petals, 'one more than woman.' He selects a primrose with its 'true number five,' as one that has not been 'by art [or] nature falsified.'

'And, woman, whom this flower doth represent, with this mysterious number [five, must] be content:' content if less than five, 'less than woman,' to improve her mind by thought, and to falsify her body by art, so as to appear to be a true, perfect woman, physically and mentally; content if more than five, 'more than woman,' to be physical as well as mental and spiritual.

Here are two women who by the processes of nature and art come to represent the perfect primrose with its 'true number five;' the two extremes, 'four' and 'six' (ten), have become 'five' and 'five' (ten); and 'Ten is the farthest number' that $4 + 6$ or $5 + 5$ can possibly make. The poet seems also to have had in mind that the flower with its 'true number five' which represents perfect physical womanhood, and the woman who is content to be physical, as well as mental and spiritual, are 'the farthest number,' the objects most to be desired by him who walks 'to find a true love.'

Now, 'if half ten [$4 + 1$] belongs unto each woman, then each woman may take half us men; Or—if [they] will not serve their turn, since all numbers are odd [one woman], or even [half us men],—since they fall five thus in each [$4 + 1$ and $6 - 1$], women may take us all.'

To put it another way: a woman who is 'scarce anything,' ('four'), being falsified by art or nature (one), becomes perfect ('five') in the eyes of 'half us men,' and, therefore, 'may take half us men.' The other half of 'us men' would prefer the 'more than woman' ('six') who is willing to be natural ('five'), or artificial, as the case may be, and so 'women may take us all.'

The next example to be cited, has undergone such great change that it may never be perfectly restored, unless the matter can be cleared up by those MSS. in England which I have not yet seen.

The Progress of the Soul, Stanza xxxix:

381. Nature's great masterpiece, an elephant,
 The only harmless great thing, the giant
 Of beasts, who thought none had, to make him wise,
 But to be just and thankful, loth to offend
 —Yet Nature hath given him no knees to bend
 Himself he up-props, on himself relies,
 And foe to none, suspects no enemies—
 Still sleeping stood; vex'd not his fantasy
 Black dreams; like an unbent bow carelessly
  His sinewy proboscis did remissly lie.

The first two lines are as Donne wrote them:

Nature's *greát* masterpiece, án elephánt,
Thé only harmless *greát* thing, thé giánt.

but the next line is corrupt. The editions of 1635, '39, '49, '54. and '69 have the line as above; 1633 gives it:

Of beasts, who thought no more had gone to make one wise.

but this makes an Alexandrine of it, and only the final verse was intended to have more than five accents.

Grosart's note (i, 94) throws a little light on the subject: 'Our MS. [Addl., 18,647, Plut. 201 H.] reads "though noe had gone," which is somewhat bewildering. The usual printed text which we have accepted [the same as Chambers] is poorly expressed yet intelligible—the elephant did not seek to be intellectually or cunningly wise after the world's wisdom, and like a tyrant, great one, or statesman, but sought to be morally wise and good.'

In this poem mention is made of Adam, Eve, Cain, Abel, Seth, Siphatecia ('Adam's fifth daughter'), and her brother Thelemite.

The elephant relying on himself (386) seems to indicate that he formerly had some one on whom to rely. The Addl. MS. 18,647 reading, 'though noe had gone' seems to mean, giving the Greek form of the word (See Matthew, xxv., 37), 'though Noe had gone.' This gives 'Noah' pronounced as one syllable, as it is in Donne's *Satire* IV, 19, and in arsis to vary with *no* which appears twice in thesis in succeeding lines.

Line 385 seems also to be corrupt. Such an elision as *Nature hath* is uncommon even in the poetry of Donne.

Lines 385-6, as here punctuated, are foolishness : ' Yet Nature hath given him no knees to bend himself he upprops, on himself relies. . .'

Every other line in *Donne* in which a compound, with -*self* or -*selves* is repeated, shows the arsis-thesis variation of the syllables. Donne must have written this line :

<blockquote>He up-props h*i*msĕlf on h*i*msélf relies.[1]</blockquote>

With the limited information, at hand, no more can now be done with this stanza.

Application of Donne's *measure* to the verse-letter *To Sir Henry Wotton* (2), (19-21) seems to improve the lines and render them less obscure,—and possibly less poetic.

<blockquote>Suspicious boldness to this place belongs,
And to have as many ears as all have tongues;
Tender to know, tough to acknowledge wrongs.</blockquote>

To scan line 20 there is an elision, *to have*, which does not occur, under the ictus, in any of Donne's lines that seem uncorrupted. 'Tender' (21) is 'Tends' in Stephens MS., while in the

---

[1] See verse 117 of this poem :
That they thĕmsélves break and do thĕmsélves spill.

same MS. 'tough' is 'loath.' My idea at present is that 'tough' was originally 'though' and that some transcriber dropped the first 'h.' Some succeeding copyist seeing 'tough' thought 'Tends' should be 'Tender,' and so made the change. Therefore, the lines may be conjecturally reconstructed:

> Suspicious boldness tó this place belongs;
> Tŏ háve as many ears as all hăve tongues
> Tends tó knŏwlĕdge, though tó acknówlĕdge wrongs.

XVI. *When Arsis-Thesis Variations do not Occur.*

Having presented the matter as strongly and as earnestly as possible, it only remains now to point out when Donne does not give his words, syllables, and sounds arsis-thesis variation.[1]

(1) *In Internal Rime: Middle, Sectional, and Inverse.*

> And háte with háte again retaliáte.[2]
>
> *The Prohibition*, 12.
>
> Which if in héll no other pains there were,
> Makes me fear héll, because he must be there.
>
> *Elegy* IV. *The Perfume*, 35–6.
>
> If we love thíngs long sought, age is a thíng
> Which we are fifty years in compassíng.
>
> *Elegy* IX. *The Autumnal*, 33–4.
>
> O! to confess we knów not whát we should,
> Is half excuse, we knów not whát we would.
>
> *To the Countess of Bedford* (3), 33–4.
>
> But thy right hánd, and chéek, and eýe, only
> Are like thy other hánd, and chéek, and eýe.
>
> *Sappho to Philænis*, 23–4.
>
> If mán be therefore mán, because he cán
> Reason and laugh, thy book doth half make mán.
>
> *Upon . . . Coryat's Crudities*, 13, 14.

---

[1] The poems from which the following examples are taken contain,—each and all of them,—the characteristic 'knot' of words, and 'twist' of arsis-thesis which prevent any confusion as to authorship. Only a few examples are necessary under each head.

[2] 'Hate' occurs, however, in thesis in the same stanza.

> But they are oúrs, as fruits are oúrs,
> He thát but tastes he thát devours.
> > *Community*, 19, 20.
>
> Thou árt not góne, being góne; where'er thou árt.
> > *Eclogue, etc.*, 202.

(2) *Sometimes a word is repeated in arsis or thesis when other words are being varied.*

> So may thў love and courage né'er be cold;
> Thў son né'er ward; thў loved wife né'er seem old.
> > *To M(r). I. P.*, 17, 18.
>
> That wé may lóck oŭr ĕars, Lórd, ópen Thíne.
> That wé may ópen oúr ĕars, Lórd, lŏck Thíne.
> > *A Litany*, XXV, 225; XXVI, 234.

(3) *In Inverted Phrases.*

> Because thŏu árt not frozen, árt thŏu warm.
> Seĕst thŏu all good, because thŏu seĕst no harm.[1]
> > *Eclogue, etc.*, 59, 60.

(4) *In Refrains.*

> Thou leavest ĭn hĭm thў watchful eyes, ĭn hĭm thў loving heart.
> > *Eclogue, etc.*, 203.

Sometimes, however, there is variation in words of a refrain, as in verse 137 of this *Eclogue*:

> The fire óf thý inflaming eyes, and óf thў loving heart.

(5) *When Arsis-Thesis Variation is Impossible or Impracticable.*

It is patent that, in the iambic movement, repeated words or syllables cannot always receive this arsis-thesis variation. With all Donne's peculiarities, it would be folly to expect to find him doing the impossible, or putting in meaningless words or syllables, or leaving out words or syllables essential to the sense of a line, even in the execution of his pet 'rule.'

---

[1] It is quite likely that Donne did not write 59 as it here stands. The variations in 55-6-7 are quite as marked as in 60.

XVII. *When Arsis-Thesis Variation is Possible.*

This variation is possible under several conditions:[1]

(1) When a monosyllabic word is repeated with no intervening word:

    Temper, O fair *lŏve, lóve's* impetuous rage.
                         Elegy XVII. *His Mistress*, 13.

(2) When a monosyllabic word is repeated with an intervening even nember of words or syllables:

    That *oúr* souls no more than *oŭr* eyes disclose.
                                   Ode, 18.

(3) When dissyllabic words, or two monosyllabic words or syllables with a similar sound, are repeated, with an intervening odd number of syllables or monosyllabic words:

    That they *thĕmsélves* break, and do *thĕmsĕlves* spill.
                         The Progress of the Soul, 117.
    In *drésstng*, mistr*ĕssĭng* and compliment.
                         To Mr. Tilman, etc., 30.
    If thou *stăy hére*. O *stáy hĕre*, for for thee.
                         Elegy XVII. *His Mistress*, 43.

(4) When trisyllabic words, or three monosyllabic words are repeated with an intervening even number of syllables:

    Lĭke á kĭng's favorite, or *lĭke ă kĭng*.
                             Satire II, 70.

(5) When four monosyllabic words are repeated with a single intervening monosyllabic word:

    Lŏok tó mĕ, fáith, and *lŏok tŏ mý fáith*, God.

XVIII. *When Arsis-Thesis Variation is Impossible.*

This variation is impossible and impracticable,[2]

---

[1] The principle here presented is sufficiently illustrated without attempting to give all the conditions under which such variation is possible.

[2] By 'impracticable' it is meant that the movement of the thought in certain verses requires some words to take their places without reference to arsis-thesis variation.

(1) When the conditions are the reverse of those mentioned in the preceding categories. A few examples, by way of illustration, will suffice:

> Sŏ pale, sŏ lame, sŏ lean, sŏ ruinous.
> I lose mў guard, mў ease, mў food, mў all.
> Elegy XI. The Bracelet, 26, 50.
> Bĕfore, bĕhind, bĕtween, above, bĕlow.
> Elegy XX, 26.
> And unto her *protĕsts, protĕsts, protĕsts.*
> Satire IV, 212.
> Ănd ăt mĭne eyes, ănd ăt mĭne ears.
> Twickenham Garden, 3.

(2) In certain fixed phrases, such as 'as well as,' 'as good as,' 'as rich as,' etc., which can be understood, without citing examples, as not lending themselves to arsis-thesis variation.

XIX. *Lack of Arsis-Thesis Variation Due to Corrupt Text.*

In lines where elision, or lack of it, indicates that the text may be corrupt.

Elegy . . . Prince Henry, (84, 97):
> By th' oaths, which only *yoú twŏ* never broke,
> So much as *yoú twŏ* mutual heavens were here.

Conjecture:
> By thĕ oaths which onlў *yŏu twó* ne'er broke.[1]

A Litany, (17, 18):
> Părt not from ĭt, though ĭt from Thee would părt,
> But let ĭt be by applўing so *Thў* pain,
> Drown'd ĭn *Thў* blood, and ĭn *Thў* passion slain.

Conjecture:
> Drownèd ĭn *Thў* blood, ĭn *Thў* passion slain.

> Whom and her race *onlў* forbiddings drive.
> The Progress of the Soul, 87.
> By thy right hand, and cheek, and eye, *onlў:* eye.
> Sappho to Philænis, 23.

The Canonization, (7):
    Ŏr the king's reál, or his stamp'd fáce.
Grosart and *Norton*:
    Ŏr the king's reál, ŏr his stampèd fáce.
Ibid., (19, 21):
    Call's whát you wíll, we aré made súch by lóve;
    We're tapers too, and at our own cost die.
Grosart:
    Call us whát you wíll, we aré made súch by lóue,
Norton:
    Call us what you will we are made such by love.
Conjecture:
    Call ús what yóu will *wĕ're* made súch by lóve.
    Wĕ're tapers too. . .

XX. *Apparent Lack of Arsis-Thesis Variation Explained.*

Sometimes when there seems to be an absence of this variation, it is because Donne has allowed himself a little wider scope. If the reader will consider each of the poems as a whole, attending carefully with the ear, and with fingers[1] too, if necessary, he will pass but few words or syllables which appear twice in arsis, or twice in thesis, till he comes to know that the variant is near by. Should his text or foot-notes fail to give these variations, it will usually be found to be the fault of his edition of the poems.

It is unnecessary to repeat the conclusions which have found their appropriate places in this study.

    I know you dread all those who write,
    And both with hand and mouth recite;
    Who slow and leisurely rehearse,
    As loath t' enrich you with their verse;
    Just as a still, with simples in it,
    Betwixt each drop stays half a minute.
    The simile is not my own,
    But rightfully belongs to Donne.
              Pope to Cromwell, *Letter* I., 11-18.

I am firmly convinced that Donne is a mine whose depths I have scarcely touched; that he possesses a richness which is not half apparent on the surface; and that, while the verses of other poets rime in the middle, or at the end, Donne's rime everywhere. Lest I be regarded as a victim of the 'editorial passion,' I agree unreservedly with Dyce: ' [Donne] was a man of great learning and extraordinary wit, and was not a bad poet.'[1]

NOTE.

I may be pardoned for announcing that I have already begun the preparation of a new edition of Donne's Poems. The work is tedious, and considerable time will be required for collating the various MSS. American students of Donne will be pleased to learn that Harvard University has just added (May, 1906), a fourth Donne MS. (the O'Flahertie) to the 'Norton Collection.'

---

[1] *Early English Poems*, London, 1863, p. 124.

BIOGRAPHICAL SKETCH.

I was born near Ripley, Lauderdale County, Tennessee, September, 1867; received my early education in public and private schools of Alabama; attended the Southern University, Greensboro, Alabama, 1886-7; the University of Nashville: Peabody Teachers' College, 1887-9, graduating with the degree of L. I. (Licentiate of Instruction), May, 1889; graduated from Blount College (Alabama), June, 1892, A. M.; Alabama State School (Troy), May, 1894, Ph. D.

I taught in the public schools of Alabama three years before and after graduation; one year in the public schools of Florida. I was president of Florida Conference College (Leesburg), 1892-5; vice-president of Nashville (Tenn.) College for Young Ladies, 1895-97; president of Tuscaloosa (Alabama) Female College, 1897–1903; student and fellow by courtesy in the Johns Hopkins University, 1903-6.

In October, 1903, I entered the English Seminary, and have pursued graduate studies in English during the years 1903-4, 1904-5, 1905-6. My subordinate subjects have been Philosophy and German.

It is pleasant to record my gratitude to President Remsen, Professors Bright, Browne, Baldwin, Wood, Smith, and Bloomfield, Dean Griffin, and Doctors Kurrelmeyer and Easter. I am especially grateful to Professor Bright for patiently and carefully reshaping my ideals.

D'Israeli, Isaac, 23.
Denham, Sir John, 124.
Dobson, William T., 117.
Dodsley, James, 35.
Done, John, 22, 111.
Donne, John (The younger), 3.
Dorset, Lord, 14, 15.
Dowden, Edward, 2, 42, 43.
Drake, Nathan, 34.
Drayton, Michael, 10, 11, 124.
Drummond, William, 8, 10, 12, 13, 27, 47, 131, 137, 139, 140.
Dryden, John, 1, 8, 9, 13, 14, 15, 23, 30, 36, 41, 44, 58, 124, 129, 186, 192.
Dyce, Alexander, 206.

Eclectic Magazine, 43.
Edinburgh Magazine (Lowe's), 24.
Ellis, John, 195.
Elwin, Whitwell, 17, 24.
Emerson, Ralph Waldo, 128.
Era, The Literary, 118.
Ezekiel, 29.

Fairfax, Edward, 10.
Farr, Edward, 35.
Fletcher, John, 10, 11, 34.
Fletcher, Giles, 88.
Franklin, Miles, 117.
Fraunce, Abraham, 10, 99, 135, 136, 137, 186, 188, 191.
Furst, Clyde, 4, 23, 46.

Garnett and Gosse, 191.
Gifford, William, 12, 128, 137, 138.
Gilfillan, George, 15, 16.
Goldsmith, Oliver, 1, 15, 16, 17.
Gongora, 186.
Gosse, Edmund, 4, 9, 13, 14, 15, 22, 25, 27, 30, 32, 40, 45, 46, 47, 49, 50, 53, 108, 110, 115, 127, 128, 133, 135, 186, 192, 195.
Gray, Thomas, 16, 41, 63, 64, 68, 69, 71, 74, 75, 76, 78, 187, 192.
Greene, Robert, 56.
Gregory, Saint, 193.
Grolier Club, 3, 4, 6, 16, 43, 49, 50.
Grosart, Alexander, 3, 4, 5, 6, 9, 13, 16, 23, 24, 27, 30, 31, 32, 37, 38, 52, 53, 65, 91, 119, 120, 122, 136, 175, 176, 183, 184, 185, 199.
Gwynne, Stephen, 54.

Hales, John W., 40, 41.
Hall, Joseph, 12, 23, 124, 173.
Harrison, James Smith, 2.
Harvey, Gabriel, 136.
Harvard University, 4, 206.
Hazlitt, William, 39, 108.
Herbert, Magdalen, 35.

Herbert, Rev. George, 34.
Herbert, Sir Edward, 37, 118, 120, 121, 194.
Herrick, Robert, 44.
Holland, Lord, 117.
Hood, Thomas, 73.
Horace, 13, 14, 186.
Hubbard, F. G., 106.
Huguenin, Julian, 1, 58, 85, 86.
Hugonius, Constantin, 24.
Hume, David, 25.
Hyde, Edward, 8.

Irenaeus, 186.

James, William, 64.
Jameson, Mrs. Anna Murphy, 29, 31.
Jessopp, Augustus, 45, 46, 49, 50, 112, 130, 131, 165.
Johnson, Samuel, 9, 16, 17, 25, 26, 29, 32, 44, 62, 105, 109, 125, 128, 129, 186, 192.
Jonson, Ben, .. 8, 9, 10, 12, 13, 25, 30, 34, 39, 41, 43, 47, 51, 54, 55, 66, 67, 68, 69, 70, 71, 72, 73, 74, 75, 76, 77, 78, 79, 80, 81, 82, 83, 84, 86, 91, 96, 98, 99, 101, 102, 118, 120, 124, 131, 137, 138, 139, 140, 163, 164, 187, 193, 195.
Jowett, B., 121.

Keats, John, 55.
Kempe, J. Edward, 39.
Key, Francis Scott, 61.
King, Henry, 108.
Kyd, Thomas, 44.

Laing, David, 9, 12.
Landor, Walter Savage, 35.
Lane, William C., 6.
Lanier, Sidney, 65, 75, 77, 78, 79, 86.
Leisure Hours, 56.
Lightfoot, Joseph Barber, 39.
Littel's Living Age, 43, 120.
Lloyd, R. J., 105, 106.
Longfellow, Henry W., 113.
Lope de Vega, 117.
Lovelace, Richard, 124.
Lowell, James Russell, 6, 14, 16, 49, 110, 174.

Macdonald, George, 37, 38, 169.
Marino, 186.
Markham, 11.
Marlowe, Christopher, 56, 124.
Marston, John, 11, 187, 191.
Masson, David, 129.
Mayor, Joseph B., 63.
Midas, 26.
Middleton, Thomas, 11.

Miller, Raymond Durbin, 1, 58, 85, 86, 87, 95, 99, 101.
Milton, John, 9, 16, 30, 32, 44, 46, 47, 55, 58, 71, 72, 74, 75, 76, 77, 80, 82, 83, 88, 89, 91, 92, 94, 95, 96, 97, 98, 99, 124, 154, 195.
Minto, William, 40.
Minshew, 10.
Mitford, John, 16.
More, Sir Thomas, 168.
More, Anna, 168.
More, George, 168.
Mosher, Thomas B., 45.
Murphy, Arthur, 26.

Norton, Charles Eliot, 3, 4, 6, 16, 24, 25, 26, 30, 31, 43, 44, 50, 101, 110, 123, 137, 140, 175, 176, 178, 182, 183, 206.
Niceron, Jean Pierre, 24.

Overby, 11.
Oxford, Earl of, 15, 17, 18.

Parnell, Thomas, 1, 15, 16, 17, 18, 23, 24, 41, 67, 68, 70, 72, 74, 76, 155.
Patmore, Coventry, 43.
Plato, 121.
Plautus, 192.
Poe, Edgar Allan, 66, 68, 70, 71, 74.
Pope, Alexander, 1, 9, 15, 16, 17, 18, 19, 20, 21, 22, 23, 24, 30, 33, 34, 41, 44, 66, 67, 68, 69, 74, 78, 80, 93, 96, 99, 100, 124, 152.
Porter, Endymion, 8.

Quaritch, 178.
Quarles, Francis, 37.

Retrospective Review, 8, 28, 35, 109, 127.
Review, The Nineteenth Century, 40.
Review, The National, 50.
Review, The Church Quarterly, 50.
Review, Quarterly, 108, 195.
Review, Fortnightly, 110.
Richter, Rudolph, 5, 51, 52, 53, 54, 136.
Roe, Sir John, 11.
Raleigh, Sir Walter, 11.
Rutland, Countess of, 13.

Saintsbury, George, 12, 44, 51, 54, 110, 117, 165, 168, 182, 186, 187, 192, 193.
Salisbury, 11.
Sanders, H. M., 50, 51, 120, 122.
Sanford and Walsh, 28.
Schelling, Felix E., 187, 192.
Schipper, Jakob, 41, 42.
Sharpham, 10.
Shakespeare, 9, 10, 11, 25, 30, 33, 39, 44, 55, 65, 66, 67, 68, 69, 70, 71, 73, 75, 76, 77, 78, 79, 83, 84, 86, 87, 88, 89, 90, 91, 92, 93, 94, 95, 96, 97, 98, 99, 100, 101, 102, 124, 127, 130, 148, 155, 182.
Shelley, Percy Bysshe, 66, 72, 74.
Shedd, William G. T., 32.
Shrewsbury, Duke of, 15, 17, 18.
Sidney, Sir Philip, 11, 13.
Sievers, Eduard, 58, 85.
Skeat, W. W., 178.
Smith, Alexander, 60, 62.
Smollett, Tobias George, 16.
Socrates, 121.
Southey, Robert, 26, 27.
Spenser, Edmund, 10, 27, 34, 42, 47, 54, 78, 153.
Speaker, The, 118.
Sprat, Thomas, 124, 187.
Stephen, Leslie, 50.
Stratton, George Malcomb, 113, 116.
Surry, 191.
Sweet, Henry, 85.
Swinburne, 41, 45, 56, 155, 156.
Sylvester, Josuah, 10.
Symonds, Arthur, 110.

Tailor, 11.
Taine, H., 37.
Temple Bar, 51, 120, 122.
Ten Brink, B., 85.
Tennyson, 9, 64, 66, 69, 71, 72, 74, 75, 76, 78, 79, 80, 82, 83, 95, 104.
Theobald, Lewis, 24, 25, 108.
Thompson, Mrs. K. B., 35.
Trost, Wilhelm, 2, 41, 53, 54, 168.

University of Missouri, 6.
University of Pennsylvania, 1.

van Dam and Stoffel, 3, 99, 101.
Virgil, 13, 195.

Wakefield, Gilbert, 18.
Waller, Edmund, 124.
Walton, Izaak, 6, 125, 126, 134, 192.
Warburton, Bishop, 18, 23, 35.
Ward, Thomas H., 41.
Warton, Joseph, 23, 27.
Watts, Isaac, 104.
Webb, William, 136.
Wendell, Barrett, 13, 54, 55.
Whateley, Richard, 29.
Whitefield, George, 127.
Wilke, Wilhelm, 99, 101.
Wordsworth, William, 32, 95, 127.
World, The New, etc., 128.
Wotton, Sir Henry, 165, 184, 185.
Wyatt, Sir Thomas, 44, 188, 189, 190, 191.

LaVergne, TN USA
12 December 2009
166810LV00003B/225/A